SHAKERS, MORMONS,
AND RELIGIOUS WORLDS

RELIGION IN NORTH AMERICA

Catherine L. Albanese and Stephen J. Stein, editors

Shakers, Mormons, and Religious Worlds

CONFLICTING VISIONS, CONTESTED BOUNDARIES

STEPHEN C. TAYSOM

Indiana University Press

Bloomington & Indianapolis

This book is a publication of

Indiana University Press
601 North Morton Street
Bloomington, IN 47404-3797 USA

www.iupress.indiana.edu

Telephone orders 800-842-6796
Fax orders 812-855-7931
Orders by e-mail iuporder@indiana.edu

⊗ The paper used in this publication
meets the minimum requirements of
the American National Standard for
Information Sciences—Permanence
of Paper for Printed Library Materials,
ANSI Z39.48-1992.

Manufactured in the United States of
America

Library of Congress Cataloging-in-
Publication Data

Taysom, Stephen C.
  Shakers, Mormons, and religious
worlds : conflicting visions, contested
boundaries / Stephen C. Taysom.
    p. cm. — (Religion in North America)
  Includes bibliographical references and
index.
  ISBN 978-0-253-35540-9 (cloth : alk.
paper) 1. Shakers—History—19th century—Comparative studies. 2. Church
of Jesus Christ of Latter-day Saints—
History—19th century—Comparative
studies. 3. Christian sociology—United
States—History—20th century. 4.
United States—Church history—19th
century. I. Title.
  BX9765.T38 2010
  289.3'32—dc22

2010012634

1 2 3 4 5 16 15 14 13 12 11

For my little ones,
Rex, Reagan, and Steele,
because you will not be little for long

For Shawny, for giving me everything

CONTENTS

FOREWORD

This volume examines two high-tension religious movements in the nineteenth-century United States that adopted distinctive strategies for dealing with the definition and maintenance of the boundaries that separated them from the rest of American society. These two outsider religious groups—the Shakers and the Mormons—have attracted a great deal of attention across time from both the scholarly world and the larger American public. This is the case despite the contrast in their situations in the twenty-first century: the Mormons, or Latter-day Saints, are a worldwide religious tradition numbering in the millions, whereas the Shakers are today a mere handful of believers.

Stephen C. Taysom's volume is a creative comparative study, an exercise in historical sociology in the tradition of the work of Rosabeth Moss Kanter, author of *Commitment and Community*, although his conclusions are substantially different from hers. He accepts received notions of the importance of boundary maintenance for dissenting, alternative, or "sectarian" communities, but he demonstrates how the Shakers and the Mormons employed different options for defining and maintaining their boundaries. The two most striking social contrasts appear in the area of family arrangements, namely, the practices of Shaker celibacy and of Mormon polygamy or plural marriage. These distinctive arrangements governing the relationships between male and female members became defining features of the two communities during the nineteenth century. Both celibacy and polygamy were the focus of sustained criticism and violent opposition from other Americans in the period. These diverse sexual arrangements have also occupied historians writing about these two communities in the nineteenth century as they have sought to identify the aspects of community life that set these religious groups apart from the rest of American society.

Taysom's comparative study also involves an examination of the structural effects of particular regulations and communal statutes on religious life in these two communities. A document called the Millennial Laws governed most aspects of daily life in Shaker villages during the nineteenth century, prescribing the roles of Shaker brothers and sisters and setting their life patterns in the community in sharp contrast to the common prevailing routines in the larger non-Shaker society. Similarly, the Mormon Word of Wisdom, dietary principles articulated by the founder, Joseph Smith, set Latter-day Saints' foodways apart from those of their contemporaries, thereby contributing to the establishment of identifiable LDS boundaries. The rules governing daily activities and the regulations concerning dietary practices played major roles in enabling the Shakers and the Mormons to maintain themselves apart from other Americans. These same rules and regulations also fueled direct opposition and violence from nonbelievers, and affliction, injury, and distress frequently accompanied membership in these alternative religious communities. Both founders—Ann Lee and Joseph Smith—knew violence firsthand. Suffering and persecution have been commonplace experiences for members of religious communities that have consciously pursued a strategy of outsiderhood.

Taysom also examines the substance of the religious experiences of the Shakers and the Mormons during the nineteenth century. He investigates the effects of the Shaker Era of Manifestations, a special time of abundant outpouring of spiritual gifts among the believers. He offers insight into the Mormon Reformation and into the Latter-day Saints' deployment and redefinition of Zionic ideals. He exploits systematically the historiographic traditions surrounding these two religious communities, demonstrating how the scholarship devoted to them, generated both by members and by others outside, has contributed to an understanding of these religions but at times has also led to mistaken judgments.

Taysom's examination of the Shakers and the Mormons sheds light on the larger patterns that have characterized alternative religious communities in the past and that continue to do so in the present. In other words, although this volume is a focused historical examination of two outsider religious movements in the nineteenth century, it has implications for understanding the expanding numbers of such religious groups in contemporary America. The United States has been and remains a fertile seedbed, a secure and inviting situation for new religious movements (NRMs) that wish to prosper outside the boundaries set by historic and well-established religious communities. The principle of the free exercise of religion articulated in the First Amendment and the historical situation of open space have created a legal and geographic context conducive to the growth and development of such alternative religious communities. Yet these NRMs have faced immense challenges, including opposition from established religious traditions and from other, independent critics. In the nineteenth century, the Shakers and the Mormons were among the most successful of such religious communities. Taysom probes the reasons for that success by examining the boundaries that set them apart from other religious groups, thereby defining, distinguishing, and protecting their members. There is much to learn from what he has done, and we welcome this new volume into the Religion in North America series.

Catherine L. Albanese
Stephen J. Stein
Editors, Religion in North America

ACKNOWLEDGMENTS

The image of the lone scholar as a solitary figure grinding out learned prose in what Warren Zevon called "splendid isolation" is a popular and appealing vision. What every scholar knows, however, is that the reality is far different. This book has been helped along by a hundred hands over the years, all of them serving to lift it well above the reach of this author alone. Here, I am afforded the opportunity of thanking some of them by name and honoring all of them in spirit.

In an earlier incarnation, this book went forth as a dissertation. My committee, Stephen Stein, Philip Goff, Constance Furey, David Brakke, and David Whittaker, provided tremendous guidance and acute insight.

I am grateful to the anonymous reviewers for Indiana University Press for helping to sharpen my arguments and make the material more broadly accessible. The editors of the Religion in North America series, Stephen Stein and Catherine Albanese, each offered substantive critiques of the manuscript that boosted both the book's level of intellectual engagement and the fluidity of the prose. Dee Mortensen, Senior Sponsoring Editor at IU Press, shepherded the manuscript through the lengthy review process with unfailing enthusiasm and good humor. Her assistant, Peter Froehlich, kept me on track in a variety of ways. My copyeditor, Merryl Sloane, performed magic in her excellent and rigorous review of the manuscript.

My students and professional colleagues also merit my appreciation. I discussed various ideas from this book with my classes at Indiana

University, Franklin College, and Cleveland State University. As every teacher knows, students often provide keen insights and critiques and notice errors in logic and argument that more seasoned scholars miss. This book is stronger for the feedback my students have given me. Faithful colleagues and friends who have lent a hand to this production include Carole Barnsley, Brian Cannon, David Grua, Aimee Hamilton, Erik Hammerstrom, Jen Hart, Christopher Jones, Nicole Karapanagiotis, David Rich Lewis, Arle Lommel, Jake Olmstead, Jeremy Rapport, and Jonathan Stapley. Mario DePillis, Lawrence Foster, and Jan Shipps all provided inspiration for this project through their work and their careers. My colleagues in the Department of Religious Studies at Cleveland State University, Sucharita Adluri, Stephen Corey, Matt Jackson-McCabe, and Derwood Smith, deserve special thanks for their support and encouragement.

Portions of the book were presented at meetings of the American Academy of Religion, the Western History Association, the Mormon History Association, the Shaker Seminar, the John Whitmer Historical Association, and the Communal Studies Association. Some of the material originally appeared as "'There Is Always a Way of Escape': Continuity and Reconstitution in Nineteenth-Century Mormon Boundary Maintenance Strategies," *Western Historical Quarterly* 37 (Summer 2006): 183–206. Used by permission.

Funding for my research and writing came from a variety of sources, including the Charles Redd Center for Western Studies at Brigham Young University, the College of Liberal Arts and Social Sciences at Cleveland State University, and the Sunstone Education Foundation.

On a more personal level, my parents, Mike and Cheryl Taysom, have always been there with encouragement and kindness. Kay and Jerry Grover have become my family in the fullest sense of the term—so much so that I find it difficult and insufficient to call them "in-laws." My wife, Shawny, is my best critic and my most ardent defender, and, crucially, she knows just when to wear each hat. Our children, Rex, Reagan, and Steele, remind me of what matters, and they give me hope every day. I am indebted to JWOL and his friends for keeping me sane during the rough spots.

SHAKERS, MORMONS,
AND RELIGIOUS WORLDS

Ann Lee and Joseph Smith were larger-than-life characters who believed that they had spoken with God and, more impressively, convinced thousands of other people that they had done so. Prophets both, Lee and Smith inspired the creation of communities of believers, people willing to sacrifice the comforts of home and family, often repeatedly, in an effort to create and maintain their peculiar and particular visions of divinely sanctioned life. This book is about those people and the worlds they created. It is also about the oppositional worlds they encountered, and in fact helped to create, that provided them with stability and uncertainty, calm and crisis. In these pages, we will meet a wide variety of personalities operating in a wide range of geographic contexts. Joseph Smith will be, by turns, provocative and meek, radical and reactionary as he and his followers make their way from New York to Missouri, from Ohio to Illinois. He will talk of golden plates and angels, he will introduce plural marriage, he will preach religious tolerance and destroy the printing press of a critical newspaper. He will inspire a massive conversion of English people to Mormonism, produce volumes of new scripture, introduce esoteric temple rituals and a theology of deification. And he will die on a June afternoon at the hands of a mob in the courtyard of an Illinois jail.

We will meet Brigham Young, the stout and leonine Vermonter who succeeded Smith as president of the Church of Jesus Christ of Latter-day Saints and who propelled, almost solely through the application of his colossal will, thousands of Mormons on an epic trek across vast prairies to the shores of a great lake sheltered by towering granite cliffs. We will witness how Young, once safely ensconced in his western fortress, eventually grew uneasy with the peace he encountered there, so unfamiliar to the Mormon experience, and the spiritual malaise that he feared it bred.

Along the way, we will come to know John Taylor, the erudite English convert to Mormonism who presided over the LDS Church from "the underground" during the years of open conflict with the United States over the practice of plural marriage. Taylor defined Mormonism and its relationship to the United States in absolute terms and vowed never to relinquish a practice that God himself had instituted. Finally, we will meet Taylor's successor, Wilford Woodruff, the earnest seeker and ardent millennialist who, at the age of eighty-three, renounced the practice of polygamy on behalf of the church he led.

No less colorful and compelling, the Shakers in the nineteenth century followed and amplified Ann Lee's vision of a world free from the pollution of sexuality and marital relationships. We will observe them creating bustling villages founded on principles of economic and spiritual equality. The powerful and dynamic Lucy Wright will work side by side with the robust Joseph Meacham to direct some of their most ardent and sturdy coreligionists to strike out into the trans-Allegheny West where they will make zealous converts, individuals like Richard McNemar (who will often write as Eleazar Wright) and John Dunlavy, who will become some of the leading Shaker thinkers and writers in the years to come with great success in the wake of the religious revivals that accompanied the Second Great Awakening.

We will witness the charismatic revivals of the Era of Manifestations, a time when the Shaker world was afire with visions and revelations, and we will see how Shaker leaders attempted to tame the manifestations and the women who received them. In the process, we will see how the Shaker and Mormon worlds encountered, changed, and were changed by the larger American culture.

The broad history of religion reveals a similar pattern. Religions are born on the social and cultural margins amid feverish charismatic frenzy, but within a generation or two those passions cool and the previously fluid and inchoate tradition hardens, takes on a discernible and socially acceptable bureaucratic form, and struggles slowly from the margin to the mainstream. Sometimes, however, the movement from the outside to the inside is impeded by external and internal resistance. In some cases, religious traditions adapt to life on the margins with such efficiency that they are loath to surrender the cohesion and energy that outsider status yields in exchange for secure, and perhaps mundane, life in the religious mainstream. This book explores the creativity and innovation that abound on the outer rim of the American religious landscape through the lens of historical sociology.

Shakers and Mormons defined their communal identities over and against the religious, political, economic, and social elements of the larger culture of which they were a part. In that sense, both groups shared an orientation of outsiderhood that played a vital and central role in their ongoing definitions of self. Shakers and Mormons lived in what sociologists call "high tension" with American culture. However, the two groups sought to create and maintain very different kinds of tension. The structures of these boundary maintenance strategies influenced, and were influenced by, the kinds of boundary markers[1] that the groups chose to utilize and dictated the degree to which adjustment of the tension generated by those boundary markers was possible or even desirable. The types of boundary markers chosen also influenced the long-term feasibility of each tension model.

Even among high-tension groups, important differences exist in the qualitative nature of the tension. In other words, groups may be approximately equal in the *amount* of tension they maintain with their cultural environment and may occupy similar spots on the traditional church-sect continuum, but they may be significantly different in terms of the *kind* of tension they maintain.[2]

ONE

The Shakers in the World: Walls and Bridges

Villages are one of the most widely recognized expressions of Shaker life. Despite the massive archival material that the nineteenth-century Shakers left behind, the most dominant traces, at least in terms of connecting with twenty-first-century Americans, are their villages. Any exploration of the creation and maintenance of physical boundaries by the Shakers must deal with these villages. It is fairly simple to note that the Shakers constructed their villages in ways that reflected their theological and social systems. Shaker villages were true symbols in the Geertzian mode inasmuch as they represented "tangible formulations of notions, abstractions from experience fixed in perceptible forms, concrete embodiments of ideas, attitudes, judgments, longings [and] beliefs."[1]

It is obvious that the Shakers built villages that served as boundaries. But why did the Shakers remain heavily involved with the culture outside of their villages, despite their fiery rhetoric of physical separation? It is well known that they conducted commercial business with the world by selling products made and grown within the villages, and they also invited outsiders into their villages. I seek to provide an explanation for this disparity between rhetoric and action based on the idea that the Shakers believed in two "worlds": the one they believed was totally evil, incredibly dangerous, and dominated by supernatural forces, which I call the *culturally postulated world,* and the world that they experienced in their everyday lives, which I call the *experienced world.*

To say that the Shaker community postulated a world is simply to suggest that they held beliefs about the ultimate nature of the world which were unique to their community and which were not shared by persons outside of that community.[2] The Shakers imagined this world more than they discovered it, and they used these postulations to great rhetorical effect. These two worlds, the experienced and the culturally postulated, worked dialectically for the Shakers, and in order to grasp the apparent contradiction between the Shakers' rationale of withdrawal and their practice of engagement with the world, one must understand this dialectic.

How did the Shakers creatively adapt their practices of withdrawal, which they had perfected in the East, to the very different circumstances in the West? One way to understand the importance of the physical boundaries provided by the villages is to look at how the Shakers functioned without them. In the West, between the time they arrived in 1805 and the time that they had bona fide villages built, the Shakers existed in a state that Victor Turner called "spontaneous communitas." How and why did spontaneous communitas differ from the normative communitas that existed in the established Shaker villages? How did this impact the Shaker attempts at physical boundary maintenance?

In the process of making my general arguments, I will offer a critique of Rosabeth Moss Kanter's ideas about the nature of Shaker withdrawal from the world, and I will discuss the ordering of chaos as the chief goal of the Shaker physical boundaries. Furthermore, I will argue that physical boundaries were designed chiefly to counter exogenous, or outside, threats.

Culturally Postulated Worlds and Experienced Worlds: The Dynamics of Selective Withdrawal

During the earliest years of the Shaker movement, the adherents devised no intentionally constructed communal living system. Ann Lee and those who accompanied her from England to New York lived together in Niskeyuna for a time, but their living arrangements were communal only in the sense that they lived in the same settlement, and they lacked any theological rationale for the arrangements. During the epic Shaker missionary journey through New York and New England from May 1781 until September 1783, missionaries encountered a group that would join the Shaker movement en masse, a group that adhered to a sort of communal living arrangement, at least in the sense that they centered their religious lives in one location: the Square House in Harvard, Massachusetts. When Ann Lee and her entourage arrived at Harvard in the early summer of 1781, this group was in a liminal state, having lost their charismatic leader, Shadrach Ireland, a few years before the Shaker missionaries arrived. Ireland's followers were well prepared to hear the Shaker gospel because they already believed in celibacy and perfectionism.[3] The conversion of Ireland's followers represented an important milestone in early Shaker history because it provided a core group of converts already living in a communal setting, which could act as an anchor and, perhaps, as a template for future Shaker communal endeavors after the missionaries left New England and returned to New York.

Lee died shortly after returning from the missionary journey without instituting any official efforts toward communal living. The years immediately following Lee's death were dominated by James Whittaker, a capable and energetic English Shaker, who successfully shepherded the sect through the difficult loss of its charismatic founder. Whittaker died in 1787 without doing much to organize and systematize the rather inchoate ritual and theological legacy left by Lee. That task fell to Whittaker's successor, American Shaker Joseph Meacham. Meacham is properly considered to be the chief architect of Shakerism as it subsequently emerged as a movement of considerable size during the nineteenth century. It is entirely appropriate to view Meacham as the genius behind the Shaker village system.

Writing in 1823, Shakers Calvin Green and Seth Y. Wells described the period before the organization of the village system: "While the believers, as a people, remained in their respective natural families, scattered about in different places, possessing respectively the temporal interest inherited by natural heirship, or acquired by their own labors in their respective callings, there could not be much order among them, excepting the common order of nature." For the believers to move forward in their individual and collective spiritual quests, according to Green and Wells, "it was necessary that they should be brought into nearer connection together, and thereby be enabled to serve God in a more united capacity, as members of the body of Christ in a church relation."[4] By 1828 at least, the Shakers had come to understand the organization of villages as one weapon in the war being waged against the sinful nature of unregenerate humankind, which dominated the culturally postulated world the Shakers imagined around them. Green and Wells repeatedly referred to the "natural" circumstances of life outside of the villages and the distinct lack of any order other than the contemptible "order of nature." The Shakers were constantly admonished to put aside all that was part of the "natural, generative order" and turn instead to the purified and appropriately ordered world provided by the Shaker gospel. The association between chaos, the natural state, and life outside of the ordered Shaker village was not lost on the coreligionists of Green and Wells.[5] In 1818, John Dunlavy, in his response to Reformed theology, argued:

> As clear line of distinction . . . as there is between Christ and the world, so clear is the same line of distinction between his Church and the world. . . . This discriminating line is so manifest so the world can see it, and discern the people of God from the world, and know that they are not of them nor of their order; that they have put off the old man with his deeds, and have forsaken the world for Christ's sake.[6]

As the Shakers gradually incorporated their villages, they drafted covenants which reflected the deep unease expressed by Dunlavy. The language of the covenants from the various villages is generally formulaic and always asserts the principle of "mutual protection" as high on the list of priorities of the villages. Compare, for example, the language used in an 1828 covenant from Sodus Bay, New York, and the text of a similar covenant drawn up at New Lebanon in 1826. The first declared that the Shakers formed themselves "into a united body for our mutual protection, support and improvement."[7] The second document traced the formation of the village system to the search "for the mutual protection, support, comfort and happiness of each other, as brethren and sisters in the gospel." Article 8 of the 1826 covenant drawn up by New Lebanon's East Family amplified the theme of refuge from the world while arguing that life in the village system served to collect and redistribute spiritual power as well as material goods. In the words of the covenant, the "sole object, purpose and design of our uniting in covenant relations, as a family or body of people in gospel union was from the beginning, and still is, faithfully and honestly to receive, improve and diffuse the manifold gifts of God, both of a spiritual and temporal nature."[8] Both spiritual and material communalisms were thus practiced at God's command.

According to the 1827 covenant penned by the leaders of the South Family at Enfield, the decision to organize villages stemmed from "the light and revelation of God," who had ordained the "order and form of a Family and religious Fraternity in gospel relation" as the ideal domestic arrangement. Such a text must be read as an indication that the Shakers saw the creation and maintenance of their villages as primarily a religious, rather than an economic or social, act. The same document argued that the system of communal living enabled the Shakers "to be more useful to ourselves and each other in all things pertaining to our travel in the gospel" and was a prerequisite for the movement if it wished to "receive and more perfectly . . . improve the manifold gifts of God," to which they, as God's chosen people, were entitled.[9]

By the 1840s, the Shakers had begun linking the form of government and social relations within the villages with the situation that prevailed in the garden of Eden before the Fall. An 1841 covenant from Tyringham, Massachusetts, sketched the path from Eden to the fallen world and back again by way of the Shaker village. "When man by transgression lost his primitive rectitude," the introduction to the covenant asserts, "he then lost his true interest, both to God and his fellow creatures." As a result of the Fall, humans became "selfish and partial [and] . . . turned to exalt and build up [themselves] at the expense of the peace and happiness of [the] species, and the loss of union to [their] creator." Moving outward from such a premise, the only way to rectify the problems caused by the Fall of humankind would be to institute a system in which each person subjugated individual will to the greater good of the community "interest." Indeed, according to the Tyringham covenant, "the object and design of the consecrated and united interest of the Church, and the covenant relation of this institution, are to regain the unity of that relation to God and that social order and connection with each other which mankind lost at the beginning." Such perfect government appeared briefly during the time of Christ and the apostles, but the "falling away" of the true religious teachings and practices in antiquity resulted in the "destruction" of the true order. The opening of the final dispensation, presided over by Ann Lee, brought a restoration and "revival . . . of the true nature of order of the church," meaning, of course, the village system and its attendant governmental structures.[10]

Both the Enfield and Tyringham covenants also convey a certain defensiveness, indicating that village life had as its object "mutual support and protection . . . from the attacks of unlawful aggression."[11] The chief purpose of the village was "to gather and protect the Believers."[12] Defensive language points up the very real sense in which the Shakers regarded the outside world, culturally postulated or not, as physically and spiritually dangerous. Shaker Elisha Allen puzzled in a letter to apostate Enoch Pease about why Pease would leave the safety of village life when Pease "knew very well that our fathers and our mothers made their *escape* from that manner of life which you seem so inclined to pursue."[13]

Clearly, then, manuscript evidence from the nineteenth century provides ample evidence that the Shakers saw the creation of physical boundaries, in the form of a village system complete with family units, deacons and deaconesses, elders and eldresses, and trustees, as a rejection of the surrounding culture. Theologically, the Shakers imagined the village as a portal to the pristine prelapsarian world of Eden. The construction and expansion of this system reinforced the notion that the world was a dangerous place and a refuge was required if the believers hoped to find respite from the travails of "Babylon." Scholars have long noted, however, that a chasm existed between rhetoric and practice with regard to the Shakers' retreat away from the world and into their villages.[14]

To see the Shaker village system simply as an attempt to withdraw from the world is to miss a significant, but subtle, facet of this withdrawal. The Shakers were really involved with two "outside worlds." The first was the world that they wrote about in their tracts and railed against in their sermons, a culturally postulated world of absolute danger and absolute evil, filled with devils and sin. It was a world dominated by "enemies" and wickedness. The second world was the mundane one in which the Shakers conducted business and interacted with those outside of their village sphere. In most cases cataloged by the Shakers, however, the threats were amorphous. In other words, the constructed world was generally spoken of in terms of categories, such as enemies, natural man, wickedness, evil, and so forth. The Shakers constantly warned about these categories of danger, but they rarely made reference to specific persons or things. The following description of the postulated world, written in 1848, captures the essence of the Shaker approach.

> Our hearts are pained whenever we look abroad upon the earth, and view . . . the wretchedness and sin, which the love of pleasure, the promptings of vain ambition, the burning lusts of sensuality, the frivolities of empty, fluctuating, foolish fashion, and all the numerous train of evils which covetousness and pride have stamped upon the human family.

The Shakers, according to the author, were "hated of all men [and] all the people of the world," but found respite in the knowledge that they "belong to a better country, even a heavenly [one]."[15]

Several things are important about the way in which this author framed his description of the world. First, the author employed absolutist rhetoric. The Shakers were hated by *all* people, and *wherever* the Shakers looked, they beheld the evil and wickedness which had "stamped" itself upon the entire human family. Only a constructed world, not an experienced one, could possibly be described in such absolutes. Second, the author listed categories of "evils" rather than specific issues or persons. This tendency reflects an attempt to create community identity by fashioning a rhetorical foil against which to contrast the community generating the rhetoric, in this case an absolutely evil realm which was the functional opposite of the Shaker world in every important respect. Finally, the rhetoric of absolute separation flows freely in the text. The Shakers found themselves "so isolated from the world that the world knows us not," according to the letter, and it goes so far as to suggest that the Shakers did not exist in that world at all but, rather, lived in a heavenly "country."

Obviously, the Shakers occupied space and time in the world shared by everyone else. Such rhetoric indicates that the Shakers saw themselves as existing in two worlds simultaneously. With one of these worlds the Shakers were obliged to engage, and they developed appropriate methods for managing their interactions with that world. The other world, their culturally postulated world, could not be tampered with.

Sometimes, these worlds touched. In 1847, during the Irish potato famine, the Shakers at Pleasant Hill, Kentucky, sent "254 bushels of corn and 10 bushels of beans as a donation to Ireland, where many people are starving to death." The author of Pleasant Hill's official record continued by praising "the people of the United States . . . [for their] many praiseworthy efforts to send relief to the suffering people."[16] The same year, a Shaker sister at New Lebanon, New York, received a revelation in which she was told by the spirit of Ann Lee that "the starvation which is in Ireland is the beginning of the heavy judgments which will surely fall upon the wicked inhabitants of the earth."[17] The Shakers thus could somehow believe that the starvation of people in Ireland was both a God-sent punishment for wickedness and a cause worthy of assistance.

The Shakers, of course, would not consent to my characterization of such a world as "imagined." No doubt, they would prefer to call it spiritual or, perhaps, simply unseen. In any case, the overall effect remains the same: this world, imagined or unseen, was evil, and the Shakers did not, for the most part, employ physical boundaries to deal with the threats posed by this world. Such dangers were much too subtle and crafty to be stopped by walls. This is not to say that the Shakers did not use their physical boundaries to create some degree of separation, however.

By the nineteenth century, the Shakers strongly believed that, in order to live their faith fully and successfully, they needed the close support and supervision of their coreligionists. Even when measured against contemporary communitarian groups, the sacrifices demanded by the Shakers were exacting and their rigid lifestyles daunting. Although villages have become synonymous with the Shaker experience, the Shakers did not always center their ecclesiastical and social lives within village walls.[18] In the years between the group's arrival in America and the elevation of Joseph Meacham and Lucy Wright to the highest positions of Shaker leadership, the Shakers did not employ any systematic form of community creation. Their physical boundaries with the world were ad hoc and idiosyncratic, heavily reliant upon local exigencies. Even after the eastern villages began to flourish and thrive, the Shakers in the West found themselves deprived of the security and community-reinforcing power of the village spaces. During these years in the West, the Shakers improvised and found different, and highly effective, means of formulating physical boundaries until fully expressed villages could be constructed.

Rosabeth Moss Kanter and the Myth of Total Separation

Sociologist Rosabeth Moss Kanter argued that the "geographical isolation" of nineteenth-century sectarian groups involved a measurable degree of physical isolation—at least five miles from neighbors, not located on a waterway or a railroad, with few people residing in the community or "in the immediate community area" who were not members—and an "institutionally complete" social structure within the group itself. Kanter defined as *institutionally complete* any group that contained within it everything "necessary for dealing with all aspects of members' lives, obviating the need to leave the group for any organizational services." Kanter placed a heavy emphasis on the physical separation of all of the groups, successful and unsuccessful alike, that she studied, claiming that in each case the groups created a remarkable level of physical separation from others. "Geographical isolation," she argued, "seems to have been a fact of life for nineteenth-century groups."[19]

However, physical isolation as Kanter defined it was the exception rather than the rule in the case of the Shaker villages. Shaker villages were situated in a wide range of physical settings, some with nonbelievers living in relatively close proximity. At least some Shaker villages were located along major roadways, near railroads, and, occasionally, on waterways. South Union, Kentucky, for example, was located on the main road running between two important southern population centers: Louisville, Kentucky, and Nashville, Tennessee.[20] The village at Groveland, New York, sat on a branch of the Erie Railway connecting the village to Rochester. The Shirley, Massachusetts, village was located within two miles of a station of the Fitchburg Railroad line.[21] In nearly every case, the Shaker villages were situated on accessible thoroughfares. The Shakers did not want their villages to be difficult to find.

More important than the basic geographic facts, however, is the reality that some of Kanter's terms are sufficiently ambiguous that, when applied in the Shaker context, they present some significant difficulties. What, for example, does Kanter mean by "member"? In the Shaker case, as discussed at length below, there existed a liminal phase during which persons interested in embracing Shakerism were allowed to practice some, but not all, of the Shaker principles in an effort to decide if they were fit for full fellowship. Membership in the Shaker order, unlike many of the other groups that Kanter studied, is appropriately imagined as a continuum rather than as a binary prospect which only acknowledges the dualistic categories of member/nonmember. The continuum model of membership thus complicates Kanter's theories regarding the presence of outsiders among the group.

Further complicating the issue is Kanter's notion of "organizational services." If this is broad enough to include the generation of capital in the form of income from the world, then the Shakers certainly were not institutionally complete. As Stein and others have observed, the Shakers participated rather vigorously in the burgeoning market revolution of Jacksonian America. Complete economic separation was simply "out of the question."[22] Precisely the same case may be made for physical separation in general. Kanter's arguments notwithstanding, a complete understanding of nineteenth-century Shakerism demands that the physical boundaries employed by the Shakers be understood as a penumbra rather than a wall.[23]

The Shakers did not maintain solid and sure physical separation from the world. Instead, the Shakers developed a sophisticated and ritualized system for preserving the sanctity of their villages that did not rely on absolute physical withdrawal. While maintaining a surprisingly high level of social, intellectual, and economic intercourse with the broader American culture, the Shakers managed to generate an efficient level of specific separation.

Spectators and Performers: Shakers and Outsiders in the Village World

Shakers liked to sing that they were "bound for full salvation / with world and flesh I'm done / I'll keep you at a distance / to die it is your doom / I'll never shed a tear for you but lay you in your tomb."[24] However, as Stein notes, "From the earliest times they [the Shakers] depended on interaction and trading with the world."[25] Shaker public meetings frequently drew large numbers of visitors. The Shakers generated a great deal of curiosity among ordinary Americans as well as those of a somewhat loftier mien, including James Fenimore Cooper and Friedrich Engels. Peter Pease, an early Shaker pioneer in the West, noted that as early as 1806, less than a year after the Shakers brought their message to the

Ohio Valley, there were "very many spectators to our meeting."[26] At the larger villages in the East, scores of "spectators" came to observe the Shakers' worship. During a snowy February 1830, Rufus Bishop noted with some satisfaction that 115 sleigh-loads of visitors made an appearance at New Lebanon, New York. In warmer weather, the spectators abandoned sleighs for "four-horse carriages," 13 of which "stopped [at New Lebanon] during the time of worship" in August 1830.[27] Relatives of the Shakers occasionally came to visit, as did travelers and others who were interested in hearing about the Shaker gospel or who simply needed lodging. Shaker diaries are replete with references to the steady stream of such persons who came to call at the various villages. A few entries from Bishop's journal should suffice to document this phenomenon. For example, on 8 April 1830, two Shaker men had "nephews to see them" at the village. Two days later, "a man and a woman from Bedford [came to the Second Family] to stay over Sabbath [and] Soon after [that] a man and two women from Black River called at our office and stayed" for an unspecified period of time.[28] In an 1835 entry, Bishop noted that a nonbeliever named Abial Wood, who "came to get information about the believers," was permitted to "lodge at the office [over] night."[29]

Hospitably accommodating visitors who happened upon the villages was one thing, but the Shakers went beyond the mere toleration of outsiders. The Shakers recognized that outsiders, if properly managed, could serve useful purposes. Betsy Bates, another resident of New Lebanon, noted in her journal that the Shaker leaders were concerned that the believers might not be making a sufficiently impressive show for their spectators. On 18 August 1833, Bates wrote that "the ministry spoke to the Elders in the society and want they should speak to there [sic] families to try and strengthen and build up the public speaking [skills] to the world," something that they felt particular urgency about "at this season of the year when their [sic] is so many of the world attends to the public meeting."[30]

Such deep concern with the opinion of outsiders certainly complicates the simplistic understanding of Shakers, which many believers themselves perpetuated, as absolutely withdrawn. Bates's journal entry points up one beneficial contribution yielded by the presence of outsiders: the reinforcement of Shaker identity through performance. Under the gaze of alien eyes, Shakers tended to act more like "ideal Shakers."

In a sense, by inviting outsiders into a carefully selected slate of Shaker meetings, Shaker leaders were setting the stage for a performance with the dual audiences of the outsiders and the Shakers themselves.[31] In other words, the Shakers were reminding themselves, as well as their spectators, how true Shakers ought to behave, by putting on an ideal performance that would have been impossible without the catalytic spark provided by the outsiders. The more frequently such performances were enacted, the more deeply the image of the ideal Shaker was inscribed into the consciousness of the players. Little wonder that the Shaker leadership sought to put the best possible face on these performances.

In addition to performing for visitors, the Shakers took the time to observe their visitors. Frequently, the outsiders became the objects of moral lessons. The Shakers contrasted the sad moral state of the nonbelievers with their own superior condition. During the summer of 1832, the first of three major nineteenth-century cholera pandemics struck the United States and threatened to paralyze Albany, New York, and the surrounding areas. Rufus Bishop spent some time at the Watervliet village during that period and noted:

> Many of the respectable inhabitants of Albany press hard to board among us—some even plead for a shelter under some of our wood houses, and say that money is no object. They generally seem to be struck with terror, believing that the *Cholera* is the just judgment of God for the sins of the world. Many of them think and say that the Shakers will not have it, and consider themselves safe among us.[32]

Bishop continued to note the arrival of potential refugees, who begged for shelter from "the judgments that are daily and hourly sweeping their neighbors, unprepared, into eternity."[33] On 12 July, Bishop confided to his journal that "Eliza Wicks died with cholera this forenoon in or near Troy," adding with grim satisfaction that "[s]he lately went to the world."[34] Such a sentiment was actually quite common among most classes in the United States. Historian of science Charles E. Rosenberg noted that, in 1832, "to die of cholera was to die in suspicious circumstances," and for the Shakers the correlation between a sinful life and the cholera pandemic was obvious.[35] Bishop's entries reflect another dimension of the usefulness of the presence of the worldly among the believers. At a time of acute crisis, Bishop was able to note the ineffectiveness of the typical trappings of worldly power to deflect the judgments of God. Consider, for example, Bishop's apparent interest in reporting that the refugees from the cholera offered to pay anything for shelter among the Shakers. Even the rich, apparently, were powerless in the face of God's wrath.

Additionally, Bishop and other Shaker leaders communicated another important message to their followers: when it really counted, the Shakers were the ones with the power. Such an inversion of the typical sense of fear and danger that the Shakers expressed about the world at large held obvious appeals for the Shakers, and the presence of needy outsiders provided Bishop and others with confirmation of Shaker superiority.

Spirit, Matter, and the Experienced World

Although it is clear that intrusions upon the Shaker enclaves were common, even everyday, occurrences, despite the fiery Shaker rhetoric of separation, scholars are left to explain the disparity between Shaker rhetoric and Shaker practice. It is extremely unlikely that the Shakers were insincere in their rhetoric and simply pretended to withdraw from the world. Perhaps the Shakers attempted to sever ties with the world but found the reality of that prospect too daunting, so they made accommodations when necessary. Such a theory has the advantage of meshing nicely with the argument, common since at least the time of Max Weber, that sectarian religious groups almost always seek accommodation with the world in order to survive. Priscilla J. Brewer argued that the Shakers adhered to a strict separation from the world early on, but under the leadership of Lucy Wright entered into a "gradual rapprochement with the World." Brewer traced a continuum of Shaker involvement with the world and argued that, by 1820, the Shakers "had more difficulty living in, but not for the world."[36] Suzanne R. Thurman suggested that Shaker "attempts to remove themselves from the world" were ultimately unsuccessful because "they shared many beliefs and attitudes with their non-Shaker neighbors, which influenced their ideas of social organization and communalism."[37] Each theory has merit, and each contributes to our understanding of this complex dilemma. The Shakers did become increasingly involved with commercial and other ventures as the nineteenth century wore on, as Brewer asserted. Also, as Thurman noted, the Shakers who came into the fold did not come in as blank slates; they carried with them lifetimes of social and psychological conditioning, some of which could be adjusted and some of which was permanent. Perhaps, however, we may benefit from looking at just exactly what the Shakers meant when they talked about the "world."

In addition to the culturally postulated world discussed above, the Shakers also dealt with the prosaic world as they actually found it and experienced it.[38] The Shakers engaged with the "commonsense" world legally, socially, economically, and, occasionally, politically. In the concrete world, the Shakers dealt with individual persons and institutions, some of which they liked and others of which they found lacking, but none of which received the categorical rejection common in Shaker rhetoric.

It is this commonsense world that the Shakers managed with their physical boundaries and that they allowed into their villages under tightly controlled circumstances. The Shakers viewed the spiritual worlds within their villages as absolutely self-contained by virtue of their sacred and sanctified nature. The Shakers believed that some of their villages were designated as settling places by supernatural powers. In 1847, for example, a Watervliet resident remembered that Ann Lee had taken up residence in one cabin, but she was overcome by "a feeling to move into the little cabin . . . standing where the Church now stands."[39]

Following van der Leeuw's line of reasoning, one may argue that the Shakers considered their village spaces to be consecrated and spiritually removed in an absolute way from the culturally postulated world of evil while conceding that they were very much part of the encountered world around them. Shakers could thus sell seeds and brooms to nonbelievers and even contract with outsiders to help them build their villages, but by maintaining high levels of stringency for initiation into the *spiritual* communion of the group, they could believe that their world had not been compromised. The spiritual power of the Shaker gospel would naturally protect the group from those who sought to penetrate the religious sphere.

Sacralizing the Profane: Shaker Villages and the Ordering of Outsiders

The Shakers sought to ameliorate the permeability of their physical surroundings by working hard to ensure that they met outsiders, be they visitors, workers, or anyone else, on the Shakers' terms. The Shakers imposed "order" onto the persons, objects, and ideas that came within their physical sphere and in so doing enacted a form of sanctification on the profane intruders. Because these outsiders came from the experienced world rather than the culturally postulated one, they could be managed. As will be discussed below, pollutions from the latter could not be ordered or sacralized; they had to be completely purged.

The well-documented Shaker fixation on order also implies a deep fear of chaos.[40] Historian of religion Jonathan Z. Smith suggested that chaos is "opposed to order . . . [and] threatens the paradigms and archetypes [of order] but . . . is, nevertheless, profoundly necessary."[41] Chaos is necessary because it allows religious communities to focus on ordering their worlds, a process that generates creativity in theology, ritual, and, in the case of the Shakers, the creation and regulation of physical spaces. As Smith correctly argued, the Old Testament is shot through with the notion that sacred space is best understood "as an enclave, a strategic hamlet walled against the demonic forces of evil and chaos." It is therefore no surprise that the Shakers adopted this biblical idea as their own, but with an interesting twist.[42] Faced with the dilemma of carving out an impossible, absolute physical separation, the Shakers insisted on ordering, and thus sanctifying, temporarily to be sure, everything that came within the walls of their villages. Shaker villages functioned in much the same way that, according to Smith, ancient Jerusalem functioned for the Jews: "as an enclave against the forces of chaos."[43]

To the extent that chaos could be ordered, the Shakers could temporarily sanctify and purify profane people and things and thus allow their physical boundaries to be permeable. Only objects from the experienced world, rather than the imagined world of absolute evil, could be so sanctified, ordered, and arranged. The Shakers set about to order intruders in a variety of ways. Most basically, each village ministry was instructed to keep a close watch on what and who came within its walls. Richard Mc-Nemar noted in his journal in 1827 that "nothing of importance should be undertaken without the full and free comment and union of the ministry, otherwise evil may be brought into the Church unawares and such evil too as will be difficult to purge out."[44] The local ministries had responsibility for filtering out persons, products, and ideas that could be deleterious to the spiritual well-being of the villagers.

The importation of ideas obviously presented difficulties, but attempts were made to curb unauthorized ideas through the control of reading material. As early as 1821, the Central Ministry forbade the reading of newspapers without "the Elders' permission" and outlawed the reading or mailing of letters that had not first been scrutinized by the village leadership.[45] Village leaders sometimes found themselves behind the curve of new ideas and were thus faced with ridding their realms of unauthorized idea-bearing materials. In the mid-1820s, when Union Village had come into its own as a full-fledged Shaker outpost, village leader David Darrow held a private meeting with Richard McNemar in which he lamented the "new ideas" circulating in the village by which "Satan transformed" the minds of many of the young believers.[46] Darrow railed against the "learned beasts," who spent their time "running into their speculations," and demanded that the village leaders "keep the gospel in its simplicity and purity, free from all such trash."[47] The following month, Darrow became vexed by theological controversies, again chiefly among young believers, regarding the cause of the Fall of Adam and Eve and the "miraculous conception of the child Jesus." Darrow called a "council of elders" and "declared [that] those new ideas were totally subversive to the testimony, [and] that if such were true, the testimony must be false." In order to parry this subversive threat, Darrow ordered that "a large collection of books of various kinds [be] publicly committed to the flames."[48]

Although Darrow's book burning was apparently spontaneous and limited, by the 1830s the ministry at New Lebanon introduced a systematic censorship program designed to control the kinds of books that believers were permitted to own. In January 1834, Betsy Bates noted, "It is felt by our ministry to be the gift for our family to give up all books, that are not suitable to be in our retiring rooms, to have them all collected together, so as to form a little family library, and to have someone take care of it, so that all can be accommodated." Shakers were to turn everything over to the new village librarian except for Bibles, books "published by Believers," dictionaries, and schoolbooks.[49] While Bates's account seems innocuous enough, her contemporary Aaron Bill added a few details that Bates chose to omit. According to Bill, the Shakers were to turn all of their books over to Seth Y. Wells, who would "judge" the propriety of the individual volumes. Upon completing his inspection, Wells returned "all such as school books to their owners" and "the rest . . . to the charge" of the librarians, except, that is, for those books Wells deemed totally inappropriate, which, according to Bill, Wells burned.[50]

The public burning of books within the Shaker villages served two purposes. First, and most obviously, the book burnings physically destroyed the objects which carried the polluting ideas. More important, however, the book burnings represented a ritual expression of the Shaker attitude toward the world. Truth was not something to be debated and haggled over in the marketplace of ideas, represented most explicitly by books, but rather it was something to be revealed by God to those in whom God had vested revelatory authority and to be obeyed by everyone else.

The Shakers surrounded themselves with a purifying fire strong enough to keep them free not only from unauthorized books, but also from the subversive ideas that such books carried.[51] Such purification could never be total, of course, but the Shaker leadership sent a clear message regarding who controlled access to ideas. In the realm of ideas and books, the culturally postulated and experienced worlds merged. The subversive ideas in the books were part of the evil, unseen world, while the books themselves came from the experienced world. Thus, the Shakers used a mixed strategy of ordering, through the careful selection and review of appropriate titles, and purging, through the book pyres, to meet this unique dual threat.

In addition to ideas, persons who entered the village confines for any reason were subject to Shaker scrutiny. Visitors who came to see worship services were kept in carefully demarcated spaces and were only allowed to see carefully selected segments of Shaker life and worship. The Shakers held closed worship meetings to which the public was not admitted. Also, when visitors stayed with the Shakers, they were typically received at and lodged in the "office." For the Shakers, the office was the place where dealings with the profane world were accomplished. The office was the seat of all business transactions, for example. In the case of lodgers, the office served as a filter; and since the office was looked upon as a sort of bridge to the profane world anyway, sequestering visitors there mitigated their influence throughout the rest of the village.

One graphic example of the Shaker effort to order intruders is the many posters hung in the offices and public areas of the villages, notifying visitors from the world that certain rules would apply within. Seven "rules for visitors" were prominently displayed, "in consequence of the increasing amount of company to which we are at all times subject." The first rule informed visitors that there was no "public house" within the Shaker village. The second decreed that "those who call to see their friends or relatives are to visit them at the Office, and [are] not to go elsewhere, except by permission of those in care at the office." Rule 3 indicated that visitors residing near the village should stay no more than "a few hours," while those whose homes were "at a great distance" would be allowed to stay "from one to four days," as determined by the Shaker leadership. The fourth rule indicated that visitors were to take breakfast with the believers at 6:30 in the summer and 7:30 in the winter. Rule 5 reminded visitors that the Shakers "dislike the wasteful habit of leaving food on the plate," adding that "no vice is with us the less ridiculous for being in fashion." The penultimate rule dealt with married couples visiting at the village, informing them that "each sex occup[ies] separate sleeping apartments," and that this particular rule would "not be departed from under any circumstances." Finally, rule 7 indicated that the Shakers were not a charity organization and that "strangers calling for meals or lodging are expected to pay if accommodated."[52]

While spare in words, this "notice" provides a wealth of clues about the practicalities of the Shakers' retreat from the physical presence of the outside world. First, it dramatically demonstrates the difference between the imagined world and the experienced world. The document does not indicate that the Shakers believed that the persons visiting were evil, only that they were confused and apt to engage in chaotic behavior if not properly supervised. For example, the notice indicates that the families and friends of Shakers visited often enough to require a rule governing the duration of such visits. The presence of outsiders was thus apparently a fairly regular occurrence, something one would not expect from a group that truly sought to insulate itself physically from the larger environment. Furthermore, the Shakers were accommodating enough to provide sleeping quarters for visitors of both sexes, although those who were married were required to practice temporary celibacy. Visitors, we learn, were permitted to eat at the same table as the Shakers, provided they followed the rules that the Shakers themselves followed.

At the Shaker village in Canterbury, New Hampshire, in the early nineteenth century, outsiders joining the Shakers for meals were given a sheet of paper on which was printed a poem by Hannah Bronson, a member of the Canterbury community. Entitled "Table Monitor," the poem couched in quaint verse the Shaker mandate that guests take only what they intended to eat and admonished them not to mix different parts of the meal together.[53]

Such efforts as those exemplified by the poster and "Table Monitor" demonstrate the sophistication with which the Shakers viewed their situation: they were not trying to cut off the physical presence of the experienced world and its inhabitants. Rather, by imposing sacred order upon the outsiders, they were making every effort to neutralize the potentially negative effects that the physical presence of outsiders might pose to the spiritual world that the Shakers believed dwelled within the physical confines of their villages.

The 1821 version of the society's Millennial Laws, a code designed to provide easily accessible and explicit guidance for the believers, similarly provides a window into the Shaker view of physical separation from the world. Like the visitors discussed above, physical objects coming into the villages through trade, including "new fashions, in manufacture, clothing, or wares of any kind," could only be accepted with "the sanction of the Ministry, thru the medium of the Elders of each family." Again, it is apparent that the Shakers did not seek to cut themselves off from the world completely, but they did seek to sanctify the worldly influences that came into their physical spaces by bringing them under Shaker order.

The Millennial Laws also gave directions about how Shakers should act when leaving the confines of the villages. In some ways, it is remarkable that Shakers were allowed into the world at all. If the Shakers truly sought complete withdrawal from the physical world, one would not expect to find nearly as many excursions into it as the manuscript materials reveal. The 1821 edition of the laws decreed that it was "contrary to order" for Shakers to "go out of the door-yard after evening meeting," "to go out among the world," "to shake hands with the world, unless they first tender their hand," or "to take your place in meeting after you have been out among the world."

In 1845, the church revised and reissued the Millennial Laws, which no longer strictly prohibited interaction with the world, but rather emphasized remaining spiritually and mentally separate while among nonbelievers. The laws limited the amount of time that Shakers could spend away from the villages on church business to four weeks at a time and decreed that, when away from the villages, Shakers must be accompanied by at least two deacons or trustees. Shakers could not "blend with the wicked," which was defined as "uniting in unnecessary conversation, jesting and joking, talking upon politics with them, or disputing or enquiring into things which will serve to draw your sense from the pure way of God." Shaker journals and daybooks from all geographic locations and throughout the nineteenth century bear witness to the peripatetic nature of Shaker life.

Believers frequently ventured beyond the walls of their own villages in search of supplies, to peddle wares, to visit with other communities of believers, to deal with legal and political issues involving the society, to visit sick relatives, and for a variety of other reasons. The key was for the Shakers to avoid disorderly intercourse with those they encountered. Not surprisingly, however, Shakers had to be symbolically reabsorbed into the community by engaging with Shaker leadership upon their return. According to the 1821 Millennial Laws:

> Whenever any member of the family go out and stay overnight, or longer, when they return they must see the Elders before they take their places in the family; and give an account of their journey as it respects their protection and prosperity while absent; and then they may take their places in the family; but they must take their places behind all in the spiritual worship of God, until the Elders think proper to let them come into their ranks again.[54]

These reentry interviews would have served a variety of purposes, one of which was obviously to emphasize the potential contagion of the world and to reinforce the source of cleansing: the Shaker leadership. As with the ordering of visitors, the Shakers who had been into the world for any substantial period had to be resanctified through the agency of their "visible leads," and in so doing they were reordered and harmonized—ready to be reabsorbed into their physical and spiritual surroundings.

Another important point is that two types of disruption, endogenous and exogenous, hampered the Shaker attempts at withdrawal. Each type dictated the creation of distinct classes of boundaries. *Endogenous disruption* occurred when a member in full fellowship with the group defected. Physical boundaries could do little to defend against endogenous threats, and these had to be managed with boundary devices, which I will address in another chapter. *Exogenous disruption,* on the other hand, involved people, objects, or ideas from the outside penetrating the internal world of the Shakers. Physical boundaries acted to deflect or, more commonly, to neutralize, exogenous threats. The Shakers were actually quite successful in defending against exogenous disruption and less adept at parrying the blows inflicted by the more complex problem posed by endogenous disruption. The Shaker rhetoric of withdrawal must therefore be measured with an eye toward the complexities and subtleties of the various kinds of threats the Shakers perceived around them.

One must also keep in mind that Shakers were firm believers in the inherent corruption of any material things, a principle that has been largely distorted through an ironic and obsessive fascination with the material culture of the Shakers. The Shakers themselves, however, in terms of their attitudes toward physical human bodies and toward their physical communities, emphasized the primacy of the spiritual component. John Dunlavy, in his 1818 treatise on Shaker theology, declared, "God is Spirit; and when man fell from God, he fell from Spirit into flesh; hence the flesh is considered as being in opposition to the Spirit. God is love, when man fell from God, he fell from love into lust."[55] In the Shaker world view, then, God was spirit and love while the material world was dominated by flesh and lust.

Shakers strongly believed that the material world was separate from and inferior to its spiritual counterpart. Frederick W. Evans, a self-proclaimed "infidel and materialist" before his conversion to the Shaker gospel, clearly expressed the Shaker view on material versus spiritual worlds in his autobiography. He wrote, "I came to a conception of the inner world as being the most substantial, and of the inner man as being the real man; the outward world being only the shadow of the invisible world of causation."[56] Shakers were always heavily involved in terrestrial pursuits and were attuned to the practical realities of nineteenth-century economic life. However, Shaker theological attitudes about the ultimate purpose of life and the relationship between matter and spirit suggest that physical boundaries were symbolic of spiritual boundaries, and although the Shakers sought to separate themselves from the pernicious influences of the world through a degree of physical separation, this was the least important, and therefore the most easily penetrated, barrier that the Shakers erected.

The limitations on the outsiders within the physical confines of the Shaker villages are not nearly as important as the strength of the other types of boundaries discussed here. Particularly important is the distinction, which neither Kanter nor Brewer emphasizes, between those who were admitted, by virtue of their entering the joint-interest system, into the spiritual Shaker village and those who were merely physically present within the walls of the Shaker villages. The former group posed a major problem if they lost their sense of commitment because they were part of the "real" community. The most effective way to combat endogenous disruption in the form of apostasy was to ensure, to the greatest extent possible, that only low-risk individuals were admitted into full fellowship. The Shakers did this through an important boundary device called the gathering order, which emerged very early in the development of the Shaker village system.

Anthropologist Victor Turner's work on what he calls communitas enriches our understanding of this point. *Communitas* is a slippery term that Turner employs in a variety of contexts, but in its most basic form it refers to "a relationship between concrete, historical, idiosyncratic individuals" who, at least at first, "are not segmentalized into roles and statuses but confront one another" directly and immediately.[57] Nineteenth-century Shakers in the established eastern villages, of course, were not living in this unstructured communitas that Turner labels "spontaneous" or "existential." Turner, however, argues that communitas "soon develops a structure, in which free relationships between individuals become converted into norm-governed relationships between social personae."[58] In this type of "normative" communitas, "the existential communitas is organized into a perduring social system" in order to "mobilize and organize resources . . . [and establish] social control among the members of the group in question." Although internally structured, a system of normative communitas functions outside of the general societal power structures and thus remains in a liminal state characterized by a tendency to "partial[ly] withdraw from participation in the structural relations of the world, which is, in any case, conceived of as a sort of permanent 'disaster area.'"[59] In Turnerian terms, the Shakers over time created a normative communitas which withdrew substantially from the structures of a society that, on the culturally postulated level, the Shakers did indeed believe to be beyond redemption, but with which they remained engaged on a limited and potentially controllable basis—with individuals and smaller units of society.

Turner's work also provides an important lens for interpreting the complexities of the Shaker struggles with physical boundaries as the Shakers encountered divergent patterns in the larger culture in which they operated. As they expanded and moved beyond their eastern strongholds, where the physical and social elements of the Shaker religious system were fully constituted within a context of normative communitas, the Shakers found themselves in the West, where their changed cultural surroundings called for physical boundaries to be created in the context of existential communitas.

Settled Villages and the Gathering Order

Thus far, I have attempted to demonstrate the complexities and subtleties embedded in the creation and maintenance of a physical withdrawal from the world. The remainder of this chapter deals with the ways in which these complex strategies of withdrawal were applied by the Shakers in two distinct settings: settled villages and frontier outposts.

Joseph Meacham began by organizing a single village in New York called New Lebanon. The records of the village note that in 1788 a "gathering of believers" was undertaken under the direction of Meacham and Lucy Wright. Meacham and Wright immediately sought to establish "order in the church, by appointing Elders and Deacons for the support and maintenance of the spiritual and temporal concerns of the church."[60] Meacham and Wright did not wait long after organizing this first village before deciding to initiate "a foundation for the dispensation of order to all the Societies of Believers in the Land." Establishing order among the various pockets of loosely organized converts throughout the eastern United States involved sending trusted members of the New

Lebanon community out to take charge of village construction. In 1790, for example, "Calvin Harlow and Sarah Harrison were appointed by the ministry and sent from the Church at New Lebanon to take the ministerial charge of the people at Hancock, Enfield, and Tyringham." In 1791, Eleazer Rand and Hannah Kendal were sent to do the same thing at Harvard and Shirley in Massachusetts, and the next year Timothy Hubbard and Anna Methewson were sent to Watervliet, New York. Similar appointments followed to Canterbury, New Hampshire, and in 1793 to what was then called Sabbath-day Pond (later Sabbath-day Lake) in the district of Maine.[61]

New Lebanon remained the nerve center of Shakerism, its headquarters and home of the Central Ministry throughout the period under consideration. Although the individual villages enjoyed a fair amount of autonomy in certain spheres, the hub of New Lebanon was never far from the thoughts of the leadership in the villages. The church covenant from Harvard explicitly stated that New Lebanon was then and would "remain as the center of union to all who are in gospel relation and communion with the society."[62] On an 1832 journey to Sodus Bay, New York, Seth Y. Wells noted that, during a closed meeting of believers, one of the elders there "endeavored to impress the minds of the Believers with a sense of the necessity of feeling their faith joined to the center of union [New Lebanon] where the gift of their protection and blessing centered and from whence all of their blessings and their spiritual strength and protection proceeded." Whether the Shakers needed to be "impressed" with this information because they were recalcitrant in some way, or simply because Wells felt that important principles bore repeating, is not clear from the context of Wells's journal. Whatever the reason for the reminder, Wells noted approvingly that, for the Shakers at Sodus Bay, "New Lebanon is the fountain to which they look for strength and protection."[63] It is not inconceivable that the elder mentioned, through fear or favor currying, simply wanted to impress the autocratic Wells, and there is no question that the central authorities were frequently criticized and occasionally ignored by village leaders. The fact remained, however, that, in matters of importance, the Central Ministry wielded considerable power. Codifying a reality that had existed for many years among the local villages, in 1860 the Central Ministry declared that "those rules and regulations relative to health, economy, and such as are the attendants of local circumstances, in the social connections of society, are subject to such modifications, amendments, or repeals, as circumstances require."[64]

By allowing for some play in the joints of the Shaker village system, the Central Ministry avoided having to become bogged down in local issues while providing the village ministries with the opportunity to respond efficiently to non-essential contingencies that might arise in their particular localities. The establishment of a thriving western Shakerism after 1805 saw the introduction of a regional western headquarters and an important publishing hub at Union Village in Ohio, but New Lebanon maintained primacy even then, although many western Shakers were less than delighted with the arrangement.

Each village was governed by an elder and an eldress, who presided over all aspects of village life, with special emphasis on the spiritual elements. A deacon and a deaconess were also appointed, and they were charged with tending to the temporal dimensions of life in the village. Deacons and deaconesses held the real and personal property of all Shakers who came to the village. In 1801, the Shakers at Watervliet, followed by other villages, emended their covenant to provide "a more permanent security," and from that point on "the property was secured to the Society and held by the Deacons, in trust only, who were endowed with authority to act as agents, for the time being, in the name and behalf of the Society."[65]

The government of the Shaker order, from the general level to the local villages, was meant as a reaction to, and a critique of, the governments of the world, including the government of the United States. In the early nineteenth century, Wells penned an important statement illustrating the deep disdain Shakers held for the governments of the world and emphasizing the folly of vesting governmental powers in "the people." According to Wells:

> God, in his providence, for wise purpose no doubt, has permitted all
> earthly governments, in some way or manner, to emanate from the people
> —perhaps to let the people see, in the end, their own inability to govern
> themselves and their fellow creatures without divine assistance. And after
> practicing every kind of human government they could devise, they have
> pitched upon a representative democracy as the most equitable and the
> best that human wisdom could devise, and in which public rulers are

chosen by the sufferages [*sic*] of the people. The result is obviously a high flaming party spirit; constantly contending and striving for the preeminence. This is the natural tendency of human nature unrestrained by Divine wisdom.[66]

The political culture of the nineteenth-century United States, a culture aptly described by two historians of the period as a "tumultuous and raucous democracy," provided ample evidence for the Shakers of the chaotic failure of the American political experiment.[67] Government instituted by God, by contrast, "has always been clear and obvious to the true and faithful subjects to it" and remained "uncontaminated by human devices." The very fact that a person opposed Shaker governmental forms indicated that such an individual was not among the "true and faithful." It is also important to note the language of contamination that Wells invokes. True to Shaker form, the chaotic and the disorderly were understood as fundamentally unclean, and the chaotic political system of the world had to be replaced by an orderly and sanctified godly government.

One of the most brilliant elements of the Shaker village plan was the segregation of members into communal "families" according to their experience, maturity, and longevity in the movement. The leading family, the group from which the leading elder and eldress of the village were selected, was typically referred to as the Church Family. Other families were organized according to their experience in the Shaker faith, and each typically lived in its own dwelling house. Particularly important for the purposes of this book is the novitiate order, which served as the ecclesiastical home for new converts. Green and Wells described the process by which individuals began their journey into full-fledged Shaker fellowship by suggesting that "[new members] should prove themselves in that situation, for a suitable length of time, in order to confirm their faith by experimental obedience, before they can be admitted as members of the society in a united capacity."[68] The physical boundary created by the Shakers in the form of the village was given flexibility because the community could quarantine new converts until they had been tested and had demonstrated their commitment to the movement.

Every communal group faces the real threat of the "free-rider" problem. In a context in which goods are shared equally, an incentive to join is created for those who bring the least to the communal effort and who stand to gain the most from the community. Simultaneously, a disincentive is generated for persons of means, who stand to lose more than they will take away.[69] By creating a novitiate order, the Shakers created a semi-permeable boundary, a sort of vestibule or filter that helped to mitigate the free-rider problem and thus maintain a relatively high average level of commitment among the members in full fellowship. The gathering order was the only attempt to mitigate endogenous disruption through the application of a physical boundary maintenance device. When Kentucky passed a law that allowed apostates to sue the society for property and funds consecrated to the group, the Shakers at Pleasant Hill issued a "revision and confirmation of the social compact" of the group.

> This effort to clarify the Shaker system for outsiders pointed out that no one [is] allowed to consecrate or bestow property to the Society in any manner that would deprive creditors or natural heirs, or to amalgamate his property and services with the consecrated interest of the Church, until he has had sufficient time and opportunity in a junior order to become acquainted with the rules, manners, and general orders of the church.

Pleasant Hill leaders went on to reiterate the process by which members of the gathering order might participate in a limited form of joint interest: at the time an individual joined the order, that person's goods were inventoried and assessed a value. If "any member of such family, [chose] to remove and separate from said family, [he or she] shall be entitled to all money and property which he or she deposited."[70]

As early as 1812, the covenant at Union Village, Ohio, held that "this important relation [full participation in joint interest] cannot be immediately entered into by any, but has to be attained by a preparatory work which must require some time to be accomplished." Those individuals wishing to join the believers had "the privilege of proving their faith and love by coming into a family relation, which may be dissolved at any time without damage." Full membership would only be granted after "sufficient trial and proof [had] been made."[71]

The process of boundary creation was thus not only a matter of separating the church from the world, but also one of separating the clean from the unclean within the society itself. Eldress Rachel Spencer of New Lebanon wrote to Eldress Ruth Farrington at Union Village, Ohio, at a time when many were joining themselves to the western villages. Spencer sounded a note of caution, reminding Farrington:

> [W]hen the gospel net is spread it gathers in all, both good and bad, and then there has to be a separation between the precious and the vile. For none can abide but those who are faithful and honest hearted. . . . Some appear to be very good Believers, and a great many more have pretended that are after nothing but the loaves and fishes. But when they begin to feel the burning truth, they fall off like withered branches.[72]

The Shakers were clearly not naive about the motives harbored by many who sought refuge in their villages. Some scholars, however, have failed to detect the sophistication of the Shaker novitiate system as a boundary device. John E. Murray, for example, argued that the Shakers, "[r]ather than screen out prospective members who might be less productive . . . preferred to make membership as open as possible, to extend potential salvation to the greatest number of people."[73] But this fails to address the fact that the Shakers were actively and constantly engaged in a rigorous filtering process. Like many exclusive religious communities, the Shakers wielded a two-edged sword that consisted, on one side, of their stated mandate to spread God's truth to as many as would listen and, on the other side, of the high threshold of commitment and sacrifice that formed the core of Shaker communal identity. Murray sees only the former and can thus make the assertion that the "greater goal for [the Shakers], for religious reasons, was to maximize the number of members."[74] The Shakers did not make a practice of sacrificing quality for quantity when it came to admitting persons into the full-fledged Shaker order. Additionally, it is not at all the case that Shakers viewed their success as being contingent upon the number of converts they attracted. The Shakers did not expect many individuals to slough off sin and take up the Shaker cross. Instead, the Shakers saw their relatively small numbers as evidence of the godliness of their message.

For example, in an 1805 letter from David Darrow and John Meacham, who were struggling to plant the Shaker gospel in the West, to the Central Ministry at New Lebanon, the concerned elders wrote, "The work of God goes on here; those that have set out in the Gospel continue to increase both in power and understanding," adding, almost as an afterthought, that "they also gradually increase in numbers."[75] An 1827 diary entry by Richard McNemar, another western leader, addressed the issue head-on: "An increase implies neither change nor addition," but "[i]t is to be more and more reconciled to the order . . . [and] more perfect in all things as we have been taught."[76] Similarly, Elder William Deming from Pittsfield, Massachusetts, in an 1832 letter to Elder Benjamin S. Youngs, who was then residing in the village at South Union, Kentucky, acknowledged that "our increase and prosperity in the work of the gospel is of all things the most important to all of us," and he cheerfully related that "the gospel work is increasing in this place." Reading further, however, it becomes clear that Deming was emphatically *not* gauging this success in terms of numerical increase: "Not that I would be understood [to say that] there is a great gathering of Young Believers, for the increase in numbers is slow and gradual. But the real work of the gospel: purity, life, and love to the way of God does increase and I believe ever will to the downfall of every thing that is contrary to God and godliness."[77] Shakers certainly desired to convert as many people as possible, but they wanted true converts who could be trusted with full membership.

Liminal Individuals and Shaker Physical
Boundary Maintenance: A Case Study

An interesting correspondence between two New England villages in the 1840s illustrates both the tendency of the Shaker villages to attract persons with less-than-pious motives and the deep interest that Shaker leaders demonstrated even in the lives of the most marginal of "converts." It is clear from this case that the Shakers went beyond the gathering orders in their cautious treatment of liminal individuals. In August 1848, the Shaker leadership at Harvard wrote to their counterparts at Enfield, Connecticut, inquiring about a young woman named Ellen who had recently appeared at the Massachusetts village claiming to have been a member of the junior order at Enfield. In reply, the Enfield leadership wrote that Ellen was an English orphan and had indeed spent three months at the village. As far as the leadership at Enfield could discover, Ellen had come "from Boston on purpose to join the Shakers, being advised to do so by one turn off [apostate] from the Society, whom she had recently been living with." As they almost always did, the Shakers had agreed to allow the young woman to stay with them for a time in order to "prove herself" adequate to the task of entering into full Shaker fellowship. Unfortunately, "before she had been [at Enfield] for three months she proved herself to be a great liar." Ellen's sojourn with the Shakers was marked by "strange operations, and a number of hysteric fits," until she eventually fled after an argument with the sister who was supervising her.[78] The Shakers at Enfield were none too sad to see Ellen go, pointing out that "upon the whole she made a great deal of noise and disturbance in the family so much that we could not mourn when she took her departure." To their coreligionists at Harvard, the Connecticut Shakers expressed what might be described as a warmly pessimistic sentiment: "If you can make a good believer of her we have no objections, yet we think there is not much hope."[79]

The general situation described in this letter was a common one, if somewhat unusual in its details. Several themes that bear on the issue of physical boundaries may be discerned in this letter. First, it is typical that the problem individual was young. As has been heavily documented elsewhere, the major demographic group likely to cause difficulty within the Shaker community, at least during the antebellum period, was children under the age of eighteen. When journalist Charles Nordhoff visited the Shakers at Harvard in the early 1870s, he inquired of a Shaker woman about the practice of taking children into the village. To Nordhoff's query "Do you like to take children?" the unnamed sister replied, "Yes, we like to take children—but we don't like to take monkeys." Further conversation revealed that the Shakers believed that children coming from "religious" homes exhibited fewer behavioral problems than those who did not.[80] In any case, it is clear that the Shakers ended up with more than a few "monkeys." While the focus is often on the children brought in as orphans or by parents who could no longer afford to care for them, even the natural children of prominent Shakers occasionally succumbed to the enticements of the world. The case of David Meacham, the son of Father Joseph Meacham, provides a fine example of defection among the children of high-ranking Shakers. The younger Meacham abandoned the Shaker life in 1799 and, "with three reprobate and dissolute young men . . . renounced their privilege in the gospel." The pacifistic Shakers were further shocked to learn that the foursome "went to Albany and enlisted in a company of recruits which was then raising for the marine service in the American Navy."[81] Tension between the keenly felt need to bring young persons into the Shaker fold and the constant difficulties that this population generated for the Shaker establishment continued long into the nineteenth century. Such difficulties, as will be discussed at some length below, actually caused greater harm to the Shakers than any outside interference.

Another typical element of Ellen's story is found in the method by which she came to know of the Shakers. Ellen was apparently directed to the Shaker village by a woman who had apostatized from the sect in the recent past. The leadership at Enfield believed this part of the story because Ellen provided the name of the woman, and the Shakers remembered that she had in fact left the community. It seems unlikely that the apostate would have recommended the Shaker life to Ellen out of a sense of devotion to the community's religious principles. The most probable scenario, given that the guidance came from an apostate and based on Ellen's behavior once at the Enfield village, is that the woman explained to Ellen that the Shakers would almost certainly take her in and provide for her material needs. If the religious elements of Shaker life came up at all, the apostate would probably have told Ellen that some things would have to be endured in order to reap the material rewards.

In many respects, Ellen is representative of a large category of individuals who sought refuge among the Shakers from the turbulent economic and social dislocations common to nineteenth-century America. Although Ellen did not stay long enough even to join the gathering order, her case is emblematic of the care which the Shakers took to guard their spiritual boundaries while permitting outsiders within their physical spaces.

The Move to the West: Innovation, Existential Communitas, and Physical Boundary Maintenance

The Shaker expansion into what was in 1805 the western United States represented a Herculean effort of persistence and endurance. The area west of the Appalachian Mountains boasted a population of 150,000 in

1795, a number that had grown to over 1 million by 1810. The Shakers took part in the large migration into this region, and they shared the experiences of "expansion and the varieties of frontier" life with others who wandered west.[82] An exploration of the Shaker sojourn in the West sheds new light on the creation and maintenance of Shaker physical boundaries.

Shaker success among religious seekers in the region was impressive. Eventually, a village system would come together in the West that mirrored the older village system in the East and that rivaled the eastern villages in terms of publishing and theological creativity. In fact, it is not possible to understand the development of antebellum Shakerism in the East without viewing it as part of a dialectic with events in the West. However, the move to the West represented a shift away from the tightly structured and reasonably polished world of eastern Shakerism and thus presented challenges to the traditional Shaker approaches to physical boundaries.

For a brief period in the West, village structures were lacking, and the Shakers existed in a more primitive state of development akin to the earliest period of Shaker life in America. The communitas that in the more established Shaker villages existed in the normative or structured phase dissolved into a form similar to Turner's existential or spontaneous communitas. Existential communitas is characterized by a less fully articulated social structure in which persons relate to one another as individuals rather than as "social personae." In the Shaker case, the term *social personae* refers to the offices of leadership as well as the categories of Shaker membership. Individual personalities were masked by the categories into which they fit within the village structure, positions such as eldress, deacon, or young believer.

There are two reasons behind the shift from normative to existential communitas during the early phases of Shaker settlement in the West. The first is that new converts greatly outnumbered established members within a very short time after the arrival of the Shakers. Shakers in the West rapidly found themselves surrounded by new converts with little knowledge of Shaker history or doctrine. Shaker missionaries were swamped by the imbalance in a way that their eastern counterparts could scarcely have imagined. Old Shakers thus had to rely on young believers not only for a myriad of practical tasks, but also for spiritual assistance, which would not have devolved upon such inexperienced converts in the context of normative communitas.

The second factor that led to the move from normative to existential communitas was the lack of visible physical structures that in the East served to orient new converts by materially representing the principles and hierarchical structures of the Shaker world. One must not underestimate the impact of a built environment on the psychological experiences of those entering into it. Visitors to Shaker villages in the East were immediately impressed with a sense of order and, more important, on the place of the individual within that order. James Fenimore Cooper, while thoroughly unimpressed by the religious rituals he observed among the Shakers in New Lebanon in the 1820s, was struck by the "neat and . . . perfectly beautiful" villages with fences "of white marble."[83] Those individuals who came to the villages seeking to join themselves with the order must have been similarly impressed.

The power communicated by the Shakers to new converts through the mere presence of the impressive village structures should not be overlooked. Such structures simply did not exist in the West during the early years, and therefore a major psychological component of the ordered normative communitas could not be brought to bear on those who embraced the Shaker gospel on the frontier. Thomas Hunt, who joined the Shakers in Ohio on 6 May 1805, lived in his own house for nearly a year until, in March 1806, he moved to the site that would become Union Village and "settled on land owned by Believers." For the next five years, Hunt continued to live with his natural family and provided his own living. Not until 1811 did he and his natural family part ways and "gather into large [Shaker] families."[84]

It is striking indeed that it was not until 1822 that "the gift was ministered to give the leaders of the different orders each his and her proper title in spiritual relation" in Union Village, Ohio. At that time, David Darrow authorized "that those in the ministry be called Elder and Eldress . . . ; and the first in care of each family in the Church be called Elder brother and Elder sister."[85] The power of social personae was thus severely undercut, if not completely absent, in the period between 1805 and 1822. As in the case of the missing village structures, the absence of powerful social masks exercised a deleterious influence on the ability of the Shakers to impose traditional Shaker power relations immediately. Additionally, six years passed from the time of Union Village's first written covenant in 1810 until "liberty was granted by the parent Church, for all who desired the privilege of confirmation, and were deemed worthy of it to sanction, confirm, and establish, forever, their solemn act of consecration, in such a manner that they could never, in future, get up any legal claim to what they had given."[86]

Darrow chose to create a sort of semi-permanent gathering order in an effort to "lay a sure foundation, and have the people prove themselves well before they consecrated themselves or their property," in spite of the eagerness of new converts "to give up all in the beginning."[87] To that point, all converts followed the pattern set by the gathering orders in the East: they consecrated whatever degree of property with which they felt comfortable with the understanding that they could "renege, at any time, and redeem the property conditionally devoted."[88] Darrow used the principles of boundary maintenance that made the gathering orders an important boundary device in an expanded role to counter the paucity of more obviously physical boundaries.

One significant outcome of this restructured world was the emergence of important theologians among the young believers in the West. Had Richard McNemar or John Dunlavy, for instance, entered into a Shaker village in the East, they would have found a complete physical world created to represent a hierarchically based social structure dominated not by individuals, but by social personae. McNemar and Dunlavy would have found themselves obscured for a time by their own social personae, that of young believers, and their individual talents would have likely been subjugated to this social category. As it happened, McNemar and Dunlavy encountered a Shakerism devoid of its physical trappings and in which Shaker leaders were cut loose from the moorings of their social personae that, in the East, would have made them much less accessible. As a result, these two newcomers quickly rose to prominence as major players in Shaker theology and eventually grew into prestigious social personae of their own as the Shaker villages in the West began to coalesce and move toward the more physically grounded normative communitas. McNemar, for example, imported his position in the Presbyterian movement, including his propensity for prolix theological writing and publishing, directly into the Shaker movement in the West. Such an immediate and relatively easy ascent would have been less likely to occur in the East.

The move from one mode of life to another represented something of a trauma to the Shakers who went west. An 1806 letter from Ruth Farrington at Turtle Creek to Lucy Wright at New Lebanon expresses the sense of frustration and disorientation that typically accompanied the shift from normative to existential communitas. Farrington wrote that only someone who had actually experienced the move west "knows how it feels to go out of the Church where there is so much good order gained and go . . . where there is so much evil and so little good." Farrington noted the extra workload that devolved upon the "Old Believers" in consequence of the imbalance between experienced and new Shakers. "We have a great many Young Believers who come to see us," Farrington wrote wearily, "[and] we have to pay attention to them, for they need to be with us, in order to gather strength and information; besides we have them to cook for and wait upon continually; so our work in temporal things comes very heavy upon us indeed."[89] An 1812 letter from Cassandra Goodrich, an eldress at Hancock village in Massachusetts, to her biological sister Molly Goodrich at South Union, Kentucky, indicated that the eastern Shakers were aware of the unique and challenging circumstances facing Shakers in the West. Cassandra wrote of the "goodly numbers of Young Believers and children at South Union" and reminded her sister that she "must be patient with them and let them have time to grow for a season," even though "it may feel to you like waiting for the growth of a tree that requires many years in order to bring fruit."[90]

Despite their willingness to sympathize and dispense advice, the eastern Shakers operated in the different milieu of normative communitas in which the physical and hierarchical structures provided the order that the western leaders had to manufacture out of sheer will. The eastern believers could thus have known little of the challenges facing the believers in their existential communitas on the frontier. In such a demanding and disorderly environment, the Shakers faced a major task in the quest for physical boundaries, and their creative power was tested through the prolonged period of existential communitas in which neither physical structures nor strong bureaucratic agents were present.

Two distinct phases of Shaker life in the West, which preceded the emergence of normative communitas, occurred simultaneously for many years. These phases occurred between 1805 and the early 1820s by which time, according to Gerald Ham, "[m]ost of the [western] communities had launched extensive building programs replacing the earlier log and farm styles with the austere federal style brick and stone buildings that characterized Shaker architecture in the East."[91] The first is the *missionary phase*. In the missionary phase, Shaker converts lived in their normal homes and were only gathered together during meeting periods. This phase began in 1805, and it continued for more than a decade as the Shakers moved into new areas. Because the Shakers employed a program of rolling expansion for nearly ten years after 1805, as villages developed the missionary phase would wane at a given locality but would continue elsewhere. The second may be called the *settlement phase*. The settlement period consists of the time between the actual gathering of believers at a particular geographic site and the construction of a fully constituted village. In both phases, the Shakers faced a host of challenges to what was in the East a well-developed communal lifestyle centered on the creation and maintenance of ordered villages. How would the Shakers respond to a situation in which isolated clusters of believers, too small in number and too poor in resources to even consider the creation of multiple villages, required the sanctification and protection that only a properly ordered village could provide? The answer demonstrates the flexibility and innovative prowess of the Shaker movement.

The move west represented the most far-reaching missionary foray undertaken by the Shakers since Ann Lee's missionary journey in the early 1780s.[92] After Ann Lee's death, the Shaker movement turned inward and did not actively seek out new converts to the faith. In 1799, however, "an order was established . . . by the ministry [at New Lebanon], for a further opening of the gospel to the world of mankind."[93] Coinciding with this decision to proselytize vigorously was a major surge of evangelical revivalism with focuses in Kentucky, western New York, and New England. Later known as the Second Great Awakening, this movement rocked the foundations of the established order in American religion.

Scholars continue to debate the causes, effects, and significance of the Second Great Awakening on American culture, but for my immediate purposes a limited set of facts may be assumed. First, the awakening was driven by the engine of revivalism, which advocated an emotionally charged approach to religion that dwarfed even the relatively passionate expressions that accompanied the Great Awakening in the earlier eighteenth century. Lay preachers emerged, qualified only by their spiritual conversion experiences, and they gathered in grand outdoor meetings to call their fellow Americans to repentance. These camp meetings aroused suspicion and hostility among the more staid elements of society, persons who objected to the "promiscuous," mixed-gender nature of the gatherings and the wildly physical "exercises" in which the participants engaged. The Shakers never participated directly in the organization of the revivals but left this task to the emerging evangelical coalition of Methodists, Baptists, and Presbyterians and the primitivist Christian movement led by Barton W. Stone and others. However, the Shakers exploited the renewed interest in religious enthusiasm to great effect. In early 1805, John Meacham, Benjamin S. Youngs, and Issachar Bates were sent by Lucy Wright "to the western states to visit the subjects of the late revival and preach the gospel of Christ's second appearing to them."[94] The three missionaries, according to one minister who resented their presence, were "prepossessing in their appearance, neat and plain in their dress, grave and unassuming in their manners, intelligent and ready in the Scriptures, with great boldness of faith. They professed the power of the Spirit, and told of their miracles."[95] The Shakers met with Barton Stone, but the meeting did not go well. One of Stone's close associates recounted the circumstances in his autobiography.

> Early in the year 1805, I went to North Carolina, and was absent from home nearly two months. During that time the Shakers from New York came into our settlement. Before I came home, they were gone to Ohio. I found our people in a commotion; some of my best friends and brethren were much shaken. They represented those Shakers as a very sanctified people; filled with wisdom and godliness. Others believed they were imposters, and were warm in opposition to them. I hastened to see Stone. They had been at his house; he had examined them calmly and deliberately; he said they spoke with great confidence—that they were insidious and artful, but he was confirmed they were impostors. He said many people had the notion that they were possessed of superior wisdom and talent, and that we could not compete with them. But, said he, we must not be afraid of them—we can confute them. They came among us several times afterwards, but Stone was firm, and had fortified me. We

withstood them to the face. Some complained that we were intolerant; but being convinced that they were not building on the sure foundation, we were decisive in our testimony against them, both in word and deed. And the churches there sustained very little injury from them.[96]

The Shaker missionaries carried with them a letter from the Central Ministry to the "people in Kentucky and the adjacent states." This text functioned as a sermon and was read by Shaker elders in a variety of settings, including camp meetings. The letter introduced the Shaker missionaries as "messengers of Christ and friends to your salvation," and it portrayed the Shaker movement as the rightful heir of the original form of Christianity, which was lost "about 400 years" after Christ's death. This message found an eager audience among the Christian primitivists longing for the recovery of authentic Christianity as described in the New Testament.

The 1805 letter is relatively vague in its description of Shaker theology. Although Shaker theological tenets had yet to be fully fleshed out, something that would be accomplished in large measure by believers in the West in the coming decades, certain beliefs were well enough entrenched that their absence from this introductory letter is notable. According to the text, the "way out of all sin" involved several steps: "first, to believe in the manifestation of Christ, and in the messengers which he had sent. Secondly, to confess all our sins; and thirdly, to take up our cross against the flesh, the world, and all evil."[97]

Those associated with Shaker doctrine could, of course, immediately contextualize this language and, almost subconsciously, fill in the blanks. To those new to the Shaker gospel, including virtually all of those to whom this letter would have been read, the language of the letter is not terribly divergent from the sorts of things that many others were proclaiming. The Shaker injunction to eschew "the flesh," for example, clearly refers to celibacy in the Shaker context, but identical language was employed by others in reference to simple chastity—the avoidance of sexual relations outside of marriage.

Similarly, Ann Lee is the object of the vaguest of references, and although her position within Shaker theology was not yet firmly settled, she was controversial enough to keep mention of her under wraps in the early phase of missionary work in the Ohio Valley.[98] The missionaries met with such rapid success and faced such sincere and penetrating inquiries into the details of their faith that, by the end of March, "there was no alternative but to hold forth on the doctrine of the single life and one united interest—that self-interest and the conjugal relationship were incompatible with the terms of the gospel feast." Everywhere such a doctrine was preached, it tended to divide the listeners.[99]

Although response to the early Shaker efforts was mixed, their message appealed to a number of well-placed ministers, chiefly leaders of New Light Presbyterian congregations. According to Richard Mc-Nemar, "The first object of this important mission was to find a place where the ark of the testimony could rest and be protected for the present." They found such a place at the home of Malcolm Worley at Turtle Creek. Just as Shaker tradition ascribed to supernatural guidance the location of the village at Watervliet, the earliest Shaker missionaries in the West saw the hand of God in their discovery of Malcolm Worley and his house, something they memorialized with the following poem:

> In confidence and patience
> With weary limbs we went
> The spirit of Elijah
> We sought
> whom God had sent
> And there behold we found it
> When on the spot we came
> In one whom God had chosen
> And Malcolm was his name.[100]

While aesthetically lacking, the poem indicated that the Shakers imported to the West their association of physical gathering places with sanctified and divinely chosen locations.

In addition to the learned Worley, men like John Dunlavy and Richard McNemar converted and, in the process, brought most of their congregants with them.[101] Such defections were significant enough to cause David Purviance, a major figure in the Christian Restorationist movement, to lament that the "shock to the church was severe" when McNemar and others "joined the testimony of the Shakers." By the time Purviance arrived in the Ohio Valley in 1807, "the Shakers had entered in, 'grievous wolves—not sparing the flock'" and had "carried away" two-thirds "of the old established preachers in the State of Ohio." In the end, of course, it turned out for the best, because the Shakers were like leeches drawing out diseased blood, purging "a growing fanaticism" from the sick body of the church. "M'Nemar and some others had become somewhat wild and fantastic," Purviance remembered, adding that "their hearts were puffed up before they were caught in the Shaker snare." Purviance was left to assure himself that "Jesus Christ," at least, "had not joined the Shakers."[102]

Such statements aside, it was clear to the Shakers that they could not have chosen a more fertile field of labor. As historian Paul K. Conkin described the situation, "It was as if all the heresies that had beset Reformed Christianity had invaded Kentucky and Ohio by 1803."[103] "Heresies," such as an emphasis on ecstatic worship, continuing revelations from God, and a general Arminian theology, fit rather well with the new Shaker gospel that the believers brought into the region in 1805. The Shakers took this approach with them as they moved up and down the Ohio Valley. In 1808, for example, a Shaker missionary contingent made its way to Busro, Indiana, where the Shakers "found an opening," which was helped, no doubt, by the fact that "Robert Housten, a preacher, opened his mind to John [Dunlavy]." From this small beginning, a village would eventually rise, although it would also be the first of the troubled western villages to close twenty years later. On another occasion, two preachers, Robert Gill and William Braselton, "opened their minds" to the Shaker missionaries.[104] Converting large portions of a congregation from another faith, usually through the conversion of the group's leader, was not unheard of. The Shakers already had some degree of experience with this as they had stumbled upon, and converted, a large number of Shadrach Ireland's sectarians at Harvard, Massachusetts. Ireland's congregation was still reeling from their leader's death and remained filled with millennial expectations with no suitably structured outlet. In the case of the western Shakers, their greatest early successes came in converting preachers and congregants from among dissenters leaving the Presbyterian Synod of Kentucky, with which the dissenters had vociferous theological disagreements.[105]

The advantages of this type of scenario were manifold. First, it provided the proselytizing group with new members who knew the surrounding environment and thus provided credibility with other locals.

Second, the new converts already enjoyed an infrastructure with homes, employment, political connections, and so forth that the proselytizing group could draw upon as they sought to establish themselves. The Shakers enjoyed all of these benefits from their earliest days in the Ohio Valley. Drawbacks existed as well, however. Most important, the proselytizing groups were immediately outnumbered by new converts, who held their own, often deeply entrenched ideas about the world and who knew very little about their new faith. The result for the Shakers in the West was a move from structured, normative communitas to existential communitas. It was some time before any villages were actually constructed, and even after they were, the eastern transplants had some difficulty with their physical surroundings. The eastern Shaker pioneers to the West wrote long letters back to New Lebanon describing their hardships in "the wicked, dirty world."

In the summer of 1806, the Shaker women who had been sent west wrote back to the ministry at New Lebanon, noting, "We used to think that we knew what hardship was, and truly we did, but we knew nothing about it to what we know now." The western sisters appended a lengthy postscript to the letter containing a description of the physical accommodations in which they lived. Obviously homesick for the sturdy and sound surroundings of their New York home, the sisters described a cabin "shingled with palisades bound on with weight poles without any nails or pegs. Likewise the floor is a puncheon floor laid down without any nails or pegs about it." On rainy nights, water "comes in by streams through every direction—sometimes in the night first thing we know the rain comes down upon us." The letter itself was written in a chamber of the cabin "where no light comes in only through the cracks and a little hole cut through the logs about a foot square, and our table was a box cover laid in the lap."[106]

Rachel Johnson wrote to New Lebanon from Ohio telling a similar story. A close reading of Johnson's letter yields important clues about her concern with the disorder of the physical surroundings, and it offers a glimpse into the efforts to recreate the traditional Shaker physical separation of the sexes. "The first of our house is finished," Johnson reported, "white oak floors without planing, two lofts, four smoky fireplaces in each loft. Our garret we have for a lodging room with seven beds chiefly on the floor. There is neither door nor partition upon the loft. We have some blankets hung up between the brethren's beds and ours." It is difficult to imagine a more stark contrast with the staid and solid eastern villages, where men and women slept on opposite sides of a large house with many walls between their beds. In the West, these boundaries were reduced to flimsy blankets separating the cots by mere inches. Johnson expressed her uneasiness about the confusion, with "people coming and going frequently." Also important is Johnson's report that no gathering order was in place, forcing "all [to] mix up together, Young Believers and old."[107] Given the importance of the gathering orders for the preservation of good order and their filter-like effect, which guarded the sanctity of the village space, it is no wonder that the absence of such a system concerned the believers arriving in the West at least as much as their rough floors and crude sleeping arrangements.

The Shakers complained of poor food and strange customs, and such issues were not quickly resolved. In 1818, Molly Goodrich, still living at South Union, Kentucky, wrote back to Calvin Green at New Lebanon that she was still struggling to "gather the oldest Believers in this place into some gift and order," and that the southerners were resistant to Shaker injunctions to be "industrious, neat and clean."[108] Ruth Farrington, one of the leading sisters in the West, complained in 1819 that she had been "here in the wilderness, toting and traveling about in the mud thirteen years."[109]

Wilderness imagery figured prominently in letters from the West. No doubt, this stems in part from the fact that these Shakers were living in a relatively remote region. However, being a biblically literate people, it is also likely that the wilderness metaphors communicated the feeling of danger, confusion, and chaos that such language typically represented in the Bible. It is clear that many of the eastern Shakers never felt at home in the West. Ruth Farrington wrote to Rachel Spencer bemoaning the fact that Spencer could "see Mother [Lucy Wright] when you are in trouble but I have not that privilege. . . . I have thought many times if I could see Mother one half hour I should be willing to do anything."[110]

The manuscript evidence testifies to the centrality of the concern with physical surroundings and the disorder in their new homes in the minds of western Shakers. Shaker letters from the West signal the importance of proper physical boundaries in Shaker life and thought, as well as the failure of the existential communitas to match the expectations generated by the structured normative communitas that the eastern Shakers had always associated with the movement. Driven by their sense of religious duty, however, the Shakers set out to recreate the safety and order they had enjoyed in the villages they left behind. To do so would require creativity and religious imagination. I argued above that the physical boundaries created by the Shakers in the East were largely symbolic of, or at the very least subordinate to, less tangible boundaries. In the West, the Shakers were for a time unable to enjoy the symbols of separation, but they immediately and forcefully recreated the sharp distinction between the people of the culturally postulated world and themselves through a thoroughly Shaker emphasis on order.

During the period between the arrival of the Shaker missionaries in the West in 1805 and the construction of proper village structures (a process that took many years), the Shakers in the West faced the tasks of maintaining separation from the world while gathering converts and of living without the ordering bulwark of the village. Operating from the home of Malcolm Worley, the Shakers embarked on several years of proselytizing in difficult and often dangerous circumstances. Constant Mosely, an eastern Shaker sent by Lucy Wright as a member of the first wave of reinforcements to the West, kept a journal of his 1808–1809 missionary journeys among the Shakers scattered throughout the Ohio Valley. His writings provide an important window into how the believers maintained separation from the world without structured villages. The most obvious strategy is Mosely's persistent rhetorical segregation of all people mentioned in his journal into two groups: believers and those of the world. For instance, he and his traveling companions "went to Absalom Chisholm's, where a large body of the world were collected, John [Dunlavy] preached powerfully to them, which caused a number of them to *retreat*."

This particular entry is important because it is representative of the physical circumstances common to the early years of Shaker work in the West when meetings were frequently held at the homes of new converts, and congregations of nonbelievers were invited to attend. Additionally, Mosely's entry displays his belief in the power of the Shaker gospel to actually drive away, and thus create physical separation from, those who lacked sincerity or who were disorderly. While lacking the protection and power of a proper village, the Shakers still felt separate and protected from evil. Mosely never named nor even described individuals from the world, but rather referred to them only categorically, a move typical of Shaker descriptions of the culturally postulated world.

From their earliest days in the West, the Shakers described the supernatural separation that their preaching generated. McNemar recalled that when he first heard the letter of introduction read by the Shaker missionaries: "Few understood it, and the singular appearance of the strangers [Shaker missionaries] more immediately interested their feelings. Their appearance, dress, conversation, etc. . . . injected terror and doubt into many; Terror from an apprehension that they were more than mortal; and doubt, whether they were for us or against us." Such "terror" resulted in the fleeing of the nonbelievers, "railing as they went, and so left the despised few, with increasing confidence to pursue unmolested, the peaceful tenor of their way."[111] The ability to ward off evil personages through the apotropaic power of Shaker faith is an idea that the believers carried with them from the East. An old Shaker legend told of the devil himself being detected by the Shakers at Tyringham, Massachusetts. The ranking elder at the village purportedly "gave him chase into the cellar and about the premises and finally drove him to the highest hill back of the village where they buried him, head down, with clam shells in his hands, so that if he dug he would go deeper instead of digging out."[112] The story clearly symbolized the Shakers' belief in their very real power over the embodiment of evil.

In lieu of sacred village space, the Shakers themselves were transformed—at least in the Shaker accounts—into receptacles of terrifying sacred power sufficient to simultaneously attract the godly and repel evil. As I will argue in the case of the Mormons in chapter 2, there was among both groups a tendency to focus on the power of the body as a physical boundary when the more traditional modes of physical retreat were unavailable. On one occasion, a meeting was held at the home of a new convert, Jesse Graham, and amid fires built to smoke out the thick swarms of mosquitoes, the Shakers preached in the yard and, while "a number believed, others mocked." Similarly mixed results emerged from a meeting at which "four or five hundred people" listened to the Shakers, who "aroused great opposition [and] a mob with clubs to drive us out but did not succeed."[113] Clearly, the Shakers did not require a village fence to understand that they were not "of the world."

Even without their familiar physical habitations, the early western Shakers implemented, to a limited degree, some of the practices of the eastern villages. Most important was the policy of holding separate meetings for Shakers and outsiders. Often, this took the form of separate congregations at the camp meetings at which the Shakers would preach. Mosely records, for example, that at one meeting "John [Dunlavy] preached to the world, [while] Issacher [Bates] spoke to the Believers."[114]

Shakers on the frontier thus maintained the same type of boundaries that they so carefully crafted in the East, although they had to do so without the powerful ambience that the village spaces provided. Despite this potential weakness, it is clear that the Shakers imported to the West a mindset of physical and spiritual separation, which was cultivated and nurtured within the walls of the eastern Shaker villages, but which received new and powerfully expressed meaning in the context of a frontier world dominated by an existential communitas. The success of this endeavor is evidenced by the fact that the Shakers not only survived in the less structured world, but they thrived. By the mid-1820s, multiple villages had reconstituted the normative communitas present in the eastern villages, complete with intricate architectural expressions of Shaker order, fully constituted joint-interest programs, and the reinstitution of categories of social personae to oversee and direct village operations. Ironically, when the villages in the West entered fully into states of normative communitas, they began to rapidly decline.

Conclusion

Given the centrality of separation rhetoric to the Shaker enterprise, it is not at all surprising that part of the routinization of charisma that accompanied the ascendancy of Joseph Meacham and Lucy Wright included the creation of intentionally planned sacred spaces into which the Shakers could physically flee from the world. Orderly Shaker villages remain one of the most easily identifiable traits of the group, but these villages are properly understood as elements in a complex and subtle process of boundary creation and negotiation in which the Shakers did not simply seek to create a hermetically sealed environment and in which the Shakers conceived of two different outside worlds: the experienced world and the culturally postulated world. The boundary between the Shakers and the physical world was never absolute, and this was not simply a matter of reality subverting an ideal but rather a case in which the Shakers intentionally welcomed some degree of controlled interaction with the world for two reasons: to attract and manage potential converts and to increase group stability and collective identity through the "performance" of Shakerism for audiences of spectators. The Shakers approached these interactions with the world with at least two mechanisms: the gathering order, which acted as a filtration node for potential new members, an innovation that mitigated the material and spiritual effects of the free-rider problem, and the intentional sanctification of foreign persons, objects, and ideas through a process of ordering that occurred when such elements entered into the village spaces. The Shakers employed a mixed strategy involving a moderate degree of physical withdrawal, a partially self-sufficient and spiritually self-contained community, and an elaborate system of purification through ordering that displayed their sense of disgust with chaos as well as their ability to sanctify, however temporarily, exogenous elements that came within their physical spaces.

The Shaker move to the West represented a distinct shift not only in the physical environment in which the Shakers operated, but also in the kind of social order that they were able to create. For years after the move to the West, the Shakers existed in a more loosely structured existential communitas in which new converts greatly outnumbered older believers and in which the social personae so important to normative communitas were replaced by individual interactions. All of this was spurred on by the lack of powerful physical expressions of Shaker order, expressions that would not emerge in the West until the years after 1810 and in some areas not until the 1820s. The complexity evident in the creation and maintenance of physical boundaries in two very different contexts is a testimony to the surprisingly nuanced and sophisticated relationship that the Shakers had with their worldly context.

The physical boundaries erected by Shakers in established villages and in frontier settings were designed to mitigate the threat posed by exogenous intrusions, and they managed these threats remarkably well. The Shakers developed tactical approaches to the world that allowed them to maintain clear boundaries that were stable precisely because they were not aggressive in their attitudes toward the surrounding communities and because their boundaries were semi-permeable.

TWO

Imagination and Reality
in the Mormon Zion:
Cities, Temples, and Bodies

Nineteenth-century Mormons understood that a line existed between the righteous and the wicked, between those who had embraced the restored gospel of Jesus Christ and those who had not. Those who had adopted the new faith or, as Mormons understood it, the newly restored ancient faith, were called "saints," while those who did not accept it were collectively known as "the world." "The world," an 1829 revelation to Joseph Smith thundered, "is ripening in iniquity," and the faithful were challenged to escape that world. The Mormons adopted a two-pronged approach to the problem of separating from the world: they employed an aggressive proselytizing program in an effort to move as many souls as possible from the "world" category to the "saint" category, and they sought to create safe havens where the saints could live in peace as the calamities of the coming apocalypse rained down on the unconverted. This chapter is an exploration of Mormon efforts to create and maintain strong physical boundaries.

Thomas Tweed offers a paradigm of religious approaches to physical space that is helpful in understanding the process of physical boundary creation as a multistage process involving the mapping, building, and inhabiting of religiously consecrated physical spaces, which Tweed categorizes as the body, the home, and the homeland. Tweed's paradigm is particularly helpful in understanding nineteenth-century Mormon physical boundary maintenance. During the Missouri period, the Mormons were unable to move beyond the mapping phase. In Nauvoo, Illinois, the Mormons were able to map, build, and inhabit their "homeland," but the boundaries eventually collapsed and they were forced to abandon their city. After the Nauvoo period, the Mormons shifted their understanding of their homeland from a centralized city to a collection of decentralized temples. In connection with this, the Mormons focused intensely on the role of the body in the creation and maintenance of physical space.

In their changing efforts to establish such boundaries, early Mormons always placed a premium on the power of God to protect their sanctuaries from the dangers that existed in the world. Thus, the plans for the original city of Zion in Jackson County, Missouri, contained detailed instructions for the building and placement of a central temple complex, residential and commercial streets, and agricultural areas, but the plans failed to call for the creation of a wall around the city. Instead, the Mormons were commanded in a revelation that those who occupied Zion must be "pure in heart," and if they were sufficiently pure, God would protect them. "The rebellious," by contrast, "shall be cut off out of the land of Zion, and shall be sent away, and shall not inherit the land." For the Mormons, the protection afforded in the city of Zion was physical, but it depended on the degree to which the individual Mormons pleased God.[1]

In order to understand the nineteenth-century Mormons' physical boundary maintenance, it is first necessary to understand why they attempted to establish cities, rather than other types of physical configurations, as their strongholds. In 1830, Joseph Smith began a revision of the Bible in which he sought, by divine assistance, to correct the manifold errors that he believed had crept into the text over the centuries. Part of that "translation" included an account of the prophet Enoch, a mysterious figure who is mentioned only briefly in the canonical version of the Hebrew Bible, but who makes appearances in various apocryphal books.[2] From these scant references, Smith spun a wide-ranging Enoch mythology in which the prophet Enoch had created a glorious city in the midst of a wicked world.

Enoch's city, called Zion, provided physical and spiritual safety for its inhabitants. Eventually, the entire city—both the inhabitants and the physical city itself—were taken up into heaven.[3] Smith understood Enoch's ancient city as a model for the creation of physical boundaries with the world. In Smith's view, the only acceptable physical boundaries with the world were divinely appointed cities in which the Mormons would "gather." Smith's revelations about the creation of Mormon physical boundaries conformed to the contours of the model provided by Enoch's Zion.[4]

Between 1830 and 1846, Mormon approaches to physical boundary creation underwent significant shifts. I have identified four general phases of Mormon physical boundary creation in the nineteenth century: (1) the period 1831–1833, when the Mormons mapped plans for the creation of the original city of Zion; (2) the liminal phase, 1834–1839, in which the Mormons had not yet mapped a city to replace the original Zion and were not building or inhabiting ritually significant spaces; (3) the period of fully realized physical boundaries that saw the redeployment of Zionic rhetoric and mapping wed with the effective actions of building and inhabiting Nauvoo, 1840–1844; and (4) the final phase, in which the Mormons rejected the city as their homeland model in favor of a model based on temples as homeland with a new emphasis on the body and personal physical boundaries.[5]

Not every Mormon settlement was designed as a physical boundary per se, but in each instance the Mormons managed to incite crisis-level tension over the issue of physical boundaries. Only the earliest Missouri settlements and the settlement in Nauvoo, Illinois, qualify as true attempts to imagine, map, build, and inhabit physical boundaries within the city-as-homeland paradigm. Although the standard interpretation of Mormon history holds that the Mormon settlements in the West represented the fullest expression of physical withdrawal from the world, I argue that, by the time the Mormons arrived in the Great Basin, they had already given up their original ideas about the religious basis of physical boundaries.[6]

Eventually, the Mormons abandoned their efforts to create cities as physical boundaries with the world, and instead they focused on the boundaries associated with their temples. The physical space that the move west provided the Mormons must not be conflated with earlier efforts to create intentional physical boundaries in the form of cities of Zion. The key difference between the Mormon policies in the West and those in Missouri and Illinois was that, in the former, the Mormons did not seek out tension with the world over their physical boundaries. I will also demonstrate that Mormon physical boundaries, as opposed to Mormon settlements, had the following characteristics in common: a connection with the myth of primordial creation, a designation by revelation as a refuge from the world and as a place of gathering and safety from coming apocalyptic calamities, an association with the concept of the "sacred center," and the creation of a temple at the heart of the city.

In Missouri, the Mormons believed that the site for the perfect sacred city was revealed. Plans for its development had wafted down from heaven, and a theology was developed that called for the creation of the city of Zion as the ultimate boundary between the people of God and the world. Before the Mormons could even make a start on the creation of the city, however, they came into conflict with the inhabitants of the area, and violence erupted.

The Mormons in Missouri faced a dilemma in which they had to choose between holding fast to their ideal in the face of severe violence and possible death or working out another approach to physical boundaries. The Mormons moved to Nauvoo, Illinois, in 1839 and started again. Nauvoo was the only city that the Mormons completed that was actually founded as a physical barrier with the world. In Nauvoo, the Mormons conjured into concrete reality much of what had only been imagined and dreamed of in Missouri. When the situation in Nauvoo eventually deteriorated, Mormon conceptions of sacred space and physical boundaries underwent a substantial change in emphasis, a change that the Mormons took with them to Utah.

Over the course of the nineteenth century, Mormons moved from an attachment to a particular physical location as the center of sacred space and protection to a view in which the notion of sacred space and physical enclosure focused on temple rituals. In fact, the Mormons never saw their settlements in the West as physical boundaries in the way that they saw their settlements in Missouri and Illinois.[7] This is a useful realization because it calls into question a general assumption about the boundaries created by the Mormons when they settled in the West. In this chapter, I will cover the major historical themes of Mormon physical boundary maintenance, and I will pause to explore in sharper focus a few important and specific moments during which Mormon notions of sacred space and physical boundaries underwent significant revisions.

Mapping the Ideal: Jackson County, 1831–1833

In September 1830, Joseph Smith received the first of many revelations dealing with the establishment of the city of Zion. At that time, Smith was residing in Fayette, New York, a small village in the Finger Lakes district where Smith had converted a family, the Whitmers, in whose home he had officially organized the church (which was called the Church of Christ) five months earlier. As often happened during this period, Smith issued a call to two men to strike out on a proselytizing mission. This call consisted of a revelatory statement from God through Joseph Smith that outlined the itinerary and the ultimate destination of the missionary journey. This revelation mentioned that the location of the city of Zion "is not revealed, and no man knoweth" it, but offered the tantalizing promise that it "will be given hereafter."[8] The main purpose of this revelation was to call Oliver Cowdery, who would become Smith's longtime associate and scribe, on a mission to "the Lamanites." According to the Book of Mormon, the Lamanites were a Hebraic group that fled Jerusalem in the sixth century BCE, settled in the Americas, and were the "principal ancestors" of the Native Americans.[9] The Book of Mormon predicted that the Lamanites, in the time of the restoration of the true gospel (the time of Joseph Smith), would serve to "build up a city, which shall be called the New Jerusalem."[10]

It is within this context that the call to head west was issued and received by Cowdery and several others. They understood the importance placed on the Lamanites' role in building the New Jerusalem, and they left on their mission full of Zionic fervor. Cowdery and his companions visited with the Cattaraugus tribe near Buffalo, New York, and presented them with a copy of the Book of Mormon.[11] No other meaningful contacts were made with Native Americans during the journey. Unfortunately for the Mormons, the mission to the Lamanites failed in its primary goal. This failure did not stop talk of the establishment of Zion, however. In June 1831, shortly after the Mormons had established a new headquarters in Kirtland, Ohio, Smith issued another revelation which commanded him, Sidney Rigdon, and others to "journey to the Land of Missouri." The revelation promised that, at some point on this journey, God would "make known unto them the land of your inheritance."[12] Smith had been teaching that Zion was to be the place where the

Mormons would gather on lands, or "inheritances," provided by God, build their celestial city, and await the return of Jesus Christ.

During this period, nothing figured more prominently in Mormon teaching and speculation than the exact location of this city and the time when settlement would begin. Smith and the others set out expectantly on their journey, and when they had reached Independence, a city on the western edge of Missouri, Smith received a revelation indicating that "the land of Missouri . . . is the land which I have appointed and consecrated for the gathering of the saints. Wherefore this is the land of promise and the place for the city of Zion . . . [and] the place which is now called Independence is the center place and the spot for the temple."[13] The Mormons went to work immediately, buying land and building a community. Zion was to be the place from which the gospel would spread, and it was clear that this would be the epicenter, the home of a great temple complex, and the place where Christ would make his triumphant return to earth.

Identifying Independence, Missouri, as the site of the city of Zion was an extremely important move for the Mormons. It occasioned, according to Smith, "a season of joy to those present, and afforded a glimpse of the future, which time will yet unfold to the satisfaction of the faithful."[14] This feeling was amplified by revelations that poured forth through Smith, promising the rapid improvement of the land, the building of a temple, and the establishment of a "celestial city." Zion was to be a permanent settlement, not to "be moved out of her place."[15] Zion was also to serve as the place of refuge from the coming apocalyptic calamities soon to be poured upon the face of the earth. God, the revelations reminded the Mormons, held Zion "in [his] hands."[16]

The early Mormons, taking their cue from Smith's revelations and teachings, believed that the task would fall to them to build a city in which the faithful would gather as the world destabilized preceding the imminent return of Christ. In January 1833, Smith wrote a letter to the editor of a newspaper in Rochester, New York, detailing his reasons for building the city of Zion and linking the creation of this physical stronghold with the coming plagues of the end times. Smith explained, "The city of Zion spoken of by David, in the one hundred and second Psalm, will be built upon the land of America," and in this city the righteous would be "delivered from the overflowing scourge that shall pass through the land." Smith dramatically declared in the name of Jesus Christ "that not many years shall pass away before the United States shall present such a scene of bloodshed as has not a parallel in the history of our nation; pestilence, hail, famine, and earthquake will sweep the wicked of this generation from off the face of the land." Any who cared to avoid such dire calamities, Smith continued, would do well to join with "the people of the Lord, those who . . . have already commenced gathering together in Zion, which is in the state of Missouri."[17]

Smith's letter demonstrated with striking clarity an important principle: early Mormons understood Zion to be, first and foremost, a specific place of physical refuge and protection from very real physical dangers. The Boston-based Universalist newspaper, the *Independent Messenger,* reported that, in April 1832, Mormon missionaries had appeared in town preaching:

> [A]ll who do not embrace their faith and mode of worship, forsake their
> friends, houses, and lands, and go with them to a place of safety, which is
> in the state of Missouri, where they are about building a city, will be de-
> stroyed by famine, pestilence and earthquakes, &c., and . . . reformation,
> repentance, and faith, unless it be accompanied by a speedy removal to
> their city of refuge, will be of no avail.[18]

In the early 1830s, Mormons clearly believed that one could not claim the fullness of available protection unless one sought safety within the Mormon stronghold. This point cannot be stressed too strongly, especially given the changes in this interpretation that emerged as the apocalyptic rhetoric cooled and the city of Zion failed to materialize.

The Mormon newspaper in Missouri, the *Evening and the Morning Star,* carried stories, articles, and revelations in each issue dwelling on the calamities that were beginning to plague the world, and urged the faithful to gather in Zion. A piece from March 1833 is typical. Entitled "Prospects of the Church," the article made it clear that the whole point of the church's existence was "to bring to pass the gathering of the elect, even the righteous, preparatory to his [Christ's] Second Coming: and the place of the gathering, as has been before published, is in the western boundaries of the state of Missouri."[19]

John Whitmer, who served as the first LDS Church historian, recorded that after the Mormon contingent arrived in Missouri, they "offered their Sacraments and oblations unto the Lord," after which Oliver

Cowdery detailed the importance of the identification and dedication of Zion in Missouri:

> After many struggles and afflictions, being persecuted by our enemies, br[others] Joseph [Smith] and Sidney [Rigdon], and many other elders, were commanded to take their journey to this land, the Land of Missouri. Which was promised unto us should be the land of the inheritance of the Saints, and the place of the gathering in these last days. Which intelligence cheered our hearts, and caused us to rejoice exceedingly.[20]

Smith himself traveled to Missouri to perform dedicatory rituals that consecrated the land. On 3 August 1831, he dedicated the land on which the temple of Zion would be built. After delivering the prayer, Smith led the congregation in a reading of the Eighty-Seventh Psalm. "The Lord loveth the gates of Zion," the group recited, "Glorious things are spoken of thee, O city of God." The Mormons were flush with millenarian fervor and a sense of divine destiny leading them toward the construction of God's city.[21]

It is fitting that the Mormons engaged in ritual acts of purification and sanctification upon their arrival in Missouri. Not only had the precise location of Zion been revealed through Smith's prophetic power, but Smith believed that the area around Independence, Missouri, was the very center of creation itself. In the revelation given on 20 July 1831, the Mormons were told that "the place which is now called Independence is the *center* place." Scholars have long recognized the ritual significance of the "center," and the Mormon concept of Zion as the sacred center is a crucially important and often overlooked element of the creation of this particular physical boundary.[22] Independence was the center in a number of ways. It would be the center of the church and the place in which the temple would be built. It would also be the center point of the gathering. More profoundly, however, Zion was the center from which all creation had spread because, according to Smith, Jackson County was the location of the garden of Eden.[23] Smith's original idea of the city of Zion represented a simple but stunningly brazen ambition: he would build up Zion in the place where God began the creation of all life.

Soon after the Mormons arrived in Jackson County (the area including Independence), tensions grew with the locals. By 1833, about 1,200 Mormons had settled in the area, bringing with them the economic plan known as the "law of consecration and stewardship." According to this law, members of the church were to consecrate all of their possessions to the church's agent, who returned to individuals what was required for their "needs" and then redistributed the surplus to needy people within the church. Unlike many contemporary communitarian experiments, the Mormon effort "was designed in such a way as to retain a large measure of freedom of enterprise."[24]

While this law was actually a miserable failure because of the reluctance of members to contribute their goods and the tendency of disgruntled members to want their consecrated property back, stories about the negative impact such a practice might have on the local economy soon spread. Similar concerns surfaced with regard to Mormon political power, even though no political party had been formed by the Mormons. Intensifying these issues was the fear on the part of some Missourians that the Mormons would bring an active antislavery agenda to bear in the region. An 1833 editorial in the *Western Monitor,* published in Fayette, Missouri, provides an indication of the level of disdain in which the Missourians held the Mormons.

> Little more than two years ago some two or three of these people [Mormons] made their appearance on the upper Missouri, and now they number some twelve hundred souls in the county; and each successive autumn and spring pours forth its swarms among us, with a gradual falling of the character of those who compose them, until it seems that those communities from which they come were flooding us with the very dregs of their composition.[25]

In response to the economic, political, and racial concerns, about 300 prominent citizens met in April 1833 to discuss possible solutions to the problem. This was an important event because it was the first time that a group of well-connected citizens of the host culture met with an aim to apply substantial external pressure to the physical boundaries created by the Mormons.

A major component of this anti-Mormon cadre was the local clergy. Presbyterian minister Finis Ewing published his opinions about the Mormons in a local newspaper in 1833: "The Mormons are the common enemies of mankind and ought to be destroyed."[26] The Reverend Benton Pixley, a Christian missionary sent to convert Native Americans in the region, was even more vocal and active in his opposition to the Mormons.[27] Pixley gave frequent speeches against Mormonism and made a practice of writing letters to newspapers all over the country, decrying the "heretical sect." One such letter chided the Mormons for their refusal to participate in "Temperance societies, Bible societies, Tract societies, or Sunday School societies." Such voluntary associations were interdenominational Christian organizations, and Pixley was clearly attempting to marginalize Mormons from mainstream Christianity by pointing out their refusal to participate in the denominationally neutral societies.[28] Pixley's various anti-Mormon activities led to a second meeting, which occurred in the summer of 1833. Mormons noted with anxiety that this meeting had been attended "not only by the rabble of the county, but also by men holding official positions."[29]

The result of the meeting was the publication of a letter from several hundred Jackson County citizens to Missouri governor Daniel Dunklin. The letter complained in general terms about the "fanatics" and "knaves" who had been plaguing the region for the past two years with their pretenses to divine revelation that "openly blaspheme the most high God." A close reading of the letter reveals that, in addition to the general doctrinal issues, there were two major focuses of concern for the non-Mormons in Jackson County. One was that the Mormons "would corrupt our blacks and instigate them to bloodsheds." The other was the Mormon assertion that "God hath given them this county of land, and that sooner or later they must and will have possession of our lands for an inheritance."[30] Both concerns focused on issues dealing with physical boundaries: the presence of African Americans who, it was feared, would become the violent puppets of the Mormons in a racial/religious war as the Mormons sought to expand their landholdings, and the accompanying fear that the boundaries of the Mormon settlements would eventually encompass all of the land in the region.

The Mormon response was a swift and aggressive defense of their boundaries. In July 1833, shortly after the meeting organized by Pixley, the *Evening and the Morning Star* published an editorial entitled "Beware of False Prophets."[31] This lengthy piece was clearly targeted at Pixley and his associates in the ministry. It read, in part:

> When men, as servants of the Lord, under the sacred name of religion, instead of building up the church of Christ, by preaching baptism for the remission of sins, and the Gift of the Holy Ghost, by the laying on of hands, with a promise of eternal life, by keeping all the commandments

of the Lord, and continuing faithful to the end, are building up mite
societies, temperance societies, missionary societies, bible societies, or
any other societies wherein the scribes and Pharisees sit in Moses' seat;
or wherein money is the principal means of urging on the work of the
Lord (as it is termed) seeing that the blessed Savior never taught any such
things as the gospel, or as an appendage to it, we exclaim, Beware of false
prophets, which come to you in sheep's clothing, but inwardly are raven-
ing wolves.[32]

In this editorial, penned by William W. Phelps with the approval of
local church leaders, boundaries were reasserted with the warning about
wolves in sheep's clothing penetrating the community. Such imagery
powerfully reinforced the notion of separation. The Mormons doubtless looked to the day when they could create strong enough physical
boundaries to keep their enemies out, but they also recognized that, for
the time being, such boundaries were not possible.

Around the same time, Joseph Smith sent plans for the city of Zion
to church leaders in Missouri. This letter set out the blueprint for establishing a city that was to be, initially, one mile square. Part of Smith's
plan is quoted here to provide a sense of the extreme detail.

The plat contains one mile square; all the squares of the plat contain
ten acres each, being forty rods square. You will observe that the lots
are laid off alternately in the squares; in one square running from the
south and north to the line through the center of the square; and in the
next, the lots run from the east and west to the center line. Each lot is
four perches in front and twenty back, making one half of an acre in
each lot, so that no one street will be built on entirely through the street;
but on one square the houses will stand on one street, and on the next
one, another, except the middle range of squares, which runs north and
south, in which range are the painted squares. The lots are laid off in
these squares, north and south, all of them; because these squares are
forty perches by sixty, being twenty perches longer than the others, their
greatest length being east and west, and by running all these squares,
north and south, it makes all the lots in the city of one size.

In the same letter, Joseph Smith instructed the Mormons that "when
this square is thus laid off and supplied, lay off another in the same way,
and so fill up the world in these last days, and let every man live in the
city, for this is the city of Zion."[33] Clearly, Smith was sending a signal that
he did, indeed, plan to establish his celestial city in the midst of his "en-

emies." The details indicated that these were not hypothetical ideas to be carried out in some far-distant future but rather well-planned intentions ready for immediate implementation. The Mormons took advantage of their relatively meager, but entrenched, physical presence to project a vision of massive physical dominance onto the mental screens of their enemies. The signs they sent thus generated crisis-level tensions with those around them. It is difficult to explain the aggressive moves made by the Mormons in these months in any other way except as a concerted effort to increase tension. Those who opposed Mormon settlement in the region were more than happy to entertain paranoid fantasies of Mormon expansion, despite the fact that the Mormon settlements consisted in reality of only a few dozen homes and some small commercial establishments.

Mormon resistance to threats in Missouri continued throughout 1833. In that year, however, the citizens of Jackson County made it abundantly clear that the proposed city of Zion would not be built in Independence. In the summer of 1833, shortly after the publication of the defiant articles in the *Evening and the Morning Star,* a group of Missourians destroyed the Mormon printing press, vandalized a Mormon store, and brutalized several church leaders. In the aftermath of the violence, the local group informed the Mormons that their only course of action was to leave the area. Half of the Mormons were to leave by the end of the year, the other half by April 1834.[34]

Smith responded by issuing a defiant revelation in the name of the Lord. "Verily I say unto you," thundered the revelation, "that it is my will that a house should be built unto me in the land of Zion, like unto the pattern which I have given you. Yea, let it be built speedily."[35] In addition, Smith altered the earlier plans for the city, calling for a temple that was even larger than previously imagined.[36] Again, Smith and the Mormons responded to *physical* assaults with a vigorous expansion of the *physical* dimensions of their sanctuary. Smith was, of course, unable to expand his physical holdings, but he managed to play on the fears of those who opposed the Mormons by offering a rhetoric of expansion that served to increase tension without the expenditure of the resources required to build the physical city.

Smith's act of defiance sent the Missourians over the edge. On 31 October, Mormon settlements were attacked just west of the Big Blue River. These attacks lasted for more than a week as homes were ransacked and razed, and men, women, and children were beaten. The attacks climaxed on 4 November when two Missourians and one Mormon were killed. At this point, the rhetoric of boundaries no longer matched the reality of the situation. Faced with the prospect of dying for Zion, Mormons abandoned their defiant stance and fled northward in early 1834, abandoning plans to construct the city of Zion in the process.[37]

It should be noted here that dying for the cause of Zion was not seen as an outlandish option. Previous revelations contained imagery of dying for Zion, and Joseph Smith often spoke of what it would mean to die for the cause. In one of the first revelations received in Jackson County, the Mormons were promised that, if they died in the process of building up Zion, they "shall rest from all their labors, and their works shall follow them; and they shall receive a crown in the mansion of my Father."[38] In December 1833, as the Mormons in Missouri began to flee Jackson County, Smith wrote an impassioned letter in which he warned his followers that no matter what "sufferings" they were called upon to endure, "it is better in the eyes of God that you should die than that you should give up the land of Zion." Smith offered the advice that, in his opinion, it would be best if the Mormons would "retain your lands even to the uttermost."[39] Thus, the flight from Jackson County must be seen, in some measure, as retreat from the ideal. In addition to dealing with what appeared to be a failed prophecy, the Mormons were also left in a liminal state with regard to their physical boundaries because they did not have a full-fledged gathering place. For the next five years, the Mormons would remain in that liminal state, creating failed settlements in fits and starts, but failing to create a true stronghold.

Managing Physical Liminality, 1834–1839

After their expulsion from Jackson County, the Mormons settled in Clay County to the north, but the Missourians there soon grew uneasy as Joseph Smith initiated heavy immigration from the East into Clay County with plans to "redeem" the lands lost in Jackson County. Smith sent a letter from Kirtland to members of the high council in Clay County, instructing them to gather as many church members as possible into Clay County "in readiness to move into Jackson County in two years from eleventh of September next."[40] Within two years, the Mormons received an ultimatum from county leaders. On 29 June 1836, a meeting was held at Liberty, Missouri, at which a committee of leading citizens decided that the Mormons, because they were "eastern men, whose manners, habits, customs, and even dialect, are essentially different," could not help but arouse the "deepest hatred and detestation" of even the long-suffering Clay County citizenry.

Slavery also provided a stout stick with which to beat the Mormons, as it had since the first Mormons arrived in Missouri in 1831. The committee in Clay County pointed out that the Mormons were "opposed to slavery, which in this peculiar period when abolitionism has reared its deformed and haggard visage in our land, is well calculated to excite deep and abiding prejudices in any community where slavery is tolerated and protected."[41] Based on this evidence, the leaders present at the meeting concluded, "if they [the Mormons] have one spark of gratitude, they will not willingly plunge a people into civil war," which would, naturally, be the inevitable outcome if the Mormons continued their campaign of heavy settlement in Clay County.

In order to remedy the situation, the Mormons were called upon to leave the county "when their crops are gathered, their business settled, and they have made every suitable preparation to move." In the meantime, it fell to the Mormon leadership to see to it that "emigration [*sic*] cease, and cease immediately."[42] In order to expedite the removal of the Mormons, the Clay County leaders offered to assist them in finding another place in Missouri in which to settle. Not wishing to revisit the horrors of the Jackson County debacle of three years earlier, the Mormons in Clay County quietly acquiesced to the demands and "for the sake of friendship, and to be in a covenant of peace with the citizens of Clay county, and they to be in a covenant of peace with us, notwithstanding the necessary loss of property, and expense we incur in moving, we comply with the requisitions of their resolutions in leaving Clay county."[43] Joseph Smith, still residing in Kirtland, sent a letter of considerably sharper tone to the Clay County committee at the end of July. Smith denied all of the charges of Mormon land grabbing, abolitionism, and general disorder made by the committee, but in order not to "provoke their fellow men to acts of violence," Smith advised the Missouri citizens committee that the Mormons would "leave . . . [Clay] county . . . as fast as they can without incurring too much loss," although, Smith added ironically, "they have but little to lose if they lose the whole."[44]

In order to understand why Smith and other LDS leaders were able to absorb yet another defeat with such apparently little pique, it is necessary to examine an event that occurred in the spring and summer of 1834. In the spring of that year, Joseph Smith mounted an armed expedition to return to Jackson County and reclaim the lands that the saints had abandoned the previous winter. This expedition, officially known as "Zion's camp," sprang from a revelation received by Smith on 24 February 1834. In this revelation, the Mormons were commanded to return to Zion with at least a hundred men. Those who believed in Smith's revelations took courage in what they believed to be God's promise that the Mormons would "begin to prevail against mine enemies from this very hour. . . . [T]hey shall never cease to prevail until the kingdoms of the world are subdued under my feet, and the earth is given to the saints, to possess it forever and ever."[45] The language of boundaries is abundantly clear in this passage. The people in Missouri are defined as God's enemies ("mine" rather than simply "your" enemies), and the Mormons are set apart from the wicked "kingdoms of the world."

Something began to change with this revelation, however. The promises made here and in following revelations are conditional in a way that they were not before. Previous revelations had placed no caveat on the promises of Zion. In the February 1834 revelation, however, the Mormons were warned that "I have decreed a decree which my people shall realize [returning to build Zion] inasmuch as they hearken from this very hour unto the counsel which I, the Lord, shall give unto them."[46] If the Mormons failed to "keep my commandments," however, "the kingdoms of the world shall prevail against them," and they would be "good for nothing but to be cast out and trodden under the foot of men."[47]

In April 1834, Joseph Smith wrote a letter to Orson Hyde, who had been sent to branches of the church farther east to collect donations for the "redemption" of Zion. Smith wrote that, if the members of the church refused to contribute their substance for the cause of Zion, "God shall take away their talent and give it to those who have no talent, and shall prevent them from obtaining a place of refuge, or an inheritance upon the land of Zion." Smith tied their support of this cause to their worthiness to be part of God's chosen people. If they failed in this, Smith warned, "the blood of Zion [shall] be on their heads, even as upon the heads of their enemies, and their recompense will be as the recompense of [their] enemies."

This was an important development because it allowed for an explanation of the failure to recapture Zion, which Smith surely recognized as a distinct possibility, and it also warned the Mormons that their own impurity could result in the collapse of the boundaries that kept them safe from their enemies. The nature of those boundaries began to be reformulated as well. In the same revelation, the Mormons were given the following promise: "Inasmuch as mine enemies come against you to drive you from my goodly land, which I have consecrated to be the land of Zion . . . ye shall curse them, and whomever ye curse, I will curse. My presence shall be with you even in avenging me of mine enemies, unto the third and fourth generation of them that hate me."[48]

The Zion's camp expedition failed in its stated mission because the Mormons were met by a larger group of well-armed Missouri militiamen. Faced with the prospect of returning to Clay County empty-handed and with most of the expedition members racked with cholera, Smith provided a revelation to his exhausted followers. The church, according to this revelation, "should wait for a little season for the redemption of Zion." The Mormons were told that "the destroyer have I sent forth to lay waste mine enemies; and not many years hence they shall not be left to pollute mine heritage, and to blaspheme my name upon the lands which I have consecrated for the gathering of my saints."[49]

Beginning in 1834, Smith entered a phase of Mormon physical boundary creation that focused on the management of liminality. Smith had to explain the failure of his prophecies regarding the creation of Zion, he had to find some place for his followers to gather, and he had to buy time in order to find another opportunity to either redeem Zion in Jackson County or create it someplace else. With the 1834 Zion's camp revelation, Smith had accomplished two things simultaneously. First, he threatened his followers with exclusion from the group for failing in the effort, a threat that Smith hoped would provide an incentive for them to give their all to the creation of the physical boundaries of Zion. Second, recognizing that they might fail anyway, he provided a way to recreate the community and blame the failure on the wickedness and pollution of the Missouri ruffians. To the language of us versus them, another dimension had been added to these revelations: time. By telescoping the potential time frame through references to future generations and by acknowledging the possibility that the Mormons could again be expelled from Zion, the revelation removed some of the urgency so evident in earlier documents and created a sense of historical longevity.

The creation of this rhetorical space provided both an explanation for the failure to build Zion and a sense that, in some nebulous future, things would eventually work out. When the Mormons were faced with expulsion from Clay County, they were thus rhetorically prepared for the loss. For the remainder of Smith's life, the revelations he received regarding Zion would reflect this sense of an eventual, but unpredictable, return to Jackson County.

The Mormons in Missouri settled in the northern counties of Ray and Daviess, and lived in two main settlements, Far West and Adam-ondi-Ahman, until 1838. While Smith designated temple sites in each of these settlements, he did little to elaborate on what the role of these places would be. Much of this stemmed from Smith's preoccupation with difficulties in Kirtland. Regardless of the reasons, Smith simply paid little attention to these settlements and made no serious attempts to create true physical boundaries there. In the fall of 1838, the Mormons were expelled from Missouri at the behest of the state's governor, a major apostasy and financial scandal in Kirtland dictated the abandonment of that settlement, and for the first time the Mormons found themselves completely homeless.

Nauvoo: Mapping, Building, and Inhabiting the New Zion, 1839–1844

Although the Mormons' situation appeared dire, their difficulties actually allowed Smith to bring the group out of the phase of liminality regarding physical boundaries in which the church had languished since 1833. That phase had resulted in confusion among even high-ranking Mormons. According to Smith's journal, kept for him by his clerk Willard Richards, as late as the 1840s, church leaders were debating about "where Zion is."[50] Given the clear and direct revelations on the subject of Zion during the Missouri period, the fact that church leaders were themselves confused about the location of Zion is striking indeed.

Smith had an opportunity to eradicate the confusion in Illinois. For the first time, the vast majority of Mormons were concentrated in a single location. All of the church's resources could be focused on the creation of a single city. After the Mormons were driven from Missouri, Smith had purchased land in the tiny town of Commerce, Illinois, on the Mississippi River. Nauvoo, as Smith soon renamed it, quickly became a bustling town. "The name of our city," Smith wrote to the Mormons scattered in the East, "is of Hebrew origin, and signifies a beautiful situation, or place, carrying with it also, the idea of rest; and is truly descriptive of the most delightful location."[51] In Nauvoo, Smith introduced an ambitious new agenda that encompassed theological innovations, social experimentation, and political ambition. In the years between 1839, when the Mormons arrived, and 1844, when Smith was murdered, he introduced polygamy, eternal marriage, the temple endowment, and the secret Council of Fifty, and he ran for president of the United States. He also oversaw construction of a magnificent temple, which he was commanded to build in a revelation received in early 1841, and for the first and last time he created a sacred city of fully realized physical boundaries.

By the mid-1840s, it was becoming increasingly difficult for Smith to imagine returning to Missouri. Smith was still wanted on outstanding warrants related to the 1838 "Mormon War" in the state, and Missouri bounty hunters made a habit of coming into Nauvoo undercover, seeking to capture Smith and take him back with them. Smith was so concerned about this that, in December 1843, as mayor of Nauvoo, he issued the following decree:

Section 1. Be it ordained by the City Council of the City of Nauvoo, *according to the intent and meaning of the Charter* for the "benefit and convenience" of Nauvoo, that hereafter, if any person or persons shall come with process, demand or requisition, founded upon the aforesaid Missouri difficulties to arrest said Smith, he or they shall be subject to be arrested by any officer of the city, *with or without process,* and tried by the Municipal Court upon testimony, and if found guilty, sentenced to imprisonment in the City Prison FOR LIFE, which convict or convicts can only be pardoned by the Governor, *with the consent of the Mayor of said City.* Passed Dec[ember] 8, 1843.
JOSEPH SMITH, Mayor.[52]

Clearly, a return to Missouri would not be feasible in the near future. In response, Smith apparently made an alteration in his approach to the concept of the city of Zion. The key to understanding this shift is to appreciate the significance of the concept of the "center." As noted above, Smith taught that the place where the temple was to be built in the original city of Zion, in Jackson County, Missouri, was the previous location of the garden of Eden. The very place where the world began and from which creation spread to cover the earth was the place where Zion would be built in the latter days. Jackson County was thus the center of all creation from the time of Adam and Eve. Smith could not rescind that teaching and claim that any other location was the center of creation, so in Nauvoo the idea of the center took on a new meaning.

By the mid-1840s, the liminal phase was over, and Smith was teaching that Nauvoo was Zion. He had to put a creative spin on this teaching in order to minimize the cognitive dissonance it would likely produce among his followers. On 8 April 1844, Wilford Woodruff recorded in his journal that Joseph Smith had informed a body of church leaders that "the whole of North and South America is Zion. The mountain of the Lord's House is in the *center* of North and South America."[53] The term "mountain of the Lord's House" is borrowed from Isaiah 2:2–4, and Mormons had come to equate this with their temple. Nauvoo, Smith taught, was located in the *geographic* center of North and South America. Smith's journal entry added an important insight into this sermon that Woodruff missed. According to Smith's record, the Americas would become Zion "as soon as the [Nauvoo] Temple is finished."[54] Smith had become obsessed with temple building in these years of his life; it is no surprise that he now saw the temple at Nauvoo as the center of Zion. According to the view espoused by Smith, all of North and South America was Zion, but because "the mountain of the Lord's House is in the *center* of North and South America," Nauvoo must be the "Center place" of Zion.[55] No attempt was made to explain how this new center meshed with the earlier teaching, which held that Jackson County, Missouri, was the center place; references to the city of Zion in Missouri simply disappeared.

John Taylor published an editorial in one of the church's Nauvoo newspapers, the *Times and Seasons*, in June 1845 in which he employed the term Zion to refer specifically to Nauvoo. Taylor wrote that William Smith, Joseph Smith's unruly brother, had been appointed as patriarch of the church, "and his labors would be more especially connected with the Church in Zion; and he would take the lead, priority, or presidency of the Patriarchal office *in this place*."[56] Taylor's usage suggests a differentiation between small congregations outside of Nauvoo and Zion, by which he meant congregations within Nauvoo.

It is a mistake to overlook the role Nauvoo played in Joseph Smith's recasting of the Zionic ideal. Scholars typically skip this phase in the development of the concept of Zion, moving directly from Smith's identification of Zion in Missouri to the later dual notion of Zion both as a place in Missouri where a city would eventually, but not immediately, be built, as well as a term for any place where the "pure in heart" gathered.

Steve L. Olsen, for example, argued that Smith continued to insist upon the centrality of Jackson County even during the Nauvoo period. The problem is that Olsen does so based on a misreading of the sources for Smith's 8 April 1844 sermon discussed above. Olsen does not use either of the two contemporaneous accounts, produced by Willard Richards and Wilford Woodruff, but relies instead upon the much inferior published version of the sermon in the *History of the Church*. Even in the source Olsen used, however, the context clearly indicates that when Smith stated that "the mountain of the Lord should be . . . in the center of the land," he is referring to the Nauvoo temple, rather than the proposed temple in Jackson County, as Olsen asserts. The context of the statement regarding the geographic centrality of the temple, in both the *History* and in Woodruff's journal, clearly indicates that it is the Nauvoo temple being so designated.

In the *History*, Smith is quoted as saying that the mountain of the Lord is in the center of the land and that "as soon as the Temple and baptismal font are prepared, we calculate to give the Elders of Israel their washings and anointings."[57] Woodruff quoted Smith as saying, "The mountain of the Lord's house is the centre of North and South America. When the House is done, Baptism font erected and finished . . . then the Elders are to go through all America & build up Churches."[58] Smith never mentioned Missouri but clearly referenced the Nauvoo temple immediately after stating that the "mountain of the Lord's house" is in the center of the land.

It is a mistake to view the 1840s as a period of decentralization in Smith's thinking about Zion and the broader theme of physical boundaries.[59] My reading of the pertinent archival materials suggests that the idea that Zion could be found wherever Mormons resided came later, after the physical boundaries created in Nauvoo crumbled and eventually collapsed. In 1841, Joseph Smith, writing on behalf of the First Presidency to encourage any Mormons who had not yet made their way to Nauvoo to do so, proclaimed that "there is no other way for the Saints to be saved in these last days [except for] . . . this gathering together of all the saints [which] must take place before the Lord comes."[60] During the period between the founding of Nauvoo in 1839 and Smith's death five years later, Zion was centered on the Nauvoo temple.

Once the Mormons arrived in Nauvoo, it quickly became apparent that this was to be a stopover of indeterminate length. Even as early as 1841, an interesting shift in the Mormon concept of physical boundaries was taking place. On 15 January, the First Presidency sent a proclamation "to the saints scattered abroad." The proclamation briefly recounted the "horrid" events of the late 1830s that led the Mormons to seek refuge in Illinois, a place that Smith portrayed as a bastion of "good Samaritans" willing to "bind up the [Mormons'] wounds." Smith also noted that the city of Nauvoo, at that point less than two years old, was "increasing with unparalleled rapidity, numbering more than 3,000 inhabitants." Nauvoo, Smith continued, was well situated for success in agricultural, manufacturing, and mechanical endeavors. Without explicitly acknowledging the change, Smith signaled a major shift in LDS thinking on the subject of Zion when he wrote that in Nauvoo the Mormons had thus far been "instrumental in laying a foundation for the gathering of Zion," and he encouraged "all who appreciate the blessings of the gospel . . . [to] prepare for the general gathering [in Nauvoo]." Smith advised the Mormons scattered throughout the East to come to Nauvoo and "establish and build up manufactures in this city, [and] purchase and cultivate farms in the county." Using the same language he had used in the earlier revelations, which referred to lands in Jackson County, Smith said that in Nauvoo the Mormons would find their *permanent* inheritance."[61]

Four days later, Smith recorded a revelation that apparently conveyed God's will that a temple be constructed at Nauvoo.[62] The revelation contained language from Isaiah:

[C]ome ye, with all your gold, and your silver, and your precious stones, and with all your antiquities . . . and bring the box tree, and the fir tree, and the pine tree, together with all the precious trees of the earth. . . . And with iron, with copper, and brass, and with zinc, and with all your precious things of the earth . . . build a house to my name, for the Most High to dwell therein.[63]

In 1831, Smith had said very similar things about the site for Zion in Missouri. On that occasion, he remarked:

[I]t is recollected that the prophets have said concerning Zion in the last days: how the glory of Lebanon is to come upon her; the fir tree, the pine tree, and the box together, to beautify the place of his sanctuary, that he may make the place of his feet glorious, where for brass he will bring gold, and for iron he will bring silver, and for wood brass, and for stones iron; and where the feast of fat things will be given to the just; yea, when the splendor of the Lord is brought to one consideration, for the good of his people: the calculations of men and the vain glory of the world vanishes; and we exclaim: God will shine—the perfection of beauty out of Zion.[64]

Nauvoo was taking shape as the headquarters of the church, the new permanent place of inheritance, the place where the temple would be erected, and as the new center, not of all creation, but of North and South America. Smith believed that in this city he would live out his days in peace and power. In the absence of fanfare and theological justification, Nauvoo became Zion out of the sheer power of Smith's words. Clearly, Smith intended Nauvoo to be a sacred center and the place of gathering for the Mormons, not simply one of many potential Zions.

The creation and maintenance of physical boundaries in Nauvoo followed a pattern similar in many respects to that found in Missouri, with the significant exception of the overall initial success in Nauvoo. Smith had apparently learned something from his experiences in Missouri because he immediately sought to consolidate power and erect stronger boundaries when he arrived in Nauvoo. The first major effort in this direction was the adoption of Nauvoo's charter. The Illinois legislature had granted a spate of charters to various municipalities in the state in the years immediately preceding the Mormons' arrival in Nauvoo. All of these charters included much of the same language and provided for many of the same offices and government organizations. The Nauvoo charter differed in that it allowed for the creation of a militia, the Nauvoo Legion, which would one day become second only to the U.S. Army in size.[65] Although the Nauvoo charter was similar to those in other cities, because church leaders also held the most prominent government positions, the situation quickly came to be viewed by outsiders as a quasi-theocracy. The charter ceded to Smith all legal and police authority, which meant that he was ensconced behind a barrier of religio-legal power that was unheard of in nineteenth-century America.

On a broader scale, Smith certainly recognized the political power that he wielded, something which the Missourians had feared, but which Smith never actually used to his advantage in the 1830s. In the Nauvoo period, Smith actively promised support to various political candidates and sometimes craftily switched loyalties. The backlash was considerable, and it was exacerbated by the fact that Smith's opponents had little recourse. Complex political machinations ensued, but the results were clear: many politicians in Illinois, Democrat and Whig alike, were calling for the repeal of the Nauvoo charter, the disbanding of the Nauvoo Legion, and the extradition of Smith to Missouri. He responded to this pressure by reinforcing the power of the charter and his position as mayor. For the first time, he was able to create a true physical boundary in which he amassed all political, social, religious, and martial power within the confines of his city.

Smith clearly had no intention of backing down from the political scene, and he worked, as in Missouri, to further the tension between the Mormons and the people in Illinois. His rhetoric reflected these efforts. In late June 1843, Smith told an excited Nauvoo audience that "he had restrained the saints from using violence in self defense but from henceforth he restrained them no more."[66] Another report of the same speech quoted Smith as telling the crowd, "I will lead you to battle if you are not afraid to die and feel disposed to spill your blood."[67] He further warned that, while he had exhibited patience in the past, "I swear I will not deal so mildly with them again for the time has come when forbearance is no longer a virtue."[68] Smith also addressed the concern that Nauvoo had become too powerful. To this charge, Smith responded by proclaiming, "all the power there was in Illinois" had been given to Nauvoo.[69]

Smith had come to view Nauvoo as an equal with the state of Illinois, and he promised to "roar like thunder" at anyone who challenged this view. Thus, in the political realm, Smith reacted to pressure with increased hostility and a ratcheting up of the tensions and the rigidity of the boundaries surrounding the community. In Missouri, the Mormons had laid plans for a celestial city which had been summarily crushed. In the aftermath of that defeat, they entered a liminal phase with little connection to any sacred space or physical boundaries. By the mid-1840s, they had created a new Zion in Illinois, where they carefully cultivated the power necessary to create and maintain a true boundary with the world.

A similar set of circumstances was unfolding in the religious sphere. During this period, Smith began introducing the idea of plural marriage along with several other controversial practices. Smith insisted that polygamy remain secret, but word leaked out. Soon, he was facing opposition from former Mormons who demanded that Smith admit his "spiritual wifery" and cease the practice. These defectors formed a new church, called the Reformed Mormon Church, which "acknowledged the authority of the Book of Mormon, Doctrine and Covenants, &c. [but although they had] believed that Joe Smith was a prophet, that he is now fallen from grace."[70]

Smith responded by exercising his considerable power to regulate affairs within his city, arresting several of these men and publishing disingenuous denials of polygamy in Nauvoo newspapers. Smith also spoke of his "enemies in the city intermingling with the saints," noting that they possessed "the same spirit that crucified Christ" and referring to them as "foes of my own house."[71] Smith faced a serious endogenous threat to his physical boundaries, and this threat set off a chain reaction that would eventually destroy the city and end Smith's life.

In 1844, the members of the dissenting group published a single issue of a newspaper, the *Nauvoo Expositor,* which told readers, in purple prose to be sure, the facts about Smith's plural marriage system. William Law, a leader of the group, wrote that his disaffection from the LDS Church stemmed from the introduction of "odious traits" during the 1840s, including "false swearing, lying, stealing, robbery, defrauding, polygamy, adultery, fornication, [and] blasphemy." The purpose of the *Nauvoo Expositor* was to "place Joseph Smith and his base accomplices in crime, before the world in their true character," as "gross, dark, loathsome, and cruel" individuals.[72]

Smith had been waiting for the paper to hit the streets since at least the first week of May, when he noted in his journal that "an opposition printing press arrived" at the home of one of the dissenters.[73] On 8 May, the *Warsaw Signal,* an anti-Mormon newspaper published in a town south of Nauvoo, reported that "a new press will soon be procured [in fact, it already had been] and a paper started which will be devoted to building up the cause of the seceders, and to an exposition of Joe Smith's enormities and mal-practices."[74] In early June, two days after the publication of the *Expositor,* Smith held a three-hour city council meeting "investigating the merits of the *Nauvoo Expositor.*"[75] As he later explained in an official proclamation defending his actions, Smith and the council determined that the publishers of the newspaper were guilty of attempting "to excite the jealousy and prejudice of the people of the surrounding country, by libels, and slanderous articles for the purpose of destroying the 'Charter' of said city, and for the purpose of raising suspicion, wrath, and indignation among a certain class of the less honourable portion of mankind to commit acts of violence upon the innocent and unsuspecting."[76]

The crimes of "slandering the Municipality of the city" resulted in orders to "destroy the *Nauvoo Expositor* establishment." William Clayton noted the existence of a meaningless caveat which offered the publishers of the paper a reprieve if they moved the press out of Nauvoo within three hours. When the editors of the *Expositor* failed to accomplish that impossible task, the police were ordered to the scene and "demolished the press and scattered the type."[77] At eight o'clock, "the Marshall reported [back to Smith] that he had removed the press, type, and printed papers and fixtures into the street and fired them."[78]

There are no records to indicate that the Mormons ever engaged in book burning, but Smith's destruction of the copies of the *Expositor* and the press upon which they were printed served the same symbolic purpose. The destruction of entire libraries, single books, and the presses upon which "subversive" materials are printed all represent the enactment of the same impulses: the destruction of "all forces acting counter" to the dominant group's agenda and the attempt to eradicate "diversity of thought and critical analysis."[79] By destroying the *Expositor* press, Smith was reacting to the presence of subversive ideas within his physical boundaries. The publishers of the *Expositor* chose to set up the press in Nauvoo as a literal and symbolic breach of the physical space dominated by Smith, and Smith returned the favor with a literal and symbolic act of his own. Smith would not tolerate subversive ideas, nor would he stand for the invasion of his physical boundaries by disloyal apostates. That Smith felt secure in committing such an act is a reflection of his confidence in the strength of the physical boundaries he had worked so hard to create.

Naturally, the Nauvoo dissenters saw things differently. In an article published in the *St. Louis Evening Gazette,* dissenter Charles A. Foster explained that those in Nauvoo with opinions differing from Joseph Smith's were faced with the choice of establishing a "press of their own, or else, quietly submit[ting] to the foul and false assertions which were heaped upon them wholesale." Foster argued that the *Expositor* represented an attempt at free expression and that its publishers drew the ire of the Mormon prophet simply because "they dared to think for themselves and express their honest opinions."[80]

Smith's aggressive and impulsive act against the *Expositor* had immediate consequences. Most significantly, a warrant was issued for Smith's arrest. Initially, Smith sought refuge across the Mississippi River in Iowa. But unable to leave his followers alone in such straits for long, Smith returned to Nauvoo and then headed for Carthage, the Hancock County seat, the next day. While Smith, who was accompanied by Hyrum Smith, Willard Richards, and John Taylor, was being held over for trial at Carthage, a mob with blackened faces stormed the jail. Joseph Smith "sprung to his coat for his six-shooter," but there was no hope of escape. Hyrum leaned against the door in a vain attempt to keep the armed group at bay, but a slug blasted through the door, striking him in the face. Hyrum Smith fell to the floor muttering "I am a dead man," while his brother's pistol jammed.[81] Joseph Smith headed for the window and reached it just as the mob burst through the door and slammed four bullets into his body. Smith fell from the second-story window into the midst of the whooping crowd below.[82] John Taylor also took four slugs, but according to long-standing Mormon legend his pocket watch caught the potentially fatal ball just before it entered his heart.[83] Willard Richards, another apostle in the jail with the Smith brothers and Taylor, received no wounds. At eight o'clock, he scrawled a hasty message to the Mormons at Nauvoo: "Joseph and Hyrum are dead. Taylor wounded, not very badly. I am well. Our guard was forced, as we believe, by a band of Missourians from 100 to 200. The job was done in an instant, and the party fled towards Nauvoo instantly. This is as I believe it. The citizens here are afraid of the Mormons attacking them. I promise them no!"[84] Taylor insisted that Richards underplay the severity of his wounds, which were in fact life threatening, in order not to cause more panic in Nauvoo.[85] By the time the note reached Nauvoo the next morning, word of the murders had already reached the Mormons, but the Mormons had trouble believing it.

Most of the apostles and many of Smith's other close associates were away from Nauvoo on missions promoting Joseph Smith's bid for the U.S. presidency when the Smith brothers were gunned down. News of the murders took as long as three weeks to reach them. Amasa Lyman, a close friend of Joseph Smith's, was preaching in Newport, Kentucky, when he learned of the tragedy. After hearing the news, Lyman morosely recorded in his journal that he "waited through the day for correct information on the matter." The next day, "no information" reached him, and Lyman still "remained in suspense." As he anxiously waited for word, Lyman watched the town prepare for Independence Day and noted with bitter irony that the celebration of the "birth of American liberty . . . might better have been turned into its funerale [sic]." Finally, on 6 July, "the news was confirmed."[86]

Charles C. Rich, the raw-boned Indiana native who served as a general in Smith's Nauvoo Legion and would be ordained an apostle in 1849, simply refused to accept the news of Smith's murder when it reached him in the midst of his missionary duties in New York. Rich blandly noted in early July that "newspapers report excitement at Nauvoo," and the next day observed that "stories increase of Nauvoo and Joseph." Two days later, Rich noted with surprise that "the papers report Joseph and Hiram [sic] shot, and the people believe it." Rich, for his part, clearly did *not* believe it, and when he encountered a group of Mormons grieving the loss of their leader, he noted with satisfaction that he "succeeded in some good degree in dispersing their anxious fears and strengthened them in unbelief of newspaper falsehoods." A week later, however, Rich had broken through his denial and lashed out at the people and government of the United States, which "exulted" in the death of the Smith brothers. "They might better," Rich mused caustically, "bemoan their own pending fate and that of our own happy country in fulfillment of his [Smith's] predictions."[87] Apostle George A. Smith, too, reported his skepticism upon hearing the news of the murders. Smith and his traveling companions all "pronounced the account a hoax." The next day, however, Smith arrived at a Mormon congregation in Indiana, where the news was confirmed and "many gave themselves up to weeping."[88]

In the aftermath of the murder, the Mormon community was stunned. Vilate Kimball wrote to her husband, Heber, an apostle who, like most of the rest of the apostles, was serving a proselytizing mission in the East when the murders occurred. "I shall not attempt to describe the scene that we have passed through," the distraught Kimball wrote. "God forbid that I should witness another like unto it." Kimball sadly told her husband that she "saw the lifeless corpses of our beloved brethren" and had "witnessed [the] tears [of the men's families] and their groans, which was enough to rend the heart of an adamant." Attempting to convey the depth of loss felt by those in the community, Vilate Kimball wrote that "the very streets of Nauvoo seem to mourn."[89]

Speculation among the Mormons on why God would allow this to happen to the beloved prophet swirled. The matter generally came to be viewed as a martyrdom, with Smith voluntarily surrendering his life to "seal his mission and his works with his blood." Wilford Woodruff's reminiscence typified the standard Mormon interpretation of Smith's death. "It seemed strange to me at that time [1844] why the Prophet and his brother Hyrum were permitted to be taken out of our midst," Woodruff candidly admitted, but "on reflection, I became convinced that [Smith] had been ordained to die—to shed his blood as a testimony to this dispensation."[90] Brigham Young offered a different explanation in 1858. According to Young, Smith decided to surrender himself "through the persuasion of others," and once he did so he did not have "one particle of light" in him. Furthermore, Young argued, if Smith had "followed the revelations that were in him he would have been our earthly shepherd today."[91]

Whatever the reason for his death, by the time the bloated and bloody bodies of Joseph Smith and his brother Hyrum rolled into Nauvoo in the summer of 1844, a pall had settled over the community. Mormon physical boundaries were in jeopardy once again. Smith personally had controlled most of the regulatory mechanisms that made

Nauvoo such a secure city for the Mormons. The murder of Smith and his brother was a decapitation that resulted in a serious erosion of those boundaries.

Despite their grief and the fear of continued violence, for most of the next year the Mormons in Nauvoo attempted to carry on as before and managed to achieve a degree of stability. Brigham Young sounded an optimistic note in a letter to Wilford Woodruff in England. Young reported that the Mormons enjoyed "peace in the city," and that despite the repeal of the Nauvoo charter "by a large majority in both houses [of the Illinois legislature], we remain undisturbed, the city affairs go on as usual." Young even held out hope that the Nauvoo charter might be restored through an appeal to the U.S. Supreme Court. The letter closed with Young's assurance that "union, love, and peace were never more universal among the saints at Nauvoo, than at the present time."[92] Construction on the temple continued, and the turmoil that had dominated 1844 had calmed sufficiently for one Mormon woman to note in April 1845 that "Peace and Prosperity reigns in the City [along with] good order and br[otherly] love."[93]

In May 1845, Young wrote to Apostle Parley Pratt that "we are pretty well satisfied that the Mob are frustrated in their plans, and either have not courage enough or are unable to raise an excitement sufficient to make a breeze." Young also cheerfully reported that the "Temple is progressing rapidly," along with a building that had been planned as an arsenal but that the church leaders now wanted to use as an "academy," owing to the forced disbanding of the Nauvoo Legion earlier in the year.[94]

On the first anniversary of Smith's murder, Young wrote again to Woodruff, and his letter practically bubbled with good news, including Young's opinion that the environment in Nauvoo was so serene that it seemed "like a foretaste of celestial enjoyment and Millennial glory."[95] In July, church trustees Newell K. Whitney and George Miller sent a letter to Parley Pratt, releasing him from his mission in New York and assuring him that "the most perfect union still prevails in our midst and especially in our little councils."[96] The letter concluded by encouraging Pratt to "bring all the temple funds that you can possibly raise, as we shall want a great amount of money this fall to purchase oil, paints, nails, etc. [for the temple]."[97] The allocation of money to the construction of the temple indicates a sense of security that would not last.

The Collapse of the Physical Boundaries, 1845–1846

It did not take long for the picture to darken considerably. Just below the apparently calm surface of life in Nauvoo, serious trouble brewed as the inevitable consequences of Smith's death took their toll on Mormon power in Nauvoo. The Illinois legislature had repealed the Nauvoo charter on 29 January 1845. Later that year, arrest warrants were issued on charges of counterfeiting against Brigham Young and eight other apostles by the U.S. District Court in Springfield, Illinois.[98] In March, Apostle John Taylor wrote a letter in which he pleaded with the governors of several states to "furnish us an asylum where we can enjoy our rights of conscience and religion unmolested."[99] Not surprisingly, none of the governors to whom Taylor wrote offered any help. With the charter repealed, the Mormon government lost its control over local law enforcement and the courts.

By late summer, the veneer of peace over which Young exulted in his letters to England was shattered. Sensing weakness in the physical strength of the Mormon stronghold, many Illinois citizens who had long resented the Mormons' presence in the state took action. Violence swelled, beginning with attacks on some of the smaller Mormon settlements in Hancock County. In September, word reached Nauvoo that "mobs" had been burning houses in Morely's settlement, twenty-five miles south of Nauvoo.[100] Solomon Hancock, a Mormon leader in the beleaguered hamlet, wrote to LDS authorities in Nauvoo explaining that the attackers had set fire to more than forty houses and nonresidential buildings in the settlement and had destroyed hundreds of bushels of wheat and other grain.[101]

Despite the renewed violence, Mormon leaders worked hard to stiffen their flock's flagging resistance. Young and his advisors concluded that the mob was "intending to burn out the Brethren until they had driven in all the Branches that lived out[side]" of Nauvoo.[102] Young dispatched a letter to Solomon Hancock, ordering him to allow the mobs to burn as many houses as they wanted in order to keep them busy while the women and children were evacuated to Nauvoo. Young suggested in his letter that the outlying settlements might have to be sacrificed in order to spare Nauvoo. "What is a little property or a few lives," Young mused, "compared with the properties and lives of a great [number of] people, and the house [temple] and ordinances upon which the salvation of that people depend?"

Young's letter indicated that the Mormons still believed that they had a chance of maintaining a permanent residence in Nauvoo if they could make a sufficient case against the behavior of the mobs and renew public support for the Mormon cause. To this end, Young instructed Hancock to "employ the best scribe you have, or half a dozen of them if necessary, to pen minutely all the movements of the enemy and . . . what houses are burned, by whom, at what hour, who were present, and who saw them do it, etc."[103] Young clearly clung to some degree of hope that, once the violence subsided, attempts at legal redress could be undertaken.

Two days later, John Taylor met with "one of the brethren deputed by Col. Williams the Chief Mobocrat," who promised to stop burning Mormon properties in the county if the Mormons would agree to leave in the spring of 1846. Church leaders, according to Taylor, "paid him no attention," firm in the belief that the "persecutors" were "heaping up to themselves wrath against the day of wrath, and that justice will speedily overtake them, and they will be taken in their own snare."[104] The same day, Brigham Young confidently predicted that "the saints would have a winter of peace."[105]

The tough rhetoric notwithstanding, the Mormons were running out of options. Back-channel negotiations between prominent opponents of the Mormons and LDS leaders had been moving in fits and starts for several days. Finally, Young issued a proclamation to Levi Williams and others in which Young flatly stated that the Mormons were planning to leave Nauvoo if the "mobbers" would cease "destructive operations" against Mormon settlements.[106] Although the recipients of this proclamation welcomed the promised evacuation of the Mormons, they objected to being referred to in the document's preamble as members of a "mob," and they felt that agreeing to the truce in its present form would be tantamount to making a "tacit confession that they were engaged in 'burning the houses, etc.'"[107] Young refused to make any move toward softening the language of the proclamation, and the matter was dropped.

Four days later, no doubt intrigued by the Mormon offer of withdrawal, delegates from nine Illinois counties gathered at Quincy, Illinois, to discuss plans for removing the Mormons from Nauvoo. The Quincy committee decided that the Mormons would have to leave, either by choice or by force.[108] Young faced a monumental decision. He could allow his actions to follow the rhetoric emanating from the Mormon leadership, which would involve digging in and using what was left of the Nauvoo Legion as a military force in the siege of Nauvoo that would inevitably follow. Young and the other leaders would almost certainly be killed or captured in such a battle, church property would be seized, and the Mormon church would be dissolved. On the other hand, Young could acquiesce to the demands of the committee, leave Nauvoo, and save the Mormon church. The price would be the complete collapse of Nauvoo as a physical boundary.

As the history of alternative religious movements has demonstrated, "end times" scenarios frequently shape up in just such a fashion, with the group provoking a final battle between good and evil that they expect to win through God's intervention. It is extremely telling that the Mormons, for neither the first nor the last time, avoided such a scene.[109]

Late on the evening of 24 September, after an emotional visit to the room where the Smith brothers had been murdered, Brigham Young responded to the request of the committee and declared that the Mormons were prepared to leave Illinois for "some place where the peculiar organization of our Church will not be likely to engender so much strife and contention as unhappily exists at this time." Young assured the Quincy committee that the Mormons would "leave this county next spring, for some point so remote, that there will not need be any difficulty with the people and ourselves."[110] Not surprisingly, the committee accepted Young's proposal, noting that it was "too late to attempt the settlement of difficulties in Hancock county upon any other basis than the removal of the Mormons from the State."[111] Almost immediately after the decision to flee west was made, a new interpretation of the stay in Nauvoo emerged. Although Mormon reactions to the committee were conciliatory to the point of obsequiousness, Young and others remained defiant.

Two days after Young wrote his letter of capitulation to the Quincy committee, he told a meeting of the Nauvoo Legion that he would never spend another "winter in the United States except on a visit—we do not owe this country a single thing." More important, Young confidently assured the assembled group that the church had "calculated to go [out of Nauvoo] all the while for I do not intend to stay in such a Hell of a Hole."[112]

At the church's general conference in October, the recasting of the purpose of the Nauvoo sojourn continued. The fall 1845 conference represents a watershed moment in Mormon history, although it has received little attention from scholars. During the conference, the leadership of the LDS Church engaged in a performance that would modify the group's collective memory regarding the entire purpose of the Nauvoo experiment and long-held notions about the nature of physical boundaries in general. In a powerful set of discourses lasting three days, Mormon apostles offered a new narrative in the guise of long-held beliefs.

Apostle Amasa Lyman drew parallels with the Missouri experience in a sermon in which he reminded his audience that God "said in Missouri he would sustain the saints for a time; and he did it. And when we came here, the Lord said, that if the people of the state of Illinois would maintain us in our rights they would be blessed; if not we might find it to our advantage to leave them."[113] No extant revelation contains such a caveat as Lyman described in this sermon, and it appears that he projected the justifications made by various church leaders for the expulsion from Missouri onto the situation in Illinois. Heber C. Kimball simply asserted that he was "glad the time is come to go; I have looked for it for years."[114] Kimball did not elaborate or explain why he might have been expecting it for years, nor why he did not mention it before. Parley P. Pratt also claimed to have "waited long to leave this land of *Liberty* and go to a place where God owns the land," and he saw in the exodus from Nauvoo the hand of God guiding the Mormons to a place where "there will be more room for the saints to grow and increase." In one of the first attempts to shift the idea of Zion from one focused on a particular city to a truly diffuse notion which located Zion wherever members of the true church lived, Pratt added that God sought to take the Mormons from Nauvoo to teach them that the people of God "cannot always live in one small town or country or state."

Pratt speculated that the root cause of the continued difficulties for the Mormons was their inability to remain equal. When the Mormons first arrived in Missouri, Pratt argued, everyone was more or less on the same footing. Eventually, divisions began to show, with some Mormons becoming prideful because of their "riches." In order to humble them, God allowed persecutions to come upon the Mormons. Pratt discerned the same pattern in Nauvoo. "When we landed in Illinois, we were all about alike," Pratt remembered, but "we now find many wealthy and many poor."[115]

An issue of the *Times and Seasons* containing a report of the conference also included a circular sent to the various LDS communities, declaring that "a crisis of extraordinary and thrilling interest has arrived." The circular continued the theme that had been so popular at the conference, casting the impending evacuation of Nauvoo as a long-expected opportunity and none too subtly reminding the Mormon readers, "You all know and have doubtless felt for years the necessity of a removal," if conditions in Nauvoo deteriorated. In the months before the decision to evacuate was made, many church leaders expected that God would intervene on their behalf and destroy their enemies before an evacuation was necessary. Nevertheless, the reconstitution of what the entire Nauvoo period meant to the Mormons had begun in earnest.

Nauvoo, according to the new interpretation, was a brief stopping place, not the center of Zion, and merely an opportunity for God to test both the mettle of his saints and the intentions of the American nation. According to Mormon rhetoric, the saints passed, but the nation failed. The circular compared the Mormons with Jesus Christ, who was "delivered up into the hands of the Jewish nation to save or condemn them—to be well or mal-treated by them; according to the determinate counsel and foreknowledge of God." Just as the Jews demonstrated their true colors by executing Jesus, the argument went, so the American nation had sealed its fate through its "bigotry, intolerance and insatiable oppression" of the people of God. The Mormons were advised not to view this turn of events as a "catastraphe [*sic*] wholly unlooked for," because "[t]he spirit of prophecy has long since portrayed in the Book of Mormon, what might be the conduct of this nation towards the Israel of the last days."[116] Erastus Snow, a mid-level general authority, apparently internalized the message being sent by higher church leaders. Snow rejoiced that the decision to leave Nauvoo "was unanimously resolved in the councils of the church," and he saw it as a providential door "which the Lord God had opened before us by which we could make a peaceable exit from this corrupt nation and establish ourselves independent of them."[117]

Wilford Woodruff got word of the evacuation of Nauvoo in a letter from Young while the former still labored as a missionary in England, isolated from other church leaders and unaware of the reinterpretation of the Nauvoo period that leaders in Illinois were constructing. Contra the new rhetoric emanating from his brethren in Nauvoo, Woodruff offered no hint that he expected the outcome described in Young's letter. Woodruff seemed stunned, noting that "the Saints having built the Temple of the Lord & the City of Joseph [Nauvoo] are now about to be drove out of it by the American Nation," a turn of events that prompted Woodruff to conclude, "This is a Strange Age we live in." Woodruff's surprise is not terribly shocking given his firmly held belief that God would deal ruthlessly with Mormonism's opponents.

Less than three weeks before learning that the saints were leaving Nauvoo, Woodruff had reflected on the teachings of the Book of Mormon regarding the end times. For Woodruff, the Book of Mormon message was crystal clear: the "American nation and all the Gentile nations of the earth" need to be warned that "unless they speedily repent of there [sic] sins & humble themselves before God they will be destroyed from off the land." Zion, according to Woodruff, "must arise and flourish for the Lord has spoken it." The nations of the earth that persecuted Zion would soon be defeated "for the bitter branches of the tree are about to be cut off to make room for the good fruit."[118] Little wonder that the news of the flight of the Mormons from the "city of Joseph" rocked Woodruff so. True to his particularly potent millennialist approach to life, Woodruff absorbed the bad news and ominously concluded that "American liberty with her proud eagle found a sepulcher" and that "the State of Illinois And the whole United States have filled up there [sic] Cup of Iniquity And well may the Saints go out of her midst As did Lot out of Sodom for her Judgment and destruction is equally sure."[119]

Woodruff's reaction is important because it demonstrates the power of collective thought and action in the creation, maintenance, and reformulation of the entire concept of physical boundaries. With a critical mass of leaders operating in Nauvoo, a new rhetoric emerged in which the Mormons pulled off a masterstroke of narrative inversion. In order to make this new interpretation work, however, the leaders had to reinforce a collective memory that was literally false but was fashioned into a remembered, functional truth. Leaders in Nauvoo accomplished this during the critical early period after the decision to leave was made through their addresses at the general conference and in the circular they published. Woodruff's personal journal records a much different reaction, largely because of his inability to consult with other Mormon leaders, who were busily reminding each other that they had always known that Nauvoo would be abandoned. The Mormon leaders at Nauvoo were engaged in a modification of their own tradition in order to maintain stability. They were scrambling to find a version of the past that would motivate and energize their community in the present in a way that the old story would not.[120] Nauvoo, in the fall of 1845, was the birthplace of a new tradition posing as an eternal tradition.

The power of the effort to rework Mormon collective memory that began in the fall of 1845 is borne out in the increasingly frequent references to Joseph Smith's prophetic foreknowledge of the Mormon move out of Nauvoo and into the West. In the months following the decision to abandon Nauvoo, more specific "recollections" emerged regarding what Joseph Smith and other church leaders supposedly knew about the fate of Nauvoo. In April 1846, after the decision had been made to head west, Apostle Orson Hyde suddenly remembered that "Joseph Smith declared in council that it was the will and mind of God to go to the West."[121] In 1847, Brigham Young announced, "it was the design of Joseph to leave Nauvoo and flee to the mountains."[122] In August 1847, Orson Pratt delivered a sermon in which he argued that "this very place, point, and spot the pioneers have found [Salt Lake]" must be the "City of Zion" spoken of by Isaiah.[123] In 1848, Young claimed that Smith had known about the Mormons' eventual settlement in Utah as early as 1831. "From the days of Oliver Cowdery and Parley Pratt on the borders of the Lamanites," Young reminisced, "Joseph Smith had longed to be here. They would not let us come but at last we have accomplished it."[124]

Young was beginning to argue for an interpretation of Mormon history that suggested that the Mormons had always wanted to head to the Rocky Mountains but had been prevented from doing so by their enemies. Young continued to hammer on Smith's foreknowledge of the West throughout his life. By 1850, the concept had become so ingrained in Mormon collective memory that many Mormons simply took for granted the fact that Smith had predicted the move to Utah. Jonathan Duke Oldham, who joined the LDS Church in 1839 and lived in Nauvoo, wrote in his 1850 autobiography that, in early 1845, church leaders "made known to the church" the "grand plan of the church to move to the west, which had previously been concocted by Joseph Smith."[125] In 1858, Young could simply assert, almost as a footnote to a discourse on a different subject, that "Joseph intended to go west; he designed to raise a company to come to the very country we now occupy."[126]

Joseph Smith was thus remembered as the one who always knew that Zion in Missouri would not be redeemed in his lifetime, that the strong physical boundaries he had created in Nauvoo would be breached and end in his death and a destroyed temple, and that the Rocky Mountains would be a place of rest for the Mormons. As time went on, recollections in this vein grew more prevalent and more detailed. The stories and reminiscences conform to a typical pattern. They always involve a memory in which Joseph Smith spoke very specifically about a time when the Mormons would end up "in the Rocky Mountains." This phrase is replicated in many stories, which is important to note because in no extant manuscript does Joseph Smith ever use the phrase "Rocky Mountains" to designate a possible gathering place for the Mormons.[127] Oliver B. Huntington, for example, recalled that in 1840 Joseph Smith's father visited Huntington's home and said that "the Lord" had informed Joseph Jr. that the Mormons would stay in Nauvoo only "seven years," after which time they would go "into the Rocky Mountains."[128] In 1897, Huntington claimed to have met "Hopkins G. Pendar an old Nauvoo Mormon," at the "Hall of Relicks [sic]" where he learned that "Joseph Smith, just before he was killed, made a sketch of the future home of the saints in the Rocky Mountains, and their route or road to that country as he had seen in a vision."[129]

Others claimed that Smith communicated this information to them in the form of blessings. In 1902, seventy-six-year-old Paulina Eliza Phelps swore out an affidavit in which she claimed that, when she was five years old in 1832, Joseph Smith gave her a blessing in which he "said that I should live to go to the Rocky Mountains. I did not know at the time what the term 'Rocky Mountains' meant, but I supposed it to be something connected with the Indians. This frightened me for the reason that I dreaded the very sight of an Indian."[130]

Church leaders helped to cement this folklore firmly in Mormon collective memory. Perhaps the most famous of such high-ranking leaders "remembering" Smith's foreknowledge of the exodus was Wilford Woodruff. In 1898, just before his death, Woodruff told the church's general conference that, in 1834, Joseph Smith had told him:

[T]his Church will fill North and South America—it will fill the world. It will fill the Rocky Mountains. There will be tens of thousands of Latter-day Saints who will be gathered in the Rocky Mountains. They will there build temples to the Most High. They will raise up a posterity there, and the Latter-day Saints who dwell in these mountains will stand in the flesh until the coming of the Son of Man. The Son of Man will come to them while in the Rocky Mountains.[131]

Based on the reminiscences recorded during the Utah period, one would be forced to conclude not only that Joseph Smith knew that the Mormons were destined to end up in the Salt Lake Valley, but he apparently never stopped talking about the future awaiting the saints in the Rocky Mountains.[132] The historical records from Smith's lifetime are, however, bereft of any but the most vague notions of a mission to the "West" to preach to the Lamanites—a notion that Joseph Smith almost certainly believed to be associated with Missouri, not the intermountain region of the Far West. On the date that Wilford Woodruff later said Smith gave his 1834 prophecy, Woodruff's journal states only that, at a Sunday meeting, "Brother Sidney Rigdon, Orson Hide [sic], Orson Pratt and others spoke—Joseph Smith closing—during the meeting. It appeared to me there was more light made manifest at that meeting respecting the gospel and Kingdom of God than I had ever received from the whole sectarian world."[133] Woodruff often made anticlerical and sectarian comments indicating his general displeasure with the mainstream American Christian landscape, and there is no reason to read these comments any differently. There is certainly no evidence to support Woodruff's 1898 assertion that Smith made plain his knowledge of the Mormons' future home in the West. The same is true of all of these recollections. More typical of contemporary accounts is that of Levi Jackman, a member of the vanguard company led by Brigham Young to Utah in 1847. In his journal, Jackman recorded that he left home with a group of "pioneers to find a location for the saints some where in the west."[134]

It is not the point of this discussion to ridicule Smith or his followers, to attack his prophetic claims, or to suggest that the Mormons never entertained any idea of a possible move west in the years before 1846. There is evidence to suggest that Smith was looking for possible places for the Mormons to settle over a wide swath of territory. In the 1840s, he commissioned expeditions to the Oregon and California territories and to Texas.[135] Smith was killed before action could be taken on any of these proposed moves, and it is clear that they never got beyond the earliest stages of discussion. What appears to be evidence of premeditation of the eventual move to Utah actually undermines, by its nebulous and vague nature, the specific and exclusive nature of the later accounts about Joseph Smith's foreknowledge of the move. It is not possible to construct, using contemporary sources, a reasonable narrative that includes specific prophecies about the Mormons' move to the Great Basin before the death of Joseph Smith.

Invented, or modified, communal memories are deeply significant to those seeking to understand the mental world of a religious community. Whenever a story is invented and presented in the form of a memory, it tells us much more about the religious climate of the story's inventors and retellers than a true story would. The historical record suggests that these stories about Joseph Smith's knowledge of the fate of the Mormons after Nauvoo were invented, and they were invented for a reason. The important issue then is what cultural work these reminiscences performed. The exodus from Nauvoo, which might be viewed as the failure of God to keep his promises to the Mormons, and the unexpected collapse of Mormon physical boundaries were transformed into a necessary and blessed action that Joseph Smith knew about from the very beginning of his ministry. As in the case of the abandonment of the original city of Zion, the issues were redefined to reflect a divine hand in the apparent failures. In the process, the Mormons engaged in a modification of their collective memory. The Mormons then used this collective memory to fuel their new approach to physical boundaries.

Homelands: From Cities and Temples to Temples and Bodies

Although before Smith's death, Nauvoo became the most complete expression of a fully articulated Mormon physical boundary, in the last years of his life he was laying the foundation for a radical shift in Mormon conceptions of what physical separation from the world meant. Smith probably did not realize the impact that the introduction of temple rituals, with their focus on the sacredness of the human body, would have, but when these new ideas were coupled with the changing rhetoric about Nauvoo that emerged after Smith's death, the stage was set for a massive paradigm shift.

During the 1840s, Joseph Smith introduced complex new rituals to selected members of his most trusted inner circle. The form of the rituals closely resembled those of Freemasonry, a fact not lost on Mormons then or now. Smith and members of his family had been involved in Freemasonry for some time, and in the 1840s, Smith established a lodge in Nauvoo. According to LDS apostle Heber C. Kimball, Smith taught that Freemasonry represented a corrupted, vestigial trace of the rituals of the true and ancient religion. Kimball wrote, "Brother Joseph says Masonry was taken from the priesthood [meaning, ancient performances of temple rituals] but has become degenerated." Critics charged Smith with pirating Masonic rites while Smith taught that it was the Masons who stole the rituals from an ancient source and corrupted them.[136]

Whatever their origins, these rites, Smith taught, should properly be performed only in a dedicated temple. He grew impatient with the slow pace of temple construction in Nauvoo, however, and, sensing a growing danger from individuals who wished him ill, decided to perform some of the new rituals on the top floor of his store in Nauvoo. In May 1842, Smith gathered a group of nine men in his store and introduced them to what he called the temple "endowment." This constellation of rituals, collectively referred to as "temple ordinances," had as their main objective the ultimate deification of men and women, who would live together in eternal marriage relationships as gods and goddesses. In Smith's words, the endowment represented "the order pertaining to the Ancient of Days [Adam] and all those plans and principles by which any one is enabled to secure the fullness of those blessings which have been prepared for the Church of the Firstborn and [allow] them to come up and abide in the presence of the Eloheim [gods] in the eternal worlds."[137] As he did when selecting the sacred site of the original city of Zion, Smith tied these sacred rituals to Adam and Eve. The endowment was preceded by a washing and anointing ritual in which the initiate was symbolically cleansed from sin and anointed with consecrated olive oil. A special garment was then placed upon the body of the initiate as a symbol of the spiritual status of his, and later her, newly anointed status. The garment also functioned as a protection against evil. Following the initiatory ritual, the men engaged in a reenactment of sacred history from the time of Adam and Eve to the final apotheosis of the faithful after death. During the ritual, the men entered into covenants that governed their behavior and that carried with them the promise of godhood. Brigham Young recalled:

> [W]hen we got our washings and anointings under the hands of the Prophet Joseph at Nauvoo we had only one room to work in with the exception of a little side room or office were [sic] we . . . [performed the rituals]. Bro Joseph turned to me and said Bro Brigham this is not arranged right but we have done the best we could under the circumstances in which we are placed, and I wish you to take this matter in hand and organize and systematize all these ceremonies. I did so and each time I got something more so that when we went through the Temple at Nauvoo . . . we had our ceremonies pretty correct.[138]

From 1842 until Smith's death in 1844, the temple ordinances were performed for only ninety persons.[139] Called the Quorum of the Anointed, this group functioned as one of three separate elites, along with the general authorities and the Council of Fifty, in Nauvoo during Smith's lifetime. Smith's Anointed Quorum met regularly in the store, in Smith's home, and in other private homes. During these sessions, Smith instructed the group in his new theological ideas, and they engaged in special prayer rituals. Also during the meetings, new members were initiated, and a period of instruction usually followed. In late 1843, for example, a quorum of thirty-five met in Smith's store for five hours during which five persons "received their endowments," and the entire group "received instructions on the Priesthood from Joseph [Smith]."[140]

Gaining entry into Smith's highly selective group usually marked a high point for those so chosen. Members voted on prospective initiates, and those chosen were notified in person. William Clayton could hardly contain his enthusiasm as he recorded in his journal that "a vote had been taken on my being admitted into the quorum and I was accepted. This filled my heart with joy, and gratitude for truly the mercy of the Lord and the kindness of my brethren have been great to me."[141] Smith indicated in 1842 that the temple ordinances would not remain an experience for the elite. "There was nothing revealed to these men," Smith wrote of the original initiates into the temple rites, "but what will be made known to all the Saints of these last days, as soon as they are prepared to receive them, and a proper place is prepared to communicate them."[142]

After Smith's death, the temple rites were democratized, as he had indicated that they should be, and 5,583 Mormons received the endowment in the Nauvoo temple between December 1845 and February 1846.[143] Smith had originally presented the endowment as a lecture, but after his death the ritual was performed as a sacred drama, with those already initiated playing a variety of parts, including God, Christ, Satan, Adam, and Eve.[144] Brigham Young and other leaders frequently worked around the clock, sleeping in spare rooms in the temple, to ensure that as many Mormons as possible received the temple ordinances. William Clayton, assigned to keep a journal of the events in the Nauvoo temple, recorded that, at one point, Brigham Young had spent "the whole of three days" administering the temple rites until he was "entirely overcome by fatigue through his constant labors to forward the work."[145] On the final day of temple work, George A. Smith reported, "upwards of six hundred received the ordinances."[146]

Scholars are divided over just what the introduction of these rituals represented. At one end of the spectrum are those who believe that the theology and ritual changes introduced by Smith in the 1840s represented a major break from Mormon thinking of the 1830s. Richard L. Bushman, for example, argued that the Nauvoo temple rites were "more akin to Kabbalah, the alternative Jewish tradition that flourished for centuries alongside rational Judaism," than to the simple Christianity preached by Smith in the early years of his ministry.[147] Opposing this view are scholars like Thomas G. Alexander, who argued, "the temple [ritual introduced in the 1840s] is an expansion of the new covenant theology revealed early in the church's history," but set within a new symbolic context.[148] Historians Jan Shipps and Kathleen Flake have both argued that, in the twentieth century, long after the Mormons lost their ability to create true physical boundaries with the outside world, LDS temples became the primary expression of Mormon sacred space.[149] The introduction of the temple ordinances surely represented a major shift in Mormon concepts of sacred space, but this shift occurred *before* the Mormons arrived in Utah and long before the turn of the twentieth century. Additionally, the importance of the body in these new temple rites and the change that the emphasis on the body signals in Mormon notions of sacred space and physical boundaries had yet to be addressed.

From 1830, the time of the first revelations about a city of Zion, through the founding and building up of Nauvoo, Mormons conceived of the highest expression of sacred space as a holy city with a temple at its center. The potential size of what might be termed "greater Zion" increased over time, but the general schema of concentric circles moving out from the center point of the temple, to the ring representing the sacred city, and finally to the largest circle representing the larger Zion, remained intact. By the time the Mormons crossed the freezing Mississippi and headed for the West in 1846, that ideal had been eclipsed by a new one in which the temple itself replaced the holy city as the outer cordon of sacred space while the individual within the temple replaced the temple itself as the particular center of Zion. Consider Brigham Young's temple sermon delivered in early 1846. He made it clear that only in the temple could the Mormons "have liberty," because there they were safe from the "wicked world." Young then made a subtle but profoundly telling remark when he said that, even though they would be forced to abandon the temple in Nauvoo in the near future, "there will be thousands of men that can go into any part of the world and build up the kingdom and build temples."[150]

For the first time in Mormon history, the idea of sacred physical space was not centered on the construction of a single sacred city with a single central temple in which all would gather, but rather on a decentralized vision of multiple temples spread throughout the world where individual Mormons could go and receive the sacred rituals.[151] Moreover, Young described the temples of Mormonism, not as centers of Zionic cities on earth, but rather as "the gate[s] into the city where the Saints are at rest."[152] Earthly temples were now gates to heavenly Zions.

One of the most important pieces of evidence for this shift is the focus on the temple garment. As part of the initiatory ordinances connected with the endowment, Joseph Smith provided members of his Anointed Quorum with underclothing that bore several small marks "of orientation toward the gospel principles of obedience, truth, life, and discipleship in Christ."[153] When the temple was finished and the endowment performed for Mormons in large numbers, they were expected to make their own garments, and the sacred markings were placed on them in the temple. Smith taught that the "coats of skins" prepared by God for Adam and Eve when they were expelled from the garden of Eden were identical in function to the holy garment received by Mormons at the time of their endowment.[154] Endowed Mormons were, and are, instructed to wear this garment night and day.[155] Apostle George A. Smith told a group of Mormons in the Nauvoo temple in late 1845 that "we should wear those garments continually, by night and by day, in prison or free and if the devils in hell cut us up, let them cut the garments to pieces also."[156] The garment was intended as a permanent fixture and, almost, as an extension of the body.

While the promises of protection attaching to the garment are chiefly of a spiritual nature, almost immediately after the endowment began to be performed in Nauvoo stories of the supernaturally protective power of the garment against physical harm began to circulate. At a meeting in the Nauvoo temple not long before the Mormon evacuation of the city, one Mormon recalled that, in the hostilities of the preceding autumn, "he was shot at, and the Sentinel who was near him was killed, but he escaped unhurt, having on his garment." At the same meeting, John Taylor, who had been severely wounded at the time of Smith's murder in 1844, recalled, "Joseph and Hyrum and himself were without their robes [garments] in the jail at Carthage, while Doctor Richards had his on."[157] Willard Richards, the only man of the group to wear his special temple garment in the Carthage jail, was also the only one to escape without a scratch.

The fact that Smith did not wear his garment on that day caused considerable consternation for decades afterward in some circles, indicating the increasing centrality of the garment in Mormon ideas about physical barriers against the world. Brigham Young granted an interview in 1877, the year of his death, in which he chastised Mormons who "remember it against Joseph that he . . . forgot to put on the regulation Mormon underclothes. They think that if he had had his garments . . . he would not have got bullet holes in his body."[158] Young scoffed at such an idea, probably in a simple effort to defend Smith's memory, but he granted no such quarter to Mormons who sought to alter the garments to make them more comfortable. After the move out of Nauvoo, church leaders generally gave no leniency to endowed Mormons who neglected to wear them or who altered the heavy, long-sleeved and long-legged undergarments. In 1846, Young wrote a letter instructing each endowed member of the Mormon Battalion never to "be without his under garment," suggesting that the clothing would operate as a means of separation from the worldly influences surrounding the soldiers.[159]

By the early twentieth century, the importance of the garment as a physical barrier against the world had become so entrenched that church president Joseph F. Smith could forcefully state:

> The Lord has given unto us garments of the holy priesthood, and you know what that means. And yet there are those of us who mutilate them, in order that we may follow the foolish, vain and (permit me to say) indecent practices of the world. In order that such persons may imitate the fashions, they will not hesitate to mutilate that which should be held by them the most sacred of all things in the world, next to their own virtue, next to their own purity of life. They should hold these things that God has given unto them sacred, unchanged and unaltered from the very pattern in which God gave them. Let us have the moral courage to stand against the opinions of fashion, and especially where fashion compels us to break a covenant and so commit a grievous sin.[160]

Most Mormons took the injunction to wear the garment at all times very seriously. On two separate occasions, for example, William Smart expressed his discomfort with being asked to remove the garment for medical reasons. In 1912, Smart wrote that, "while being treated for rheumatism hot packs were applied to my hip and I had been requested or advised to remove my leg from [the temple] garment, and ... I felt uneasy and discontented until it was replaced."[161] Twelve years later, Smart was less pliable, refusing to remove his garment when undergoing emergency treatment after being struck by an automobile.[162]

When the Mormons left Nauvoo, they literally wore a physical boundary on their bodies, a sacred shell that tied them to the first scene of creation and insulated them from the world in which they had to live, and it increased in importance as the memory of their sacred cities grew more distant. In 1879, Apostle Charles Penrose summarized the essence of the shift in Mormon ideas about physical barriers when he told a congregation in Provo, Utah, that endowed "men can go forth in the midst of the wicked, enwrapped in ... *the garments they wear,* and be separate from the world, and they can carry an influence in the world which other men cannot carry."[163] After the move west, the Mormons introduced the practice of burying endowed persons in their temple garments and temple robes, indicating the increased importance of these items. Also in 1879, at a meeting with stake presidents, LDS president John Taylor expressed his concern that "in clothing the dead a carelessness was often manifested in allowing the clothing to be exposed to view [of] Jew, Gentile, and Apostate, who might be present at our funerals." Taylor was offended at the casual attitude among some church members toward the sacred garments and reminded the assembled leaders that "it is the duty of the Priesthood to guard sacredly those emblems which God had given us, and avoid 'casting pearls before swine.'"[164] Garments thus had become an important boundary that extended even to the grave.

Salt Lake City is protected by the Wasatch mountain range and a thousand miles of prairies, but it never held a place in the Mormon world view of a true "city of Zion" along the lines of those in Missouri and Nauvoo. In the earlier cities of Zion, the temple was the center and represented a singular sacred presence. The temple in Salt Lake City, although magnificent when finally completed, was the fourth temple dedicated in Utah. Over time, "Zion" came to hold an increasingly complex place in Mormon discourse, as different definitions were added and emphasized. From the original sense of the term as a specific and eschatologically charged designation of a central gathering place, it also came to mean the settlement of the Mormon-dominated regions of the Great Basin and to refer to any place where the "pure in heart" found themselves. In fact, these definitions operated simultaneously. Consider the following sermons delivered by Brigham Young during 1853. In the course of one year, he used every definition of the term at least once. In January, Young remarked that "the Latter-day Saint, who is far from the bosom of the Church, whose home is in distant climes, sighs, and earnestly prays each day of his life for the Lord to open his way, that he may mingle with his brethren in Zion."[165] Obviously, Young is here referring to Utah. In the same sermon, Young used another definition, which severed the concept from any particular geographic place.

> Whenever we are disposed to give ourselves perfectly to righteousness, to yield all the powers and faculties of the soul (which is the spirit and the body, and it is there where righteousness dwells); when we are swallowed up in the will of Him who has called us; when we enjoy the peace and the smiles of our Father in Heaven, the things of His Spirit, and all the blessings we are capacitated to receive and improve upon, then are we in Zion, *that is Zion*.[166]

In October, Young made reference to Zion in Missouri: in "Jackson County, Missouri, Joseph [Smith] commenced to lay out a city to be called Zion; and not now, but after a time, when the Lord has accomplished His preparatory work, it will be built, even the New Jerusalem."[167]

There is, then, a subtle but crucial contrast in meaning between the use of the term in the 1830s and 1840s and later uses. This shift is clearly illustrated by a footnote inserted in the published version of the LDS Church's minute books kept in Missouri in the 1830s. The original manuscript simply records that, on 24 August 1831, Hyrum Smith "spoke of Zion and the gathering of saints into her." When the manuscript was published as *Far West Record*, the editors clarified for modern readers what was plain to those in the 1830s and 1840s by including a footnote that read: "'Zion' means Jackson County, Missouri."[168] One must therefore use caution when interpreting Mormon sources that employ this term. Mormon discourse, in the past and in the present, often shifts from one sense of the word to another without overtly signaling a change.

Salt Lake City never functioned as Zion. I am not suggesting that the term was never applied, but rather it was used in a distinct and different way. Joseph Smith's Enochian vision of Zion as the heart of creation, centered on the sacred city of Zion, which first referred to Jackson County and, later, to Nauvoo, was never applied to Salt Lake City. The more general idea of Zion, drawn from the history of ancient Israel, as a "promised land" where the people of God could dwell in peace, was certainly used in reference to the Mormon culture region in the West. It is this latter definition that Catherine Albanese uses when describing, correctly, that in Utah the Mormons "founded their own Zion in the mountains, the state of Deseret."[169] However, these are two significantly different ideas. If, for example, Salt Lake City had been conceived as a city of Zion in the same way that the earlier Mormon headquarters were, it is impossible to imagine that a temple would be built elsewhere in Utah first. In addition, sermons during the first few decades of the Utah period increasingly focused on the future return to Jackson County, something that had almost disappeared from the rhetoric of the Nauvoo period when Nauvoo itself had eclipsed Jackson County as the city of the saints. By the 1850s, Zion, in its definition as a city of isolation and physical protection from the world, was something to be looked forward to, an ideal that had been eclipsed by a more practical reality symbolized by the temple garment.

Conclusion

The process of establishing Zionic cities in Missouri and Illinois represented a genuine attempt by Mormons to create and maintain physical boundaries against the world. The city of Zion in Jackson County, Missouri, and the "City of Joseph" in Nauvoo, Illinois, were each seen by the Mormons as sacred sites, chosen by God for the refuge and prosperity of his people. The fact that neither place of refuge functioned as the Mormons believed it would provides historians and scholars of religion with a rich opportunity to observe the boundary-remaking process at work.

In Jackson County, the power that the Mormons projected and that their neighbors imagined stretched their boundaries to the breaking point; in Nauvoo, *actual* Mormon power eventually led to bloodshed. In both cases, the Mormons managed to create crises relative to their physical boundaries. Nauvoo replaced Missouri as a physical stronghold, was proclaimed in revelations as the place of gathering, and functionally replaced Jackson County as the city of Zion. When the Mormons lost Nauvoo, they never really replaced it, although the Mormon settlement of the Great Basin represented a Herculean accomplishment, and they managed to remove themselves from the rest of the country for a little more than a decade before "gentiles" once again found the Mormons. In Utah, however, no revelations were given establishing Salt Lake City as a divinely appointed center for gathering. In fact, almost as soon as the Mormons arrived in Utah, they began employing a rhetoric of longing for their return to Jackson County. In Nauvoo, church leaders rarely spoke of returning to Missouri because they did not need to; they had founded a new Zion in Illinois. The presence of such strong longing for Missouri during the Utah period reflects the absence of a truly Zionic sense attaching to the settlements in Utah. Mormons referred to Utah as Zion, to be sure, but, as I will discuss in the next chapter, this meant something different from what it did either in Missouri or in Nauvoo. In Utah, as in the latter stages of the Nauvoo period, Mormon notions of physical boundaries against the world moved from the concept of the divine city to an intense focus on the individual. Individuals could only be sanctified through the temple rituals introduced by Smith in Nauvoo, and the garment they received as part of the endowment served as the real physical boundary from the world.

It is interesting to note that the Mormon temple in Nauvoo, as grand as it was, looked like a very large version of a traditional meetinghouse. The temple in Nauvoo was not designed to function as a fortress because the city itself served that purpose. The temples built during the nineteenth century in Utah, however, looked more like medieval castles than American churches. The nineteenth-century Utah temples in Logan, Manti, and Salt Lake City stood as imposing fortresses, complete with battlements and turrets. Architectural historian C. Mark Hamilton described the nineteenth-century Utah temples as "a compromise between the massive load-bearing qualities of the Romanesque round-arch style, and the soaring verticality of Gothic architecture."[170] These temples had no Zionic cities to protect them; they, and the garments that persons received inside them, had become the physical boundaries.[171]

THREE

Godly Marriage and Divine Androgyny: Polygamy and Celibacy

Of all the potential points of comparison between Mormons and Shakers, the groups' approaches to marriage are perhaps the most obvious. Gross examination would indicate that the groups employ opposite strategies when it comes to sex and marriage. The Shakers are perhaps best known for their strict enforcement of celibacy, consisting of prohibitions on both sex and marriage; and even today, more than a hundred years after officially discontinuing the practice, Mormons still are closely associated with the practice of plural marriage.[1]

Although the Mormons and Shakers appear to rest on opposite ends of the spectrum of possible marital arrangements, close inspection yields a more complex situation. The field of cognitive anthropology provides some helpful interpretive tools for this particular comparison. Cognitive anthropologists have argued that the structures underlying an individual's motives, what they call "schemas," are hierarchically arranged. At the top of the hierarchy are "master motives," or goals related to the most fundamental ideas about the purpose of existence.[2] Individual and group behaviors may be understood through reference to the master motive. An examination of the schemas employed by the Shakers and Mormons relative to their sexual and marital arrangements reveals that, while the particular behaviors enacted are nearly perfect opposites, the structures motivating those behaviors are nearly identical.

The master motive, or the ultimate goal, for the Mormons and the Shakers was to behave in ways that imitated God. In both Shaker and

Mormon theologies, there was a direct link between behavior that was sanctioned by God and behavior that was imitative of God. It is significant that both the Shakers and the Mormons believed that the correct knowledge of God's attributes was lost to humankind and could only be restored through direct communication with the divine. The Shakers believed that "God can only be known through the medium of Divine Revelation." Through correct knowledge of God's attributes and by doing what God does, one may draw "nearest to him."[3] Compare that approach to Joseph Smith's teachings about the importance of a correct knowledge of God. In 1835, Smith taught that one must come to a "correct idea of [God's] character, perfections, and attributes."[4] Later, Smith taught that the object of humanity's existence was to live "as God" in the presence of God.[5]

When it came to marriage, mainstream Protestants and Catholics did not posit a link between God's nature, which they believed to be ultimately mysterious, and the path of behavior for human beings. All Christians, by definition, seek to emulate Christ in some sense, of course. What set Mormons and Shakers apart was their insistence that the marital status of God and Christ represented the ideal marital arrangement for human beings.

The Mormons taught that God was married, and from 1843 to 1890, they taught that he was a polygamist. Moreover, Joseph Smith taught that God possessed a "body of flesh and bone as tangible as man's," which he would use to create spirit children throughout all eternity. In January 1841, Smith revealed that spirits came to earth for the express purpose of gaining "a body and present[ing] it pure before God in the Celestial Kingdom." "The great principle of happiness," Smith continued, "consists in having a body." Smith added, "[T]he Devil has no body, and herein is his punishment."[6] It is clear that, from the time of Joseph Smith, Mormons viewed the body as a completely positive object, whose desires and appetites had to be tamed and channeled into righteous expressions, but should never be snuffed out.

The Shakers, by contrast, held a view of an androgynous God that transcended all physicality. Celibacy for the Shakers represented the symbolic performance of androgyny. The Mormons and Shakers shared structurally identical master motives (to be like God), as well as identical secondary motives (to be like God, one must enact a God-like practice).

The difference between the two systems is found not in the upper levels of the motivational schemas but in the particular theologies, which posited very different ideas about the nature of God. Shaker celibacy and Mormon polygamy, then, reveal fundamental similarities relative to their underlying assumptions about the role of ritual, praxis, and the ultimate destiny of the human soul. The fact that the particular practices each group deployed in response to their master-motive structures are opposites is perhaps the least important feature of the comparison.[7]

Because the structures that motivated Shakers to be celibate and Mormons to be polygamous bear such fundamental similarities, it is not surprising that both groups put their practices to similar cultural use. Indeed, celibacy and polygamy formed the core boundary markers for these groups during the nineteenth century, and these boundary markers were so effective that they reveal a rare point of contact between outsider and insider views. If nineteenth-century Americans knew anything about either of these groups, it would most likely have been that they were celibates, in the case of the Shakers, or polygamists, in the case of the Mormons. Likewise, nineteenth-century Shakers and Mormons in their sermons, public and private writings, architecture, rituals, and conversations with each other and outsiders always placed their practices and beliefs about sex and marriage at the center.

In this chapter, I will explore the contours of Shaker celibacy and Mormon polygamy, with an eye toward their functions as boundary markers and their roles in the overarching tension models for each group. This is not a comprehensive history of either Shaker celibacy or Mormon polygamy. Such studies have already been carried out in other contexts. Rather, I will make specific and limited points about the practices, including the costs and benefits of them and the relative flexibility of celibacy and polygamy as doctrinal/ritualistic boundaries. As with other elements here addressed, clear patterns emerge suggesting that the Shakers and the Mormons, while both maintaining relatively high tension with the outside world, employed qualitatively different applications of their boundary maintenance strategies.

Any practice that serves as a boundary marker also acts as a "sign" in the semiotic sense. That sign is then assigned value by those to whom the sign is directed. In this case, the Shakers and the Mormons directed the signs of their sexual arrangements to Victorian American culture.[8] Both groups understood clearly that any variation from monogamous marriage would naturally elicit a negative reaction from the American public at large. Both celibacy and polygamy thus posed a general challenge to the order of the young republic, which was closely tied to monogamous marriage.[9]

Although both plural marriage and celibacy generated negative responses from the American public in general, celibacy carried a significantly less negative sign value than polygamy, while managing to accomplish the purposes of a tension-generating boundary marker, i.e., setting the community apart from the outside world and driving the community itself closer together. Because outlawing non-marriage was not a possibility, Shaker celibacy provided a marker that was beyond the reach of official legal machinery. Celibacy nevertheless provided negative feedback to the community through cultural vehicles like magazines and books. Such negative cultural feedback was an essential element in the dialectic of boundary maintenance in that it reinforced the Shakers' view of their difference from, and moral superiority to, the culture at large. Celibacy thus provided a high-visibility boundary marker with a moderately negative sign value, which was not likely to induce crisis-driven tension from the outside.

Polygamy, on the other hand, carried a potently negative sign value and was firmly within the grasp of American legal retaliation. These factors contributed to the high potential for crisis-level tension. Historian David J. Whittaker has astutely argued that the period of open Mormon polygamy represented the "high tide of Mormon nonconformity."[10] This nonconformity not only included Mormon marital practices, but also surfaced in the tone of Mormon rhetoric. Polygamy was flexible, however, and the Mormons followed a familiar pattern of rising tension followed by boundary adjustment over the course of their fifty-year history of plural marriage.

This chapter is not simply another argument about how outsider groups deviate from the norm in their marriage and sexual arrangements. Rather, it is a look at some underexplored elements of the boundary maintenance strategies that informed the choices made by these two groups relative to their sexual practices.

Shaker Celibacy and Mormon Polygamy as Rituals

Nineteenth-century Shaker celibacy and Mormon polygamy functioned as ritually enacted boundary markers. Mormons performed plural marriages as a formal ritual that involved the groom, the new bride, and the groom's first wife. While plural marriages were marked by discrete ritual moments, the very act of living in a plural marriage represented a ritual act of another kind. It was an ongoing ritual of cultural separation, a constant reminder of the Mormon prophetic connection to the Hebrew patriarchs and thus a sign of the sacred in the midst of everyday, mundane life. Catherine Bell suggested that a key function of ritual is to "bind the immediate local community together by virtue of a heightened intimacy and a sense of being a distinct community in opposition to so much around them." Polygamy certainly filled that bill for segments of the Mormon population.

Not all Mormons were polygamists, of course. Most Mormons never entered into a polygamous relationship, despite the establishment of polygamy as the ideal type of marital relationship. Nevertheless, the fact that the Mormon hierarchy was almost completely polygamous meant that polygamy acted as a ritual sign, what Jonathan Smith argues is one of ritual's central functions: "a means of performing the way things ought to be in conscious tension to the way things are."[11]

Shaker celibacy may be understood as belonging to the category of "rites of affliction," one of Bell's six "genres of ritual action." Bell argues that rites of affliction "attempt to rectify a state of affairs that has been disturbed or disordered; they heal, exorcise, protect and purify."[12] The Shakers viewed the natural state as one of profound disorder that could be traced to the disturbance caused by Adam and Eve's sin of fornication in the garden of Eden. Green and Wells summed up the general Shaker doctrine of the Fall when they wrote that Adam and Eve engaged in "the act of sexual coition; and thus they partook of the forbidden fruit."[13] Celibacy functioned as a rite of affliction since it was an effort to undue the damage done in the garden of Eden. Celibacy functioned ritually to protect the Shakers from their own fallen natures, to exorcise the nature of the "serpent" which had insinuated itself into the souls of all of Adam and Eve's posterity, and to purify those fallen souls to make them fit for life in heaven. Thus, for the Shakers, celibacy represented more than simply avoiding sexual activity. It was not seen as the mere *absence* of action, but rather as the intentional *enactment* of the divine model of behavior.

Although Bell's rather fluid approach to ritual seems preferable, one need not assume that Shaker celibacy only qualifies as a ritual on such inchoate grounds. Setting aside the issue of ritual as a discrete act, Shaker celibacy fits rather well into more specific definitions. Edward Muir, in cataloging some of the definitions of ritual that scholars have offered through the years, lists the following: ritual as a "communication that allows people to tell stories about themselves," as a "collectively created performance," and as a "specific kind of practice that constructs, maintains, and modifies society."[14] As I will demonstrate below, for the nineteenth-century Shakers, celibacy functioned in all of these ways and more.

Shaker Celibacy

Few Shaker topics have drawn the interest of scholars as persistently and intensely as that of celibacy. Such attention is only natural given the centrality that nineteenth-century Shakers themselves assigned to this practice. As a religious phenomenon, celibacy is found among most major traditions. Typically, celibates represent a unit of a larger, noncelibate polity, as in the case of Roman Catholicism, or as part of a life cycle that includes both celibate and noncelibate phases, as in the case of some forms of Hinduism and Buddhism. Daniel Gold, a scholar of South Asian religions, noted that "smaller, extreme groups with radically negative views of life in the world may prescribe celibacy as an ideal for all."[15] The Shakers adopted a theological position that required celibacy of all practitioners, based largely on their negative views of both the world, as we saw in chapter 1, and the physical body itself. The Shakers shared with many other celibate groups a tendency to view, in Gold's description, "the physical body as disgusting and ultimately worthless."[16]

The origins of Shaker celibacy are cloudy. As with nearly every aspect of Ann Lee's life, few contemporary documents exist that bear witness to it. Too many scholars and popular authors have relied uncritically for their narration of the history of Shaker celibacy on the *Testimonies* collected after Lee's death and published in 1808.[17] These *Testimonies* were collected from those who claimed to have heard Ann

Lee teach on a wide variety of subjects, including celibacy. Due to the remoteness of the recollections from the time in which they were supposed to have been originally heard and the probably high degree of editorial manipulation during the collection and compilation process, the only sound historical conclusions that may be drawn from this body of recollections bear on the time of their collection rather than on the time of Ann Lee. The exception to this is when some teaching or event described in the *Testimonies* can be corroborated by a contemporary eighteenth-century source.

The *Testimonies* tell us that, at least by the first decade or two of the nineteenth century, the Shakers had come to believe that Ann Lee had been introduced to the concept of celibacy by her mentor in England, Jane Wardley. According to the early nineteenth-century view, Wardley told Lee that the older woman and her husband, James, shared a bed but were as innocent as "two babes." Nineteenth-century Shakers also believed that Ann Lee experienced a vision of the divine while in prison in 1770 in which she was told that sexual intercourse was the sin committed by Adam and Eve, allegorized in the Bible as the story of the forbidden fruit, and that the sex act had to be avoided by any who sought salvation. According to the published account by Lee: "[I] saw the Lord Jesus in his kingdom and glory. He revealed to me the depth of man's loss, what it was, and the way of redemption. Then I was made able to bear an open testimony against that sin which is the root of all evil."[18]

Setting aside the *Testimonies,* there is contemporary evidence to suggest that Ann Lee personally adopted celibacy at some point, perhaps due to her enormous difficulties with pregnancy and the premature death of four children.[19] Less clear is the degree to which Ann Lee developed a theological underpinning for the practice of celibacy and the scope of the practice among the Shakers before her death. As early as 1781, a published report recorded that the Shakers were teaching persons desiring to join the community that they must "renounce and abstain from all works of the flesh" and that the world was "ruined" by the "carnal copulation" that constituted the original sin of Adam and Eve.[20]

It is important to emphasize that the Shakers understood sex to be not only the first sin committed by humans, but also the source of all the evil that existed in the world. Shakers commonly used the word "lust" to describe a range of behaviors and attitudes quite apart from those associated with sex, but they always traced any evil back to sexuality. In 1843, for example, Thomas Stebbins, a Shaker living at Enfield, Connecticut, wrote that he was relieved to have remained sexually pure and "grateful to God that I was called to take up my cross and follow Christ while young... for I have been saved from the pollutions that are in the world through lust."[21] The eradication of sex, not only in practice but also in desire, thus constituted an effort to reverse the effects of the Fall.

The Shakers came to view the practice of celibacy as part of the reconstitution of true Christianity, which had been corrupted and plunged into apostasy in the centuries following the death of Jesus. One of the earliest published statements of Shaker belief, the 1790 *A Concise Statement of the Principles of the Only True Church According to the Gospel of the Present Appearance of Christ,* sketches out the Shaker view of the apostasy. The author of the tract, Joseph Meacham, stated:

> [T]here was a falling away from that faith and power that the Church then stood in [during the time of Jesus] which falling away began soon after the apostles and gradually increased in the church, until about four hundred and fifty-seven years from Christ's birth (or thereabouts) at which time the power of the holy people, or Church of Christ, was scattered or lost by reason of transgression and anti-Christ got to be established.

Meacham took a swipe at traditional Christendom when he identified "anti-Christ" as any religious body "falsely called the Church of Christ."[22]

The first fully articulated discussion of the relationship among celibacy, true Christianity, and a general apostasy was offered by Green and Wells in their *Summary View of the Millennial Church,* published in 1823 and revised in 1848. By this time, the Shaker authors had taken the basic principles of celibacy outlined by Lee and had woven a historico-theological tapestry that placed celibacy in a much broader context. Green and Wells argued that celibacy was not practiced by all early Christians, because they were endowed with only a degree of truth, but that the Christians in Jerusalem did practice it.

One of the more interesting pieces of evidence offered by Green and Wells for this view is the presence of celibate orders within the Catholic Church. "These measures being adopted at such an early period in the apostacy [*sic*]," Green and Wells reasoned, "shows that the purity of the primitive church at Jerusalem was well known in the church of Rome."

The Catholics adopted a limited degree of celibacy, according to the Shaker view, in an attempt to "make a show of sanctity and deceive the world by counterfeiting this purity."[23] Ann Lee, as head of the fourth and final dispensation of time, had reintroduced the true doctrine and practice of celibacy in connection with other elements of the true gospel, including the principle of confession and the communitarian efforts that the Shakers called "joint interest."

Green and Wells not only appealed to revealed truths to defend the practice of celibacy, but they also made an effort to demonstrate that the sinfulness of sex was evident in nature. Green and Wells challenged their readers to ask any person who had remained a virgin "till the nuptial ceremony had sanctioned the deed. What were the sensations which succeeded the loss of their purity?" The authors confidently asserted, "[T]he candid and honest answer will, invariably, be, *disappointment, shame*, and *disgust*." These feelings, according to Green and Wells, provided "incontestable evidence of its [sex's] filthy nature and deceitful influence."[24] Green and Wells provide no evidence for their opinion that feelings of disgust and shame would automatically be attached to sex by many of their readers. What is important, however, is that the Shakers interpreted this widespread guilt as evidence of the dark and degrading nature of sexuality.

Among the extant nineteenth-century Shaker manuscripts are dozens of published and private explanations and defenses of celibacy. Calvin Green, in addition to his published work, also produced holograph manuscripts that dealt with the issue. In one such undated manuscript, entitled "A Virgin Life," Green set forth five "plain and conclusive evidences given by the Savior" suggesting the "necessity of a virgin life."[25]

Green argued that Christ was born of a virgin "without the generative cooperation of man," which demonstrated, according to Green, "that the generative progress in the work of God ended in him." Not only was Christ born of a virgin, but Christ himself "lived a perfect virgin life." Green pulled back the curtain on the Shaker master-motive schema when he wrote that because a true disciple of Christ must follow Christ and because "we cannot follow him where he never went," those who "marry in the flesh are not his disciples." Green explained that no persons could truly be "subjects or professors of [Christ's] heavenly kingdom" unless they have "utterly forsaken" sexual activity in all of its forms. Drawing on the New Testament, Green argued that those persons worthy to enter heaven "neither marry nor are given in marriage."[26]

In both his published and unpublished work, Green went to great lengths to tie celibacy back not only to Ann Lee, but to Christ himself. This interpretation of Christ became deeply engrained in Shaker theology. An 1881 editorial in the monthly periodical the *Shaker Manifesto* declared that one looking for models of celibate living need look no further than "the grand exemplar Christ—a CELIBATE."[27] The Shakers believed that celibacy was the most heavenly of all potential approaches to sexuality and family life. "The power to live in purity and innocence," a Shaker sister wrote, "is found in the conviction that a spotless, virgin, angelic life is the order of the kingdom of Christ, and is higher, better, and happier than a sensual, worldly life."[28] The Shakers viewed celibacy as a shining, heavenly light introduced into the suffocating darkness of a sensual and fallen world.

CELIBACY AS AN INTERNAL BOUNDARY

Shaker authors spent a good deal of time explaining the doctrine and practice of celibacy to outsiders. This fact alone is a testament to the importance of the practice as a boundary marker. Decades after Green and Wells published their *Summary View,* a Shaker named John Lyon penned a remarkably detailed theological treatise that spun a vast and complex defense of celibacy.

Lyon expanded upon many of the points made by Green and Wells, and he detailed the Shaker belief in two creations: an old creation that was responsible for conditions before the Fall and a new creation that was partially achieved by Christ's mission and which would be further accomplished by individuals who "take up the cross" of the Shaker gospel. According to Lyon's theological argument, Adam and Eve were tempted by Satan, who "found access to them" through their flesh. Succumbing to the serpent's wiles, Adam and Eve became corrupted and received "the whole of the serpent's nature, which is the nature of lust." Their very natures were altered, and they were transformed from creatures in the likeness of God to creatures after "the nature of the serpent, or lust."[29]

Lyon's prose is evocative in its grotesque description of the effects of the corruption of humankind. Satan, according to Lyon, "ensconced himself in man's nature where he lay protected and sheltered so that whatever was projected by the nature of man came in contact with the serpent." Adam and Eve, instead of "producing a progeny upright and innocent according to their pristine order, . . . brought forth a race of serpents, a brood of vipers which have overspread the earth."[30] Lyon accurately represented nineteenth-century Shaker ideas about the fundamentally evil nature of human beings. True Shakers were those who recognized that the "old creation" had become corrupted and who sought to be created anew by "hating the element and principle of the flesh in which the serpent has fixed his habitation" and by carrying an equally fervent hate for "their own lives with all of the lusts of their father [Satan]."[31]

Celibacy thus functioned, in part, as a boundary internal to each individual. The practice of celibacy allowed Shakers to erect a buffer between the nature of the serpent, which had become ensconced in every human born into the family of Eve and Adam, and the new creature of spirit, which the Shakers were striving to nourish. The Shakers imagined deep spiritual crevices within the natural human soul, and they viewed celibacy as a boundary between the regenerate soul and the darkness within.

Quite apart from external factors, the Shakers recognized that the "manifold weaknesses in the flesh pose a constant [threat] to the progress of souls in this purifying work of the cross."[32] Oliver C. Hampton, a prolific Shaker poet and hymn writer, expressed the urgency felt by many Shakers concerning the corruption they carried within themselves. In a hymn entitled "Right Feelings," Hampton proclaimed:

> Yea I will keep a constant strife
> Against the man of sin
> O Mother give me strength and life
> To do my work within
> Then by a proud and fleshly sense
> Be bound I never will
> For will I make a vain pretence
> And keep my idol still.[33]

Continuing the theme, Hampton penned another hymn warning his fellow Shakers: "No one need be mistaken / They'll find the foe within / For in our camps be taken / The lofty man of sin."[34] Celibacy was the chief barrier protecting individual Shakers from the internal threats attendant to their serpentine natures. The Shakers had to practice constant vigilance against their own spiritual doppelgängers, and celibacy was seen as the only effective weapon in that fight.

An apocryphal quotation attributed to Lucy Wright indicates the extent to which nineteenth-century Shakers viewed celibacy as an internal boundary device. The statement, which the Shakers who published it clearly believed was authentic, portrayed Wright as teaching, "Some think they have harder times, and their crosses are greater than others, but such ought to consider whether there is not something in *them* which needs greater crosses to subdue."[35]

CELIBACY AS SIGN

In 1873, Shaker elder Harvey Eads drew up a list of questions and answers designed to explain Shaker beliefs and practices to the outside world. One of the questions asked whether celibacy was not an "unnatural" standard "which scarcely any can adopt and if lived up to would depopulate the world?" Because Eads constructed the questions as well as the answers, there is much one can glean from the inquiry itself, quite independent of the answer that Eads offered. Eads was not simply posing a question that occurred frequently; he was also framing the question to reflect what he hoped outsiders would notice about celibacy. Eads was shaping the sign that celibacy was sending to the culture at large. Posing as the nameless inquisitor, Eads communicated within his question the idea that celibacy was a practice to which relatively few persons could successfully adhere. The implications were that those who managed to do so represented a spiritual elite and that outsiders questioned the practice in part because of their own inability to shoulder the cross of self-denial. Obviously, the Shakers would consider the fact that "scarcely any" could adopt celibacy as a tribute to their own spiritual superiority.

It is telling that Eads, in his response to his own question, simply ignored this part of the inquiry. Perhaps he felt it would be gauche to gesture so explicitly to the spiritual superiority of the Shakers to their noncelibate neighbors. In any case, the careful wording of the question allowed Eads to signal one important element of celibacy's function as a boundary marker: those who successfully lived a celibate life in the Shaker order were morally superior to those who did not.

Eads was more forthcoming in his discussion of the "unnatural-
ness" of the practice. Eads, again acting as the anonymous interlocutor,
chose his words carefully. The introduction of the issue of naturalness, if
nothing else, signals that the questions presented by Eads are simply too
good to have been crafted by an outsider. The wording of the question
allowed Eads to unload with both theological barrels. "While [celibacy]
is unnatural," Eads began, "it is not *unspiritual.*" With this, Eads began
a lengthy and quite standard Shaker discussion of the superiority of the
spiritual order, as taught and practiced by the Shakers, to the natural
order, as practiced by the world. The natural order, and the world that
practiced it, "lies prostrate before you, wounded and bleeding at every
pore." Eads ended his response by suggesting that celibacy was certainly
not "adapted to the masses."[36] The signals sent by the Shakers were clear:
no, celibacy is not natural, and yes, it is so difficult that ordinary persons
probably cannot live that way.

Eads's questions and answers effectively summarized an entire genre
of Shaker writings designed to demonstrate one of the signs that celibacy
was intended to broadcast. The Shakers frequently used celibacy as a
mark of their spiritual superiority. In 1879, Alonzo G. Hollister gave a
backhanded endorsement of marriage, offering his opinion that it was
"good for those who own no higher purpose in life" and stating that it
was marginally preferable to "licentiousness and self-abuse [masturba-
tion]."[37] An 1872 article in *Galaxy* magazine quoted an unnamed Shaker
sister who emphasized, "A virgin life is strictly believed to be essential
to be a true follower of Christ." The sister added her judgment that "only
the children of the world marry and are given in marriage."[38] Shaker
celibacy thus functioned as a boundary between the spiritually weak
and the spiritually strong.

Outsiders reacted in varying ways to the practice of Shaker celibacy
as well as to the defenses of the practice that the Shakers put forward.
Some saw the Shakers as a delightfully exotic sect, a sentiment that
caused one author wistfully to imagine a life among either the Gypsies
or the Shakers, either of which would provide a "taste of the queerness of
things."[39] Another observer commented on the harmless "semi-monk-
ish" qualities of the sect.[40] The Shakers suffered in some quarters from
a comparison of their celibate lifestyles with the celibacy of the Roman
Catholic clergy. The virulent anti-Catholicism of the mid-nineteenth

century sometimes spilled over onto the Shakers. Nicholas Summerbell, a primitivist Christian and the president of Union Christian College in Indiana, wrote that Shakerism was "only Romish monkery broken loose from popery."[41] Another observer, writing in the 1840s, argued that the Shakers "are bound together by precisely the same means as the Catholics." In addition to celibacy, he continued, the Shakers and the Catholics shared a propensity for mindless followership, and both could be described as "mere automatons, having no mind of their own—mere passive slaves to the will and control of their superiors."[42] More intellectually inclined commentators viewed Shaker celibacy as part of the generally benign and widespread "follies, weaknesses, and insanities" generated by the principle of free and open religious expression.[43] Still others found the Shaker sexual arrangements, or lack thereof, troubling, but held a high opinion of the farm and craft skills demonstrated by the sect. In an 1835 article discussing the career of Matthias, a prophet who emerged from New York in the early 1830s and briefly led a small group of followers in various religious experiments, W. L. Stone noted that Matthias had not learned from the Shaker example that a group could be as "strange" as it wished but could be tolerated so long as it possessed the sort of "good husbandry" skills exhibited by the Shakers.[44]

In general, celibacy tended to draw fewer criticisms than did some contemporary experiments in sexual arrangements, such as Mormon polygamy or the "complex marriage" system practiced by John Humphrey Noyes's Oneida Perfectionists.[45] On one level, Americans tended to value the discipline required to live a celibate life over what they viewed as the sexual indulgence and even perversion of other practices. Charles W. Shields, writing in the quarterly magazine the *Century,* described the Shakers as the founders of "peaceful retreats of harmony and virtue."[46] In 1829, a visitor to Watervliet, New York, published his impressions in Baltimore's *Niles' Weekly Register.* In contrast to nuns whom the author had met previously and who "were the pale victims of celibacy," the Shakers appeared healthy and happy. "The two sexes together bear the burden, if burden it may be, of celibacy," according to the author, who added that the Shakers "enliven the dullness of it by the amenity of their intercourse together."[47]

O. A. Bierstadt published a short story in 1886 in which a young woman named Agnes was convinced by her boyfriend to leave the Shaker village in which they both lived. After leaving the village, the couple was wed and Agnes soon became pregnant. Agnes's new husband promptly fled and she was left to ponder "the present and all its woes." In the midst of her depression, "all the years of her life among the Shakers rose up before her mind," and reflecting on her "happy [Shaker] home," populated by "angels of heaven," she wondered "why she had ever left such an earthly paradise." Agnes decided to return to her unnamed New York village in the dead of winter and upon arrival, she discovered that her child had frozen to death. Of course, as befitted the ending of a story written for middle-class American fireside reading, Agnes lived happily ever after among the Shakers.[48]

In addition to the rosy picture of Shaker life presented in the story, one can hardly miss the rather unsubtle symbolism employed by Shields to link sex, procreation, and death in a way that would have resonated deeply not only with the Shakers, who would have been unlikely to read the story, but also with women who feared the very real dangers of childbirth in the nineteenth century. Although fictional, the story suggests that some Americans had developed a soft spot for the Shakers that manifested itself in saccharine stories of life among the believers.

Harper's magazine made a visit to the Shakers at New Lebanon the subject of the "Editor's Easy Chair" feature in April 1860. The editor was impressed with Shaker cleanliness and industry and, although he purported to discern "something of the woman yet smoldering in the ashes of renunciation" when he looked into the eyes of a young Shaker sister who was showing him a lamp stand, he finally acknowledged that, "although they had renounced love forever, they did not seem very envious of those of us who were not yet saintly enough for such renunciation."[49] The editor's comment about the superiority of those who practiced celibacy is telling. Either the Shakers were sending that signal, or he believed that they were. In either case, the effect was the same. That the editor couched his remarks about the relative spiritual fitness of celibates in dismissive and sarcastic terms is ultimately beside the point.

Obviously, the Shakers did receive their share of criticism from outsiders. In January 1872, the popular periodical *Scribner's Monthly* published a scathing article that castigated "the Shaker" for believing that "he leads a purer life than the world around him, in consequence of the fact that none marry or are given in marriage within the circle of his sect."

The individual Shaker, according to the author, thinks "that he merits something for the voluntary surrender of these loves and satisfactions." The problem, the author continued, was that the Shakers were actually incurring God's wrath by "fighting a passion which God made strong that his institution of the family might be well-nigh compulsory." The article concluded with an attempt to reveal the hypocrisy at the heart of Shakerism by pointing out that, while the Shakers might "believe they live more purely for their celibacy, we know better, and the world knows better." The Shaker life was one of "torture and meager satisfaction," which all Shakers would give up if not for their "sensitive personal pride."[50]

In August 1879, the same magazine published an opinion piece entitled "Marriage as a Test." The author of the article argued that marriage between a man and a woman is simply a law of nature and that within such a domestic arrangement the "human virtues are best cultivated, the finer affections are most naturally developed, and those attachments are formed and those sentiments engendered which make life a beautiful and significant thing."[51] The "test" from which the article's name is drawn should be applied to every "enthusiast in religion" who "begins to tamper with marriage." According to the author, "there is no better test of a new system or scheme of life than its relation to Christian marriage." While *Scribner's* readers had apparently expressed some interest in seeing the test applied in print to the Oneida community, the magazine's editors decided against it, citing the "amount of dirt involved in an exposure of the Oneida Community's views of marriage and the practices that go with them." The Mormons, too, were rejected as subjects for the test because their views on marriage were "just beastly."[52] The practices of those two groups were apparently too negative to be dealt with in a respectable middle-class periodical.

No doubt to the great disappointment of many readers, the editors decided not to venture into such a "sea of irredeemable nastiness." Instead, they trained their sights on the less risqué Shakers and their celibate rejection of the marriage relationship in toto. The problem with celibacy, which the article judged a "dirty substitute for marriage," was that it represented a "rotten foundation" that sought not only to pervert the traditional family but to "destroy it root and branch." Universal adoption of Shaker principles would result in "the suicide of the race," and since "a race has no more right to commit suicide than a man," the

Shaker rejection of marriage was immoral. More importantly, the article contended, the Shaker concern with avoiding sex served to emphasize "in the mind the passion it is intended to suppress, and fixes the attention upon it."[53] Thus, the Shakers, in their own way, must be as depraved as the "beastly" Mormons and Oneida Perfectionists because one cannot constantly avoid sex without becoming obsessed with it. The final judgment of the article was scathing indeed. The celibate Shaker, the author concluded, "disgraces himself and his own father and mother by his gross views of an institution before whose purity and beneficence he and his entire system stand condemned."[54]

Other voices expressed more than indignation about the questionable morality of celibacy and argued that the practice was potentially corrosive to American society in general. An 1844 article linked Shaker celibacy and the dreaded "Romish" orders, asserting that celibacy was "destructive to religion and good morals."[55] Nineteenth-century American intellectual gadfly Charles Astor Bristed, a grandson of John Jacob Astor, frequently contributed to *Galaxy* magazine under the pen name Carl Benson. In 1870, Bristed wrote that Shaker celibacy was an effort to "subvert legitimate matrimony."[56] In 1882, an anonymous author argued that the Shakers had as one of their "principle [*sic*] objects the extinguishing of the human race by devoting themselves, and persuading others, to celibacy and the strictest chastity."[57]

Other outsiders worried that America's reputation would be sullied by the fame of Shaker celibacy. In an anonymously penned *Scribner's Monthly* review of Charles Nordhoff's book *The Communistic Societies of the United States,* the author fretted that Nordhoff's book gave the impression that "abnormal phases of social life [such as the Shakers and their celibate lifestyle] are characteristic of American civilization."[58] Nordhoff should have made it abundantly clear, admonished the reviewer, that the United States "only furnished the field into which the fanatics and enthusiasts and crack-brained ignoramuses of other lands enter with their various schemes." The author reminded his readers that Ann Lee and her first followers came from England, despite Nordhoff's annoying habit of describing the Shakers "as Americans."[59]

More than twenty years earlier, an article in the *United States Democratic Review* had expressed similar concerns about the "American-ness" of the Shakers. "The feeling of individuality is too strongly developed in the American to render him a fit subject" for communal, celibate life. The Shaker enterprise, the article concluded, was bound to end "in the *reductio ad absurdum*" because it was based on a faulty and most un-American premise.[60]

Sometimes, even the allies whom the Shakers attracted served to strengthen the boundaries between the Shakers and mainstream American culture. In 1889, for example, the *North American Review* published an article by Minot J. Savage that mentioned the Shakers. Savage was a former Congregationalist minister who had left his post and taken a leadership position in Boston's Church of the Unity. Savage championed the new field of higher biblical criticism, openly praised Darwin's evolutionary theories, and advocated the comparative study of religion. Little wonder that Savage gained few friends for the Shakers among mainstream Protestants when he wrote:

> It has been the custom of the Protestants to condemn severely the Romish doctrine and practice as to the celibacy of the clergy. But the teaching of the New Testament is explicit and clear as to the superior holiness of the single as contrasted with the married state. This would seem also to apply to the laity as well as the clergy, so that the Shakers are doubtless right in their contention.[61]

The responses generated among the larger American public were thus varied. Some were positive, although it is important to note that the Shakers rarely mentioned those assessments. More often, they focused on the negative comments that occasionally appeared in the American media. This negativity generally focused on the challenge that celibacy posed to the institution of marriage and to America's reputation, rather than on the negative effects that celibacy had on those who practiced it. This stands in stark contrast to Mormon polygamy, which was not only viewed as a threat to institutional marriage but which also spawned a discourse of victimization in which certain segments of U.S. society expressed deep concern about the physical and psychological impact on the women and children in polygamous families.

Such negative reactions, of course, were what the Shakers expected. A letter written at Mount Lebanon, New York, in 1848 warned that anyone pursuing a life of "virgin purity" could expect nothing but "persecution and oppression, and we must prepare to meet it manfully, valiantly, and cheerfully." Being "hated of all men for [Christ's] name sake" was evidence, according to the letter, that the Shakers were God's people "chosen out of the world" and served to "confirm our identity."[62] The Shakers used the negative attention that celibacy garnered as a solidarity-generating device.

Successful religious tension models, as I discussed above, serve to redirect criticisms and attacks intended as disintegrative and to channel them into integrative energy that strengthens the commitment of the individual to the group and the group's overall sense of identity. This key dialectical relationship is an essential element in any comprehensive boundary marker system.

Mary S. Russell, a Shaker sister living at Enfield, Connecticut, demonstrated this tendency in her 1843 autobiographical "testimony." Russell wrote that ridicule over her celibate lifestyle, coupled with her experience of "having seen many fall by the way" because of their inability to practice celibacy, "increased my zeal more and more to be faithful, and stand fast, for I knew that they could not deprive the faithful of any good for they were corrupt at heart."[63] Russell's language is suggestive of the important function that the criticisms and defections caused by celibacy served for the Shakers. Most obviously, Russell identifies those who criticize or fail to practice celibacy as "corrupt at heart," a judgment that logically leads to the conclusion that those who endure criticism and keep the faith are purer in heart than those who do not. Russell saw in her sufferings for celibacy an imitation of "the holy anointed parents and leaders in the New Creation who have passed through heavy sufferings and tribulation to maintain . . . purity agreeable to the requirements of God."[64] This sort of stylized narrative, which was generated at the "request of the beloved lead" at Enfield, suggests that the Shakers were taught to see celibacy not only as a practice of personal purity but also as a practice that would bring criticism and difficulty that could be worn as a badge of honor linking the individual Shakers to their most highly achieving spiritual forebears.[65]

The link among celibacy, "persecution," and community identity apparently took little time to sink into the consciousness of new Shakers. Samuel Rollins, an early Shaker convert in the West, wrote a letter to New Lebanon in which he acknowledged that the "trials and persecutions" that came as a result of mortification and celibacy "make Shakers more wise than the wisest natural man on earth."[66]

The Shakers made much of the criticism leveled at them, and it fueled their sense of identity and sanctity. They tended to ignore praise, however, largely because it undermined their identity as outsiders.

CELIBACY, THE EMBODIMENT OF TRADITION, AND SYMBOLIC VIOLENCE

In considering the role of celibacy in nineteenth-century Shakerism, we have explored how it functioned as a boundary between the members of the community and the world beyond that community as well as the function of celibacy as a boundary between each individual Shaker and her or his internal sinful self. There are other features of Shaker celibacy that rendered it a remarkably stable boundary marker. The cost for this stability, however, was intransigence manifested in a deep resistance to adaptation.

Historian of religion Gavin Flood's work on the phenomenon of asceticism provides helpful insights into the relationship between the stability of Shaker celibacy and its inflexibility. Flood argued in his book *The Ascetic Self* that ascetic practices, including celibacy, involve a process in which "the ascetic conforms to the discipline of the tradition, shapes his or her body into particular cultural forms over time, and thereby appropriates the tradition."[67] Asceticism is a means through which practitioners perform their theologies and, with their bodies, enact the highest values of their religious traditions. According to Flood, as the "ascetic self [is] constructed in ritual, the ascetic is performing the memory of tradition. . . . The 'I' of the ascetic, through an act of will, conforms to the 'I' of tradition . . . [while] the indexical 'I' of the everyday self is eroded by contact with the structure of tradition and is subsumed by it."[68] Flood's observation that ascetic practices, or "corporeal ritual performances," tend to erode "the distinction between the sign, the signifier, and the interpretant [the sense made of the sign by the interpreter]" has implications for the study of nineteenth-century Shaker boundary maintenance.[69] For the Shakers, celibacy came to be viewed as an essential component of identity. To be a Shaker meant to be celibate; if one violated the prohibition against sex, one did not simply transgress against a commandment, one transgressed against personal identity. The Shakers believed not only that celibacy qualified them for a place in God's kingdom after death but that it also set them apart from their contemporaries and linked them with important figures from the past, including Jesus Christ and Ann Lee. Celibacy thus became a way for the Shakers to become living texts, inasmuch as they performed and transmitted sacred history through their behavior. In addition, the entire community came together as something resembling a sacred text because their refusal to engage in sex in any form reinforced their theological and historical foundations. All Shakers thus enjoyed access to the sacred through their performance of tradition. To tamper with celibacy, therefore, would be tantamount to attacking both scripture and tradition, which of course constitute major sources of sacred power in any religious tradition.

The embodiment of tradition was only one feature of Shaker celibacy. Another was the violent imagery that Shakers typically attached to the practice. Nineteenth-century Shakers, as devoted pacifists who refused to take up arms even to defend themselves against mob violence, did not employ violence even figuratively in most of their writings. The single exception to this trend is found in Shaker descriptions of the effect of celibacy. The Shakers frequently deployed language of hatred and violence in their narratives dealing with the goals of celibacy. In 1792, for example, Daniel Goodrich told a group of Shakers that "you have been believers long enough to hate the flesh." Goodrich warned his audience, "[I]f you do not wake up and hate the flesh you will sink in the flesh at last."[70] More than fifty years later, John Lyon wrote that true Shakers must "hate the element and principle of the flesh in which the serpent has fixed his habitation . . . and hate their own lives with all the lusts of their father [Satan]."[71] Lyon continued by reminding his readers that, by following the Shaker program of celibacy, they would be able to invoke "that fire which will melt and consume the old order of the flesh where the serpent has his habitation to carry on his works of lust."[72] Calvin Green made it abundantly clear that all believers should be actively engaged in the process of "crucifying and destroying" their "fallen natures."[73] Samuel Rollins, a young believer in Ohio, stated the same position with considerably less volubility than Green. "There is no escape for the flesh," Rollins wrote, "it must die."[74]

Although the Shakers probably borrowed this language from Catholic literature, it is significant that they chose to make it such an important theme. One could speculate about the possible stimuli that would induce the Shakers to place an act of symbolic violence at the heart of their belief and practice. Beyond the general observation that most marginal religious movements feel a sense of frustration with the dominant culture, there is little one can do to trace the root of the violence. It is clear that the Shakers imported the most important symbol of violence in Christianity, the crucifixion of Jesus, into their own ritual system. Unlike other Christian communities, which ritually experience the crucifixion through rites of communion such as the consuming of sacramental food emblems, the Shakers chose to crucify themselves symbolically through the mortification attendant to celibacy. It is interesting that, in the early Christian world, Tertullian viewed celibacy as a substitute for the "majestic shadow of a martyr's death," which not everyone was fortunate enough to merit.[75]

The Shakers did understand that a central element in their ritual practice of celibacy was the mortification—the killing—of a version of themselves. The surrogate victim upon whom the symbolic violence was inflicted was called by the Shakers "the man of sin," the person of the "old order" or the "old creation," or the "son of Adam." It is important to note that the Shakers generally did not speak of killing a part of themselves, but rather employed anthropomorphic language to suggest that they were killing an entire person. René Girard suggested that the selection of a surrogate sacrificial victim is based on the lack of a "crucial social link" between "these victims and the community."[76] The Shakers selected as the victim of sacrifice their own old "selves," which not only lacked a link to the community, but presented a major endogenous threat to the community dynamic—a threat that could not be countered effectively with external boundaries.

THE COST OF CELIBACY

Religious boundaries can help certain kinds of religious traditions maintain an outsider status, which in turn may yield beneficial results. However, there comes a point when the tension generated may usher in a situation of diminished returns. Often this comes in the form of actions taken by outsiders who threaten the marginal group with legal or extralegal force beyond the power of the group to resist or successfully absorb the pressure. In the case of the Shakers, however, the diminishing returns attendant to the practice of celibacy were largely generated internally. The Shaker experience with celibacy raises an important question: why would a group that believed in continuing revelation and the possibility of religious change refuse to make changes to a policy that was clearly resulting in diminishing returns?

The number of Shakers declined from a zenith of around 4,000 at mid-century to 1,849 in 1880 and 855 in 1900.[77] Obviously, celibacy per se cannot be the cause of this decline because the Shakers practiced celibacy throughout their history in America, including the period during which they enjoyed their greatest numerical growth. Celibacy did, however, exert a greater impact as time wore on than it did initially.

The problems associated with celibacy had several dimensions. First, of course, is the simple matter of demographics. Even in the mid-nineteenth century, when infant mortality rates were high, natural reproduction in a group like the Shakers would have yielded geometric increases within two generations.[78] Compounding the problem of a lack of natural reproduction was the lack of emphasis on person-to-person proselytizing. With the exceptions of Ann Lee's 1781–1783 missionary journey through New England, the 1803–1804 itinerant missions on the East Coast, and the Shaker expansion into the West beginning in 1805, the Shakers deployed no systematic proselytizing effort, beyond their substantial publication ventures, to attract converts. Giles Avery, writing probably in the 1870s, gave two reasons for the "very limited" missionary activity among believers. First, "the general Shaker mind has not considered outside society prepared for Shaker testimony, in its entirety." Second, "suitable missionaries" were scarce, given the labor-intensive "burdens and duties" of Shaker village life.[79] Even in explaining a lack of interest in proselytizing, this particular Shaker author could not resist making an assertion of Shaker outsiderhood through the trope of moral superiority.

More important even than the issue of sheer numbers was the problem of socialization and commitment. In an effort to minimize the numerical costs of celibacy, the Shakers actively took in orphans and children whose parents lacked the means or the desire to care for them. In an era when state-run social services for children were nonexistent, the Shakers presented an attractive option for those responsible for the disposition of homeless children. While the Shakers managed to take in many children and adolescents throughout the nineteenth century, few of them remained committed to Shaker life after reaching adulthood. In fact, the Shakers expended tremendous resources in their efforts to keep young people "orderly."[80]

It is axiomatic that religions flourish when new generations are socialized from birth into the tradition.[81] It follows that the younger an individual is when socialized into the religious world, the less external legitimation is required to maintain the plausibility of that religious world. Similarly, the presence of parents who espouse the belief system upon which the religious world is built also contributes to the relative plausibility of that world for children. The Shakers, in contrast, were faced with the more difficult task of constantly socializing adult converts and children with no natural ties to the community.

Finally, because celibacy's costs resulted from the natural circumstances attendant on nonreproduction, they could not be mitigated successfully through the use of persecution narratives in the same way that general cultural criticisms could be. Thus, there was no benefit to offset that particular set of costs in that the lack of naturally born members could not be interpreted as a sign of the world's disfavor.

Celibacy's dual nature as both an external and an internal boundary made it both extremely stable and very difficult to change, even in the face of severe numerical decline and the increasingly disproportionate age and gender ratios within the Shaker world.[82] Celibacy became a permanent, continuous, and multivalent ritual act that served to increase group solidarity and communal identity, to protect the believers from vestiges of their unregenerate selves, to provide an outlet for symbolic violence, and to use their bodies as a text that received and transmitted tradition. Because celibacy served so many functions within the Shaker community and because it was a universal requirement, it was extremely difficult to make adjustments to the practice in response to changing circumstances. Had the Shakers abandoned celibacy, or made even less dramatic adjustments to the practice, they would have lost a major component of Shaker identity, they would have forfeited an important outlet for frustration through the symbolic violence inherent in the mortification rhetoric of celibacy, and they would have lost the protection against their own evil tendencies that celibacy was designed to provide.

Although no adjustments to celibacy were ever effected during the nineteenth century, apparently an effort was made to do so in the 1840s. The Era of Manifestations will be discussed at length and in a slightly different context below, but one incident from that period must be addressed in connection with celibacy.

In the spring of 1842, Philemon Stewart, who had become one of the most prominent "instruments" for receiving heavenly visions at New Lebanon, New York, claimed to have received and recorded a lengthy series of revelations. The collection of revelations was so long that when it was published it ran to more than 400 pages. The book caused quite a stir throughout the Shaker world, but it was embraced by a majority of believers of all ranks in the eastern and western villages alike. Despite the book's popularity, or perhaps because of it, Shaker leaders objected to several issues raised in the revelations.[83]

These objections eventually led to the insertion in the published version of editorial comments affirming the primacy of Shaker leaders.

One issue that has apparently escaped the notice of historians but did not pass unchecked by Shaker leaders in the 1840s was the controversy over the "law of grace" versus the "law of nature." Stewart's revelations contained several obscure references to the notion that persons unable to live the law of grace, which included celibacy, could find some favor with God by living the law of nature, as given to Adam and Eve in the garden of Eden. In chapter 21, for example, the revelation stated that "such as do not feel themselves called upon by the awakening flames of conviction, in their own consciences, to obey the law of gospel purity, must return to the moral law of nature, saith the Lord, or they cannot escape the heavy hand of my awful judgments."[84] Some Shaker leaders resented the implication that anyone not living the full Shaker laws of celibacy and joint interest could hope to "escape the heavy hand" of God in any degree.

In October 1843, Seth Y. Wells attended a "conference meeting concerning the Sacred roll, lately printed."[85] Wells reported a "difference of opinion respecting the doctrine of restoring mankind back to the order of nature from which man fell by disobedience." Some Shaker leaders objected specifically to the idea that those who would return to the order of life prescribed by God to Adam and Eve, including the injunction to multiply and replenish the earth, "and prove faithful to it, should be blessed in their order, according to their faithfulness, as well as those that live under the law of grace." It is not surprising that this concept "seemed not to meet the feelings of some then present." Wells, however, felt the need to offer a defense of the ideas contained in Stewart's revelatory book. In a letter to Rufus Bishop, an extremely powerful member of the Central Ministry, Wells argued that recent revelations from the spirit world indicated that "it was the purpose of God to overthrow Satan, and restore mankind back to the order of nature; and that he is determined to effect this work by establishing a law and order for that portion of the children of men, who do not embrace the gospel of Christ, and come under the law of grace." The law to which these persons would be subject was "the law of nature, given to man at the beginning." Those who kept that law "strictly and faithfully" would not "fall under the judgments prepared for the rebellious and disobedient."

In his letter, Wells painted a picture of a three-tiered hierarchy of righteousness: those who lived the law of grace, who would be blessed by God in the fullest sense; those who lived the law of nature, who would be blessed but in a diminished degree; and those who "will be subject to no law." The third group would fall under "Divine Judgment."

The first tier, which consisted of those who were "specially called" by God to come out of the world and live the full law of grace, and the third tier, those who would be damned, represented nothing new. The Shakers had always believed and taught that salvation came only through the successful bearing of the celibate cross. Everyone else would be damned.

The provocative element of Wells's letter is found in his discussion of the middle tier. This second group consisted of those well-meaning souls who were inadequately prepared to meet the requirements of the full law. "The largest portion of the human race" would find themselves in this cohort. He argued that "prophetic inspiration" had revealed that "those who shall freely submit to the [natural] law and order, shall have their leaders of their own order, chosen from among the most faithful of their order." Moreover, they will "greatly honor and respect those under the law of grace, and look to Zion for counsel and instruction."

Wells emphasized that the introduction of the new three-tiered schema lay in the future for "altho God has declared that it shall be, yet he has not revealed the time when, nor in the manner which it will be brought to pass." He cautioned that the particular practices connected with the law of nature had "not been revealed," but he drew from unnamed sources to provide the "general terms" that any persons living the law of nature might be expected to obey. All but one of those terms corresponded exactly with the laws that already governed the Shakers. Wells specifically identified pacifism, abstention from "all contention and strife," honesty in "all dealings," and strict adherence to the principle of doing unto others as "they would have others do to them." All of this, of course, was standard Shaker behavior.

Wells saved for the end of his list the rather surprising requirement that those under the law of nature should "come to their wives only for the purpose of procreation, and that only once in eighteen months." Viewed from the perspective of mainstream American culture, of course, such strict regulation of marital relations surely must have seemed draconian. As I have documented at length above, however, by the time this letter was written the Shakers had already developed a dense theological justification for celibacy as the only acceptable arrangement. From the antebellum Shaker vantage point, the ideas advanced in Wells's letter must have seemed blasphemously permissive.

It is no surprise that the balance of the letter focused on a defense of this explosive theological innovation. Wells centered his defense on two points. Wells first noted that Christ, Ann Lee, and Father Joseph Meacham all taught the principles Wells discussed in his letter. Moreover, Wells offered a pragmatic defense. Wells wrote of his "reasonable expectation that these people will furnish Zion with a constant supply of innocent members, who will not be so sunken and lost in pollution and defilement, as the present race, from which we are in the practice of gathering members." Implicit in the defense that Wells offered was an additional cost of celibacy: the Shakers were forced to pick their new members from the ranks of unregenerate humanity. Wells apparently hoped that allowing moderately righteous persons to reproduce would result in spiritually superior offspring who would more likely be able to shoulder the full Shaker cross.

Despite Wells's ability to view the introduction of the law of nature as a "bright prospect," he was keenly aware that this was not a position with which most Shakers would agree. Wells expressed his concern about the loss of "unity in one faith" and observed that the believers were "divided in sentiment" over the issue. In an apparent effort to quash dissent through his personal gravitas, Wells closed his letter by suggesting rather strongly that "fair" and "enlightened" Shakers could have no objections to "the going forth of the law of nature and the law of grace . . . simultaneously . . . from Zion."

Few records exist that help to contextualize Wells's letter to Rufus Bishop. I was able to locate only two additional items bearing on the debate. The first is a short exposition by Richard Bushnell, a trustee at New Lebanon. Bushnell sharply criticized Wells's position:

> [T]o have such a law [of nature] run parallel with the gospel, for souls to choose either it, or, the law of grace, makes void, to my understanding, the worth of [Christ's] Second Appearing, as coming to destroy the man of sin and blending, in a measure, flesh and spirit, [it] makes no distinction between seed time and harvest, the work of the Sower and the work of the Reaper.[86]

Bushnell expressed the simplest of Shaker principles when he insisted on complete separation between the "man of sin" and the pure regenerate soul. He also seemed to suggest that, given a choice of practicing celibacy or not, many would choose the latter. Finally, Bushnell argued that only those who behaved as God did in matters of sex could be true Shakers. He pointed out that Jesus was a lifelong celibate.

The second item I located was penned by John Lyon of Enfield, New Hampshire, and it was written as a direct response to the Bushnell essay. Lyon sided with Wells and offered a lengthy five-point rebuttal to Bushnell's shorter piece. Lyon's argument basically restated the points made by Wells in the 1843 letter, but he added an interesting theological twist. Lyon argued, contra traditional Shaker doctrine, that the original sin committed by Adam and Eve was not sexual intercourse. It was, rather, an act of "positive rebellion," "wholly an act of the soul" in which "man set himself up as God, to do his own will and be his own lead."[87]

To my knowledge, no scholar has yet cited the Wells letter, much less dealt with its implications. Obviously, it raises some perplexing and provocative questions. Why would Wells, an ensconced leader with every reason to defend the status quo and someone who had already expressed objections to some of the material in Stewart's revelations, go to such lengths to defend what was a radical challenge to Shaker theology? What were the other sources he was using to develop the rules that were to govern the law of nature? Why is there such a paucity of other records documenting the divisive debate that Wells sought to quell with his letter? What happened to the debate? The ideas seem to have evaporated from the archives. It is impossible to know the extent to which the notion of a modified celibacy rule had spread among the Shaker villages. The Bushnell and Lyon manuscripts were copied into a packet that apparently circulated through some villages, although the only copy I could find was in the materials dedicated to the Enfield, New Hampshire, village.

While we cannot answer many, perhaps most, of the questions raised by the Wells letter, the thundering silence that followed it tells us something important: even an individual as powerful as Seth Y. Wells could not put a dent in either the theological or the practical elements of the juggernaut of Shaker celibacy.

Although the Shaker practice of celibacy remained remarkably stable throughout the nineteenth century, one should not conclude that all of the elements of the Shaker social and religious worlds enjoyed such stability. In the final chapter, I will examine just such an episode of instability when I look at the crisis that brought about the Era of Manifestations.

Origins of Mormon Polygamy

Like the Shakers, the Mormons in the nineteenth century placed their practices regarding marriage at the heart of their boundary maintenance strategy. Introduced by Joseph Smith to a few key followers beginning in the early 1840s, the practice of polygamy, or plural marriage, was instituted on a much more general level once the Mormons became ensconced in the intermountain West. Although Smith may have experimented with the practice as early as 1832, it was not until the summer of 1843 that he committed the doctrinal justifications for the practice to paper.[88] In July of that year, Smith issued a revelation linking plural marriage with exaltation and eternal family relationships. Apparently, the catalyst that led Smith to introduce the practice of plural marriage was his belief that a restoration of all things must include "the doctrine of having many wives." Smith's reading of the Hebrew Bible led him to conclude that God had justified the taking of multiple wives by "Abraham, Isaac, and Jacob, [and] also Moses, David, and Solomon."[89]

Smith wrote the revelation down in an effort to convince his first wife, Emma, that the practice of plural marriage was from God. Smith's clerk, William Clayton, noted that this effort failed miserably, and "Emma did not believe a word of it and appeared very rebellious."[90] Throughout the Nauvoo period, the practice was limited to members of Smith's Anointed Quorum but remained an open secret.

Polygamy generated two general types of tension: cultural and legal. The cultural tension was not unlike that endured by the Shakers in relation to celibacy. Polygamy was a favorite topic of the newly popular national magazines and was always guaranteed to sell newspapers. But crisis tension of the sort that the Mormons seemed to seek only derives from legal or vigilante sources. While it is true that the Mormons had no control over the initial legal machinations that surfaced in connection with polygamy and therefore could not have intentionally sought the legal tensions, they did everything in their power to exacerbate and prolong those tensions until 1890. The bulk of my discussion of Mormon polygamy will focus on the rising cycle of tension accompanying the legal resistance to the practice. The Mormons could have conceivably offered much less resistance to the legal tension, but they chose a path of aggressive resistance, which reveals a great deal about the kinds of tension that nineteenth-century Mormons used to shape their communal identity.

CULTURAL AND LEGAL TENSION

In 1852, the practice was officially announced to the world as a doctrine of the LDS Church. Almost immediately, cultural opposition to the practice grew. Mormons were ridiculed in publications across the country and were portrayed in cartoons as lecherous fiends. The first Sherlock Holmes story, *A Study in Scarlet,* featured a plot in which Mormon missionaries were scouring the streets of London looking for unsuspecting girls to bring back to their harems in Utah.

The cultural objections to Mormonism that formed the sources for tension between Mormonism and American culture in respect to polygamy were varied.[91] Some focused on the damage that the practice did to women, and others focused on the physiological impact of polygamy on children born of those unions. Newspaper and magazine articles, some by apostates, others by authors who had visited Utah, still others by people who had simply heard about the "atrocities" of polygamy, proliferated. In the interest of space, I quote here from a single article that covers almost all of the objections raised in the hundreds of other pieces written over the years. Published in the *New York Times* in 1858, the article reported:

> A very brief examination of life in the Valley presents indubitable evidence that polygamy is destructive of social comfort and peace, as well as of female delicacy, refinement, and virtue. It also induces extreme poverty. Jealousy and contention among the women is the rule rather than the exception. The children of polygamists are weakly, poor and miserable. The subjection of women to the debasing and disgusting practices of Mormonism, has been reduced to a system. The process is directed from the beginning to the destruction of their delicacy and the subversion of their free agency, so that they may become the merest slaves. As the instinctive shield of a woman's delicacy falls, she is fitted for the sacrifice.[92]

The Mormon response to such cultural tension was typically aggressive. Apostle George Q. Cannon published an editorial in his California newspaper, the *Western Standard,* in which he turned the tables on the critics. "The genius of Christian monogamy," Cannon wrote, "is to encourage prostitution."[93] Mormon children "are uncommonly robust and healthy [with] mental vigor in proportion to their physical perfection." In the Christian world, by contrast, "wives are now sickly and wretched, and are giving to the world children filled with evil passions fastened upon them by the inordinate indulgence of their begetters." Cannon noted the rise in "effeminacy and barrenness" that centuries of monogamy had foisted upon the world. His solution to these problems was simple: "Legalize polygamy, abolish whoredom by the strong arm of the law, and punish adultery with death, and numberless evils both physical and moral would disappear from the land."[94]

More than twenty years later, Apostle Joseph F. Smith gave a sermon in which he touched upon the same points, indicating that the general content of the cultural criticisms of polygamy had not changed.

> "Mormon" plural marriage cannot be degraded to the level of a comparison with the sexual crimes and iniquities of the world; there is no similitude between them. One is the antipode of the other—one is virtuous, pure and honorable, and the other is corrupt, treacherous and debasing

to the utmost degree. Our system of marriage promotes life, purity, innocence, vitality, health, increase and longevity, while the other engenders disease, disappointment, misery and premature death—that is the difference. Hence there is no resemblance for they are not allied to each other at all.[95]

It is interesting that the Mormons did not reject the eugenic arguments made against polygamy; they only objected to the particular application of those arguments to polygamy. Cannon's and Smith's thoughts are representative of a wide body of Mormon discourse that used the cultural criticisms caused by polygamy as an opportunity to reinforce Mormon superiority and purity. Cultural tension tends to be the least crushing of tensions, and if that were the only type that plural marriage created, the Mormons could have continued the practice and reaped the benefits of that tension indefinitely. However, the cultural tension soon bled into the legal arena.

The beginning of the meld between cultural and legal tension came in 1856. In that year, the Republican Party famously named polygamy and slavery the "twin relics of barbarism."[96] Lawmakers in Washington soon began to push legislation that, they hoped, would put an end to the practice of plural marriage. The leadership of the church strenuously rejected these moves, employing various methods of subterfuge to escape U.S. marshals who came to Utah to arrest them. Many Mormons did end up in jail, and they considered it an honor to be persecuted for their beliefs. Rudger Clawson, who would later become a member of the Quorum of the Twelve Apostles, wrote to one of his wives from prison, "[I]f by this and other sacrifices made from time to time, we can secure an eternal association together, happy indeed are we."[97]

Mormon rhetoric regarding polygamy was pitched higher as the external pressure mounted. The negative cultural and legal reactions to plural marriage were interpreted by the Mormons as evidence of the principle's correctness. In the face of opposition, church leaders remained defiant. In 1875, to cite one of many examples, Apostle Wilford Woodruff chided those members of the church who refused to enter into polygamous marriages and reminded them, "This law of the patriarchal order of marriage and plurality of wives is a revelation and commandment of God to us and we should obey it."[98]

In 1882, the church's First Presidency and the Quorum of the Twelve Apostles met to discuss "the policy of yielding any principle to a state government." Church president John Taylor told the group that the church "could not swap the Kingdom of God, or any of its laws or principles for a state government."[99] Eight years later, however, under Woodruff's leadership, the church did just that. Woodruff announced in September 1890 that the time had come for him to act for the "temporal salvation of the church." He issued the Manifesto that disavowed the solemnization of plural marriages but said nothing to indicate that the theology behind the practice had changed.

Many scholars have remarked upon the jarring singularity of this move, pointing to the repeated assertions that the principle of plural marriage would never be abandoned. However, the church was acting in a well-established pattern. As in the case of their approach to physical boundaries, the Mormon approach to the legal tension generated by plural marriage revolved around an aggressive and crisis-ridden tension model. In the case of plural marriage, one can track the process quite clearly. It began with the aggressive assertion of an ideal, which was followed by an equally aggressive response from various sectors of American society. The Mormons, reading these signs as evidence of their divine mission, ratcheted up the tension through aggressive rhetoric and further entrenchment of the practice of plural marriage. Finally, when the Mormons faced annihilation, this time through the actions of the U.S. Supreme Court, they broke the tension and reformulated their boundary markers.

POLYGAMY AS SIGN

From 1852 until 1890, church leaders made plain the fact that plural marriage was required by God for exaltation, at least in theory. Joseph F. Smith, Wilford Woodruff, John Taylor, Brigham Young, George Q. Cannon, and other church leaders preached the necessity of plural marriage. Brigham Young wrote in 1863 that "plurality [of wives is] as much a part of our religious faith as the crucifixion of the Savior for the redemption of man."[100] Joseph F. Smith taught that "whoever has imagined that he could obtain the fullness of blessing pertaining to this celestial law [polygamy], by complying with only a portion of its conditions [monogamous marriage in the LDS temple] has deceived himself, he cannot do it."[101] On another occasion, Brigham Young remarked, "The only men who become Gods, even the Sons of God, are those who enter into polygamy. Others attain unto a glory and may even be permitted to come into the presence of the Father and the Son; but they cannot reign as kings in glory, because they had blessings offered unto them, and they refused to accept them."[102] In the fall of 1885, the church's First Presidency issued an "epistle" to the general church membership in which they quoted from Joseph Smith's revelation on plural marriage and warned that "the penalty affixed to a refusal to obey this law [plural marriage]" was "damnation." In the same message, church leaders argued that polygamy was "given [as] a law to His Church for its salvation and exaltation" and that the doctrine had become "indissolubly interwoven in the minds of its members with their hopes of salvation and exaltation in the presence of God."[103]

Some scholars have argued that these kinds of statements were "not as inflexible as they appear." For such scholars, the fact that not all Mormons practiced plural marriage indicates that it must not have been required for exaltation.[104] By that standard, of course, few things could be considered religious "requirements" because few principles enjoy absolute adherence by the members of any religious population.[105]

It is true that there are scattered statements by LDS leaders that seem to contradict the stricter view. Brigham Young, for example, told Horace Greeley in 1859 that he "could not say" how widespread polygamy was among the Mormons, but some church leaders "have each but one wife; others have more; each determines what is his individual duty."[106] Young's statement, while factually true, carried an implication that certainly was not, namely, that monogamous marriages for eternity held equal stature with polygamous unions in Mormon theology.

It is also true that plural marriage was not a requirement for church membership nor temple privileges. The total percentage of Mormons involved in polygamous marriages in the nineteenth century is difficult to calculate, and it varied widely from locality to locality. Even in the most polygamously oriented towns, however, such as the Mormon colonies in Mexico, the rate was probably never higher than 60 percent, and in most other areas it was significantly lower. Stanley S. Ivins provided what is probably a reliable estimate that, at the peak of the Mormon polygamous experiment, "15 or possibly 20 percent of the Mormon families of Utah were polygamous."[107] As in the case of Mormon physical boundaries, Mormons often sent signs that were more important rhetorically than they were in practice. Just as few Mormons ever practiced plural marriage, few Mormons ever lived the law of consecration or lived in Zion.

That the volume of the signs far exceeded the reality of the practices those signs represented is further evidence of the importance of dialectically produced tension in the Mormon boundary maintenance strategy. The Mormons chose to play up potential tension-building signs rather than playing them down, at least in the early stages of the dialectic tension cycle.

In any case, it is abundantly clear that the ideal was established during the 1850s that plural marriage was the best, most God-like marital arrangement and that, at the very least, men in positions of leadership at the level of bishop and above were expected to practice polygamy. When a vacancy in the First Council of Seventy opened up in the fall of 1882, Taylor publicly stated that Seymour B. Young had been asked to take the position, but could only do so if he would "be obedient to the law of Celestial marriage."[108] Since Young was already married to one wife for eternity, Taylor here equated celestial marriage with plural marriage.[109] John Taylor remarked in 1882 that God was a polygamist, and "if we do not keep the same law that our Heavenly Father has, we cannot go with Him."[110] Exaltation, as defined in Mormon theology, consisted of life with God in the highest level of the "celestial kingdom." According to Taylor, if the saints did not live the law of plural marriage, they "could not go where our Heavenly Father dwells." Polygamy was thus asserted as the ideal condition and the only marital arrangement that would open the doors of exaltation.

In 1880, as the pressure for Mormons to abandon polygamy was increasing but not yet at the breaking point, Wilford Woodruff received a revelation as he camped alone in the deep snow blanketing the Arizona wilderness. Woodruff said God reassured him:

> [M]y Purpose shall be fulfilled upon this Nation, and No power shall
> stay my hand. And I say again woe unto that Nation or House or people,
> who seek to hinder my People from obeying the Patriarchal Law of
> Abraham which leadeth to Celestial Glory which has been revealed
> unto my Saints through the Mouth of my servant Joseph for whosoever

doeth these things shall be damned Saith the Lord of Hosts and shall be broken up & washed away. Fear ye not your Enemies [for] your Enemies shall not prevail over you.[111]

In this revelation, stark contrasts were drawn between the wicked U.S. government and the righteous people of God. Obedience to the law of plural marriage was the standard of behavior that set the chosen group apart, and anyone militating against this position would "be damned." This revelation also provides an example of the tendency to take negative signs sent by the host culture and to redirect them to serve as reinforcing mechanisms for the very practice such signs were designed to destroy.

Around the time that Woodruff recorded his revelation, Apostle Franklin D. Richards mused in his journal that, even though "step by step the Saints are plundered of their liberties, they still should be thankful that their enemies are yet restrained from violence and bloodshed."[112] Richards counseled courage and sought to bolster the Mormons by reminding them that things had been worse. Resistance, not accommodation, resonated through the texts of this period and accurately captured the Mormon mood.

LEGAL TENSION AND THE CRISIS CYCLE

The legislative pressure for the Mormons to abandon polygamy began around 1860.[113] While rhetorical opposition was immediate, the legislative wheels took a bit longer to get rolling. In 1860, the *Congressional Globe* contained an article opining that "whatever differences of opinion may exist as to whether marriage is a civil or canonical contract the whole civilized world regards the marriage of one man to one woman as being alone authorized by the laws of God, and that while the relation of husband and wife exists, neither can be lawfully married to another person."[114] The first piece of anti-polygamy legislation was passed just two years later. The Morrill Anti-Bigamy Act provided for criminal penalties for anyone found guilty of plural marriage, disincorporated the church, and set at $50,000 the maximum amount of real estate that the church could legally hold.[115]

Due to the outbreak of the Civil War, little was done to enforce this legislation for the next several years. Despite the passage of the bill, Mormon polygamous marriages continued to be performed unabated. It was not until 1874 that an arrest was made which could be used to challenge the constitutionality of the Morrill Act. In that year, George Reynolds, one of Brigham Young's secretaries, was arrested. Church leaders decided that they should test the constitutionality of the Morrill Act by instructing Reynolds to offer testimony against himself. The church was confident that the U.S. Supreme Court would hold that the legislation was unconstitutional in that it infringed upon the free exercise of religion. The Court, however, disagreed. It ruled that bigamy was not a legitimate expression of religion and that, in any case, the damage done to the fabric of society outweighed the religious prerogative.[116]

Beginning in the mid-1870s, the government aggressively went after polygamists in Utah. The Morrill Act proved to be ineffective, however, because it required that the state prove that a man was married to multiple women. Proof of such marriages had to be garnered from witnesses to the ceremonies themselves, and, of course, few such witnesses were willing to assist the government. A frustrated federal law-enforcement officer said:

> The limited number of indictments which we have been able to present against the violators of the law in question is due to the extreme difficulty in getting proof of polygamy marriages. The marriage ceremony is a secret one and attended only by the interested parties and those who either counsel its performance as a religious duty or profess to believe its divine origin. Under these circumstances we feel it is unexcusable to expect us to get sufficient evidence to convict except in rare circumstances.[117]

The frustration of federal officials reached to the highest levels. President James A. Garfield, in his 1881 inaugural address, lamented, "The Mormon church offends not only the moral sense of mankind by sanctioning polygamy, but prevents the administration of justice through the ordinary instruments of the law."[118]

In an attempt to remedy these difficulties, in 1882 Congress passed the Edmunds Act, which allowed prosecution for unlawful "cohabitation," something easy to prove because it simply required that a couple be observed living together. During the 1880s, over 1,300 Mormons were prosecuted and served short jail terms for unlawful cohabitation. The Edmunds Act went further than the Morrill Act in that it barred polygamists from voting and holding public offices. It also denied them the right to serve on juries, helping to ensure fewer acquittals during cohabitation trials. The final measure was passed in 1887. The Edmunds-Tucker Act put teeth into the Morrill Act's provision for the seizure of church property with value in excess of $50,000. The church once again challenged the law, but it was upheld in a court decision issued in May 1890.[119]

During this time, church leaders made vigorous and frequently belligerent speeches reemphasizing the divine nature of plural marriage and the primacy of God's laws over the laws of men. After the very first rumblings of anti-polygamy legislation in 1856, Brigham Young gave a spirited address in which he asked rhetorically, "how will they get rid of this awful evil in Utah?" Sounding a defiant note, Young offered his vision of how things would have to unfold: "They will have to expend about three hundred millions of dollars for building a prison, for we must all go to prison. And after they have expended that amount for a prison, and roofed it over from the summit of the Rocky Mountains to the summit of the Sierra Nevada, we will dig out and go preaching throughout the world."[120] Young's hyperbole was not only memorable, but it served the important purpose of clearly defining who was right, who was wrong, and what the difference between them was.

As the years passed and serious legal action began to be taken against the Mormons, the rhetoric heated up. In response to the initial sign of plural marriage, the U.S. government initiated legal action, which the Mormons understood as persecution that, of course, validated their identity as the chosen people of God. Apostle Erastus Snow addressed an audience in Salt Lake City shortly after the Edmunds Act was passed. During his sermon, Snow denounced the "immical [sic] legislation" which was authored and passed by "the wicked" and which was designed to "deprive the saints of their liberties."[121] W. W. Phelps summarized this perspective when he wrote, "The religion of Jesus Christ, has always been persecuted. But when a saint lives to God, persecution or applause is all one."[122] In fact, persecution was better than applause not only because it served to drive the community together, but it reminded them that their actions were displeasing to the "world." In 1882, George Q. Cannon noted rather candidly that, "as for this legislation, I want to say to you, that in some respects I am thankful for it. Let persecution come if it will have a good effect. Why? Because it puts us all in the same boat and does not divide us. A better plan could not have been devised to make us one than the ruling they have made in regard to those 'in the marriage relation.'"[123]

Some even viewed the tension generated by plural marriage as an opportunity for those Mormons who missed out on the persecutions of earlier eras to have their turn. One such leader wrote to his son from a "safe retreat" in September 1885, telling him "the Lord is permitting them [anti-polygamists] to take a course that has the effect to try and prove many as they have never been tried and proven before." The faithful, however, "rejoice in having the privilege of taking part in this great work, and in passing through these scenes. They rejoice that they are worthy to suffer for the cause of Christ."[124] Thus, the Mormons took the legal and cultural opposition to plural marriage as encouragement to live the law of plural marriage, no matter what the consequences might be.

In order to make full use of the resistance the Mormons experienced, church leaders were careful to identify themselves and their community with God and his will and were equally careful to paint everyone else as being associated with evil. In an 1885 letter to First Presidency counselor Daniel H. Wells, then serving a mission in Liverpool, John Taylor's personal secretary waxed confident that the church's "enemies will gain no advantage over us, of this we feel assured." He further mused: "If this nation continues to uphold the wicked in their attacks upon us, and pursue the attitude of seeking to destroy this people and trample upon every humane right and liberty, God will come forth and hold a controversy with them, and His wrath [will] be made manifest."[125]

With regard to the mounting pressure from the government to abandon the practice, Woodruff cast the struggle, and the boundaries, in decidedly stark terms: "this warfare is between God and the Devil, Christ and Belial, Saint and Sinner, Light and Darkness, good and evil."[126] John Taylor even engaged one of his audiences in the ritual creation of boundaries when he asked:

> Do I expect to give up my religion to the devil? I think not. What shall we do? Shall we trust in God or in the arm of flesh? Shall we give up our religion and our God and be governed by the practices that exist in the nation which are contrary to the laws of God? All who are in favor of abiding by the laws of God hold up their right hand (The congregation voted unanimously).[127]

Taylor's sermon and others like it also indicate that support for plural marriage within the Mormon community was not absolute. In 1876, nineteen-year-old Heber J. Grant castigated his peers for their cavalier attitude toward plural marriage and warned them against giving up the practice in order to suit the "notions and fancies of our bitterest enemies."[128]

This internal rhetoric increased in frequency and vitriol as the anti-polygamy legislation became more pointed and effective. As the public attitude toward polygamy grew more ominous, however, Mormon leaders slightly modified the severity of the signs they projected to the culture at large. John Taylor and George Q. Cannon expressed the reasons behind such a move in an 1887 letter to a Mormon living in Washington, D.C. "It is not necessary that we should advocate polygamy," they opined, because "that is not our business." Taylor and Cannon argued that the doctrine of plural marriage was so sacred that to expose it too often to the gaze of the "wicked people" of the nation would be blasphemous. Taylor and Cannon finished the letter with a stinging indictment of both the "gentiles" and many Mormons: "There are comparatively few even of the Latter-day Saints who are in a condition to practice this system in the manner God designs, and how much less the people who do not believe the principles of the gospel!"[129]

Taylor's position was a foretaste of the cat-and-mouse game that LDS authorities would play with U.S. officials for years to come, but it was generally ineffective in its attempts to mollify American cultural attitudes toward the Mormons. The reason for this is simple. The Mormons never modified the intensity of the internally broadcast signs relating to plural marriage. Rhetoric designed for internal consumption continued to emphasize the importance of plural marriage as a theological tenet. As a result, the Mormons became increasingly committed to plural marriage, despite the slightly softer message that some church leaders were trying to send to the world outside.

Historian Thomas Alexander pointed out that Wilford Woodruff entertained high hopes of achieving Utah statehood in 1888, and during this period he tried to calm the aggressive pro-polygamy rhetoric coming from church leaders.[130] The result was a conflict in goals that led to a conflict over boundary markers. To some segments of the church hierarchy, it was becoming clear that statehood for Utah would necessitate a shift away from polygamy. Others rejected this position and insisted that, if God wanted Utah to be a state, he would open a way for that without forcing the Mormons to abandon such a central tenet of their faith.

In late 1888, Woodruff received from Mormons in Washington, D.C., a draft of a proposed statement that they wanted Woodruff to issue. The draft stated that the Mormons would henceforth "conform their lives to the Laws of Congress." While Woodruff seemed at first to be in favor of such a move, most other church leaders were hostile to it. Richard S. Van Wagoner, in his study of Mormon polygamy, briefly mentions this episode, noting only that Woodruff unsuccessfully sought the advice of his counselors and instead ended up laying "the matter before the Lord."[131] Van Wagoner does not discuss the tense meeting of the Quorum of the Twelve Apostles during which a hesitant Woodruff brought the issue up for discussion. Apostle Franklin D. Richards characterized the document as coming from "persons *supposed* to be friends" and noted approvingly that each of the apostles present "refused unqualifiedly to adopt its sentiments."[132]

Future church president and then-apostle Heber J. Grant, in a considerably more voluble account than that offered by Richards, recorded in his diary the reactions of some of his fellow apostles to the proposed document. According to Grant's account, John Henry Smith flatly stated that, without direct revelation from God, he could not "submit to such a document." Francis M. Lyman offered his opinion that he did "not feel that the Lord would justify us in abandoning any principle of the gospel."[133]

The proposed statement offered quotes from previous revelations to justify the abandonment of plural marriage and specifically cited the January 1841 revelation excusing the Mormons from constructing their temple in Jackson County, Missouri.[134] Although precisely this line of reasoning would be used by church leaders after the Manifesto was issued in 1890 (see below), at this point many apostles saw no true parallel between the disappointments in Missouri and the potential casting off of plural marriage. Lyman argued that "the revelations that say where the Lord gives a command and the people not of us prevent the saints from fulfilling same he thought referred only to temporal matters, such as the building up of the center Stake of Zion or the erection of a Temple."

Franklin D. Richards agreed with Lyman and explained that, in his judgment, "manual labor and not principle is what is referred to in the Revelation of the Lord where he speaks of work not being done and it will no longer be required of the Saints." Based on the thoughts offered at this meeting, it seems that polygamy was seen as qualitatively different from any other commandment given by God; it was not a temporal issue but an eternal spiritual principle, a stance that would be altered after 1890. Apostle Moses Thatcher took an even stronger stand, noting that "as yet we have not gained one single point on account of what we have heretofore yielded and I don't believe we would be sustained by the Lord in accepting any such a document."

Joseph F. Smith sounded a defiant note in the 1888 meeting. Referring to recent compromises made by the church, Smith lamented that the church had "been yielding and stretching our consciences so we could retain the City and County governments and not allow them to pass out of our hands." Smith had grown indignant at the prospect of trading the sacred for the approval of the profane.

> If we keep on, to be consistent we must yield everything. To my mind it has come to this point now, that we must yield no more. I feel we should take a stand right here and never yield another point or come out and say we will not in the future carry out the commands of God because we are prevented by our enemies. If we don't take a stand now I feel we will have to yield our manhood before we get through yielding.

Implicit in Smith's slippery-slope argument is the necessity and unavoidability of persecution for those who are pursuing God's ways in Satan's wicked world. He recognized that any future difficulties would result in an automatic surrender with nothing more than a nod to an old revelation if Woodruff set such a precedent. Smith clearly viewed the situation as one of extreme pressure on a tight vessel, pressure that demanded the exertion of an equal and opposite force in order for the church to remain viable as a religious enterprise. Smith imagined a complete collapse of the entire Mormon boundary system stemming from the collapse of the most important nineteenth-century boundary marker.

The tension that plural marriage generated reached a crescendo as the church used it to fuel retrenchment and more aggressive rhetoric. Although moments of uncertainty arose, such as the 1888 statehood debate, the church consistently decided to maintain its boundaries.

POLYGAMY AND THE MANIFESTO OF 1890:
ANNIHILATION OR REFORMULATION

The story of the coming of the Manifesto in 1890 has been told and retold at great length. There are no significant debates about the course of events. In 1890, the U.S. Supreme Court upheld the constitutionality of the 1887 Edmunds-Tucker Act, and the government stood ready to confiscate the church's property, including the sacred temples. On 19 May, an obviously morose Woodruff bemoaned in his diary that "the Supreme Court of the United States decided today against the Church of Jesus Christ of Latter-day Saints. They decided to escheat all property, real and personal. This is the turning of the last key that will seal the condemnation of this nation."[135]

As had happened in Missouri and Illinois, the Mormons faced a conundrum. In those cases, the church eventually came to the point in its cycle of crisis-driven boundary maintenance when it faced potential annihilation stemming from vigilante resistance. In this case, the final decision of the Supreme Court to seize church property, including temples, put the Mormons in the position of either continuing the cycle, and risking annihilation, or ending the cycle and making an effort to recast the boundaries. The Mormons could repeat their previous, defiant responses to pressure and hope that God would save them in a miraculous way, risking, of course, severe cultural and religious dislocation. On the other hand, they could follow the pattern set in the previous instances: accommodate the increased pressure and reformulate the boundaries and the narrative. Woodruff, of course, chose the latter.

The foundation for such a move was laid in a revelation recorded by Woodruff in November 1889. Church lawyers had pressed Woodruff to make some "concession" on plural marriage, and in response Woodruff "spent several hours alone and inquired of the Lord," and he received a revelation warning him not to make any concessions. This document took a stand that was not nearly as defiant as those taken in previous revelations, however. It asserted that the courts were in God's hands and that the church's enemies would not prevail, but it also contained repeated admonitions to seek further guidance from God on the subject. Apostle Brigham Young Jr. felt moved to "thank God for this revelation," in which Woodruff was warned "not to make promises to [our] enemies nor concessions," but to always "seek for His Holy Spirit by mighty prayer."[136]

The 1889 revelation may be read as a transitional statement, perched on the cusp of a major shift in the episodic crisis model. The revelation promised that the church would ultimately prevail, but made no specific promises that the practice of plural marriage would be continued. Furthermore, the revelation made it clear that further "guidance" would be needed to claim the promised blessings—just the kind of guidance that Woodruff would claim brought about the Manifesto.[137]

In December 1889, Mormon William Smart expressed his hope that the church would force an apocalyptic standoff over plural marriage, something that he doubted would happen. Rather than even consider accommodations, Smart wrote, the church should have continued to resist so that "persecution [would have] reached its climax; and sooner would God have made bare His arm in behalf of His people. Then, too, when the climax had been reached, what a history of constancy and heroism would have been left as vantage grounds to future generations."[138] Mormons had never before taken such an approach to their enemies before, however, and Smart was about to see that they would not do so over plural marriage.

In the summer of 1890, after the unfavorable outcome from the Supreme Court case, Woodruff apparently moved to put an end to plural marriages within the United States. Joseph F. Smith answered a query posed by Charles W. Nibley, a Mormon businessman who had served as a missionary under Smith in the British mission in the late 1870s. Nibley wrote asking for advice for a friend who wished to enter plural marriage. Smith replied, "I could not offer a single objection to the 'friend' concerned, but I would commend him, under ordinary circumstances, and say go ahead, but the times have changed, the conditions are not propitious and the decrees of the 'Powers that be' are against the move." Smith's close friendship with Nibley allowed him to be frank, and Smith demonstrated remarkable candor when he told Nibley, "I do not care so much for the outside powers as I do those within, although common prudence would suggest that defference [sic] should be paid to both."[139]

Smith was a tough and severe individual, known to have a violent temper, who had been totally dedicated to the practice of plural marriage.[140] Clearly, Smith was rankled at the limits Woodruff was beginning to place on the practice and frustrated at what he viewed as capitulation. In any case, Smith resigned himself to the fact that no matter how "difficult [it is] for me to say, the decree now is that there shall be no p——l m——s [sic] in the United States, and that there shall be none anywhere unless one or both of the parties remove beyond the jurisdiction of this government to make their home."

Smith sounded a cautionary note, however, when he told Nibley that once a person has "got sufficient family to fulfill the requirements of the [celestial] law"—meaning when a man has entered into one plural marriage—that person ought not "take any more chances or make any greater offering for sacrifice." As for Smith himself, he insisted that it would take "nothing short of a direct command of God that could induce me to take one more" plural wife. "What I have done I will stand by and will not 'go back on it,'" Smith affirmed, "but if the Lord wants me to do more than I have done in that direction he must command me to do it." Smith indicated that this "efectual estoppel" of plural marriage might be temporary, but for the time being such marriages were not to be risked. Although Smith believed it was possible that the "clouds [might] roll by" and the "gloom pass away," he was noncommittal about when, if ever, it might be advisable for people to contract new plural marriages. The fact that Smith, one of the most devoted practitioners of plural marriage, expressed such feelings of caution did not bode well for the future of the practice.[141]

In September 1890, Woodruff issued the Manifesto, a document that contained absolutely no doctrinal discussion of the merits of plural marriage. It simply asserted that plural marriages would no longer be sanctioned by the church. The most important sentence of the statement claimed that "we are not teaching polygamy or plural marriage, nor permitting any person to enter into its practice." In the aftermath of this decision, the church went through a period of difficulty as the membership tried to adjust to the new policy. In a move reminiscent of one performed in relation to Zion, the doctrine of plural marriage shifted from the realm of orthopraxy to the realm of orthodoxy. Plural marriages were banned, although it would be another decade before officially sanctioned polygamous unions ceased completely, but belief in the correctness of plural marriage was maintained. This construction began even before Woodruff announced the Manifesto publicly, and it persisted throughout the twentieth and into the twenty-first century.[142]

Franklin D. Richards, then president of the Quorum of the Twelve, attended a meeting of church leaders on 24 September 1890, during which the men "spoke of the President WW's Manifesto its reception by the Saints and the world. How the Lord had suspended the operations of His laws in various occasions & held the enemies of his Church responsible for the same."[143] Clearly, some of the leaders at the top of the church hierarchy recognized immediately the similarities between the "suspension" of the practice of plural marriage and previous events in LDS history.

The month before the Manifesto was issued, Woodruff, Joseph F. Smith, and George Q. Cannon traveled to a quarterly stake conference in Manassa, Colorado. At that conference, Woodruff spent a good deal of time discussing the failure of the Mormons to build the temple in Jackson County, Missouri, adding, "God will not and never will hold us responsible for not building the Temple in Jackson county, until he opens the way." No doubt thinking about the justification he would have to provide for the suspension of plural marriage that he would soon issue, Woodruff added that "God would hold the nation responsible for hindering his work."[144] It is difficult not to see Woodruff's August address in Colorado as a trial run for the arguments he would make about plural marriage in the coming months.

On 10 October, Richards made explicit what he had alluded to the previous month when, at a meeting of "60 or 70" members of the priesthood in Salt Lake City, he "spoke of the present suspension of Patriarchal marriages by Pres[iden]t Woodruff's Manifesto and gave several instances of similar doing in other things and in former times and quoted rev[elations] on the 435 & 381 pages of Doc. & C [the Doctrine and Covenants]."[145] Richards, it will be remembered, had rejected this application of scriptural precedent to the case of polygamy in December 1888, arguing that plural marriage was an eternal rather than merely a temporal concern and as such was not comparable to such an obviously terrestrial activity as constructing a temple. Less than two years later, Richards apparently found reason to adjust his thinking on the issue and reverse course, although he was only echoing what George Q. Cannon had told the general membership of the church in the meeting at which the Manifesto was read publicly. After quoting the 1841 revelation, which excused the Mormons from completing the temple in Jackson County, Missouri, Cannon argued that "it is on this basis that President Woodruff has felt himself justified in issuing this Manifesto."[146] Cannon, of course, was present at the meeting in Colorado the previous month when Woodruff had reminded his listeners that God sometimes excuses his people from accomplishing his commands when the external opposition is too great.

Cannon went on to chastise members of the church who claimed to have predicted the demise of plural marriage and who, in Cannon's words, believed that abandoning the practice of plural marriage at the first sign of pressure "might have saved very serious consequences to us all and left us in a better position than that which we occupy today."[147] Cannon set a discursive course that would become common in the period immediately following the Manifesto. Persecution, a cherished building block of boundaries with the world, would follow even on the heels of the Manifesto. In the dramatic crescendo of his address, Cannon pointed out that the devil was not pleased with what the Mormons had done.

> It is seldom I have seen so many lies, and such flagrant, outrageous lies told about the Latter-day Saints as I have quite recently. It seems as though the devil is mad every way. "Now," says he, "they are going to take advantage of this, and I am determined they shall have no benefit of it; I will fill the earth with lies concerning them, and neutralize this declaration of President Woodruff's." And you will see in all the papers everything that can be said to neutralize the effect of this. To me it is pretty good evidence that the devil is not pleased with what we are doing. When we kept silence concerning this, then we were a very mean and bad people; and now that we have broken the silence and made public our position, why, we are wicked in other directions, and no credence can be attached to anything that we say. You may know by this that his satanic majesty is not pleased with our action. *I hope he never will be.*[148]

Cannon clearly took any objections to Mormon policies as direct evidence of a satanic conspiracy, and his rhetoric served to remind his listeners that the boundary of plural marriage might be fading but the boundary between the saints and the world was as distinct as ever.

In an editorial published in the church's *Deseret News* on the same day that Cannon gave his address, the writer also sought to assuage fears that the church had bowed to external pressure. The author pointed out that the criticism leveled at the church after the Manifesto was issued—criticism that was greatly exaggerated by LDS leaders—was evidence of the futility of any

> attempt to please the world or satisfy the demands made upon them by [the church's] enemies. No matter what they may say, it would not remove their opposition to the Church and their hatred of the Saints, their encroachments will never be stopped by submitting to their clamors, but every point yielded will only encourage them in their oppressions and increase their determination to destroy.

Once again, the correctness of the decision was measured by the degree to which it offended the enemies of the church. In language reminiscent of Cannon's remarks about his pleasure at the devil's pique, the *Deseret News* editorial encouraged the Mormons to "let the wicked rage. Let the heathen imagine vain things. But be not swerved to the right or the left by what they may howl for, nor think for a moment that they will ever be satisfied."[149]

REFORMULATING THE BOUNDARIES

In February 1893, B. H. Roberts, a member of the Presidency of the Quorum of Seventy, rehearsed in his diary the events surrounding his immediate reaction to the Manifesto. He described being so shocked and dismayed at the news that he refused to vote to sustain the declaration when it was read in the church's October general conference. At length, Roberts reconciled himself to the Manifesto, although he wrote that "I do not to this day" understand the "purposes for which it was issued." On a lighter note, Roberts comforted himself with the belief that "the principle of plurality of wives is true and in connection with all other truth will eventually prevail and be established on the earth."[150]

A full decade after the Manifesto was issued, meetings of the apostles still occasionally grew heated when the topic came up. In early 1900, the apostles met to discuss a letter that Woodruff's successor to the LDS presidency, Lorenzo Snow, had sent to the world, reaffirming the church's commitment to monogamous marriages. John W. Taylor, making no effort to conceal his contempt for the move, called the letter "Snow's little love-letter to the Gentiles."[151] George Teasdale flatly stated that he was not convinced that "God had repealed this law [of plural marriage]." He told the assembled leadership that, if the church was going to abandon its principles in the face of persecution, then it "might as well [give up] the priesthood." In an unusually candid moment, Teasdale admitted that he "felt humiliated at [the church's] back-down."[152] Apostle Marriner W. Merrill also referred to polygamy, noting, "it had come to stay in one form or another," and the "principle would never be taken from the earth."[153] Brigham Young Jr. said that he had a "testimony concerning the Manifesto," and he focused his critique on the Mormons themselves. God, Young argued, abrogated the practice of plural marriage, and with it the attendant blessings, because so few Mormons had been willing to enter into plural marriages. Finally, Francis M. Lyman suggested that the suspension of the law of plural marriage was akin to the status of the law of consecration, which had been suspended in 1838 and replaced with a less stringent requirement of a 10 percent "tithing" of an individual's "increase." "We are not now under the law of consecration," Lyman pointed out, "so we are not now under the law of polygamy."[154] The implication, of course, was that both consecration and plural marriage were the ideal laws and would be reintroduced when the Mormons were spiritually prepared to receive them.

Rudger Clawson, an apostle who spent time in prison for practicing plural marriage, expressed at a 1902 meeting of the apostles his feeling that, "in selecting sisters [to be] officers of importance in the church, they should be interrogated as to their *views* and *feelings,* as were the brethren, for some who have been chosen, it seems, have no *faith* whatever in the principle of plural marriage, and even talk against it." Clawson may have been taking his cue on this from the "apostolic charge" given to Hyrum M. Smith when he was called to be an apostle on 24 October 1901. The charge, delivered in the temple by John Henry Smith, read in part: "it is presumed that you [Hyrum M. Smith] are a moral man [and] that you accept the principle of plural marriage." Hyrum Smith obviously passed the test regarding his attitude toward plural marriage, which is significant because he was then a monogamist in practice and would remain so until his death in 1918.[155]

Clawson repeatedly raised the danger of "calling some [women] to office [in the relief society] who have no *faith* in plural marriage." Clawson succeeded in establishing a policy whereby stake presidents were instructed to see that women were "carefully questioned as to their views and feelings" regarding polygamy.[156] The next year, Apostle Matthias F. Cowley expressed his hope that the church's "young people shall not lose sight of the principle [of plural marriage]," noting that, even if in the form of belief only, "plural marriage will stand."[157] In 1927, on the occasion of his seventieth birthday, Clawson told a family gathering, "I still believe that plural marriage is a true principle," adding, "I have suffered for it, believed in it, and I believe in it today."[158] This view of polygamy as a true, but abrogated, principle rapidly trickled down to Mormons outside of the hierarchy. In 1901, William H. Smart recorded in his journal that "celestial marriage is as true today as ever it was but it is simply suspended, and . . . no one can enter the highest degree of the Celestial glory unless they practice this principle."[159]

Heber J. Grant, who would eventually become president of the church, wrote from his missionary labors in Japan that "the general impression in the entire Empire of Japan was that we are still practicing plural marriage," and "most of them [the Japanese people] feel that we are still unworthy because we will not deny that we think the doctrine was all right."[160] More than thirty-five years later, President Grant told a reporter, "We never believed polygamy was wrong, and never will."[161]

Such views were increasingly scarce in Mormon public discourse, however. In 1938, James Henry Moyle mused that "the silence of our people on the subject [of plural marriage] now is nothing short of remarkable, especially to one who lived in Utah in the 1880s and 1890s when it was the most talked of and publicized subject before the public eye."[162] Nevertheless, the fact that Grant expressed his support for the ultimate correctness of the doctrine of plural marriage long after officially sanctioned post-Manifesto marriages were ended and while the church was in a pitched battle to discredit so-called Mormon fundamentalists, who continued the practice despite the practically automatic penalty of excommunication, is significant. Even though plural marriages were being contracted during this period, it is clear that Roberts, Merrill, Clawson, Cowley, and others were more concerned with the importance of belief in the doctrine of plural marriage than with its practice, even though these men and several others in the upper echelons of the hierarchy took plural wives even after 1904.[163]

In 1958, Bruce R. McConkie, then a member of the church's First Council of Seventy, wrote of polygamy that "obviously the holy practice will commence again after the Second Coming of the Son of Man and the ushering in of the millennium."[164] To this day, Mormon policy allows men who have been sealed for eternity to be sealed again for eternity once their wife has died, as long as the second wife was not sealed to another man previously. The LDS Church has rid itself of the practice, which pushed its boundaries too far, but retains a belief that the principle will be reinstated at a future time. Thus, Mormons are able to maintain a boundary based on belief that does two things: it allows a moderate level of tension by creating a boundary that allows members of the community to move more seamlessly in and out of the broader culture, and it simultaneously preserves belief in the doctrine in question.

Conclusion

This chapter has demonstrated the complexities involved in the creation and maintenance of the most prominent boundary markers for nineteenth-century Shakers and Mormons. Celibacy and polygamy represent practices that grew out of similar master-motive schemas, schemas that the Shakers and Mormons shared but that were quite different from the schemas of the dominant evangelical majority in the nineteenth century. An examination of the structure and function of celibacy and polygamy yields important insights into the qualitative dimensions of the tension that Shakers and Mormons sought to create with American culture. The Shaker approach involved a high-intensity practice that was absolutely required of all members, that generated fairly negative cultural responses that were sufficient to reinforce the Shaker self-image of outsiderhood without drawing significant negative legal action, that was a double-sided boundary protecting the Shaker from the evil outside as well as within the individual soul, and that represented a performed expression of the central tenets of Shaker theology and tradition.

Celibacy was a remarkably stable boundary marker, far more stable than any similar practices deployed by contemporary groups. The very elements of the practice that ensured stability, however, also made the practice difficult to adjust in the face of diminishing returns. Complicating the issue was the fact that demographic depletion attendant to the practice was naturally, rather than externally, imposed. This meant that the Shakers could not inscribe that particular cost into the persecution narrative that functioned to turn externally generated disintegrative pressure into integrative pressure by pointing to opposition from a wicked world.

Plural marriage followed a pattern that was as typical of Mormon boundary maintenance patterns as celibacy was of Shaker boundary maintenance. First, polygamy was ideally required for the exaltation of all Mormons, but unlike Shaker celibacy, only a relatively small number of Mormons ever lived polygamously. One could be fully included within the Mormon tradition and not be a polygamist. Mormon rhetoric concerning the requirement of polygamy for full exaltation, however, convinced most of the United States that most Mormons were polygamists. Second, polygamy carried a highly negative sign value that not only drew cultural disapprobation, but also led to the mobilization of federal law-enforcement agencies in an effort to arrest and prosecute Mormon polygamists. The story of Mormon polygamy is thus one of a dialectical crisis-driven tension that escalated from 1852 until 1890, after which the Mormons ended the crisis and reformulated their boundary markers. They crafted a new narrative to accommodate the changes. Because relatively few people practiced plural marriage, it was much easier to abrogate the practice in the face of severely diminished returns than it would have been for the Shakers to end celibacy.

FOUR

Boundaries in Crisis:
The Shaker Era of Manifestations
and the Mormon Reformation

In the preceding chapters, I have demonstrated the variety of ways in which the Shakers and Mormons used physical and doctrinal/ritualistic vehicles to create and maintain tension with the larger American culture of which they were part. By now, the differences in the models of tension that the two groups pursued should be quite clear. In this chapter, I will look at two periods of crisis that stemmed from the disruption of those tension models.

The Shakers constantly sought to avoid crisis, and their approaches to physical and ritual boundaries reflected this. The unwanted crisis of the 1830s, however, caused a rupture that demanded action. Although there are certain similarities between the period of retrenchment known as the Mormon Reformation and the resurgent charisma of the Shaker Era of Manifestations, a crucial structural difference exists. Although both periods represented important episodes of innovative boundary maintenance, the Mormons used their Reformation to generate a crisis while the Era of Manifestations was a response to a genuine crisis. Perhaps the most important evidence in this regard is that the visions that started the Era of Manifestations emerged spontaneously outside of the leadership structures of the individual villages. The Mormon Reformation was a top-down operation from start to finish. Another way to think about this is to consider the conditions of each group before the periods of retrenchment began. The Mormons were enjoying a prolonged period of peace without the tension that they had come to expect. The Shakers were in a period of tremendous stress and disorder on a scale that they had never before experienced. In each case, the group had lost touch with its usual tension model, and each group sought to recreate its model.

In the 1830s, the Shakers at North Union, Ohio, who derived their identity from the boundaries that set them apart from the world and from their belief that they were a community of shared religious vision, experienced a genuine crisis. To use Rosabeth Moss Kanter's language, they allowed a community of "negation," which Kanter defines as a community that comes together to "move away from perceived ills or discomfort rather than to share a positive vision," to penetrate their boundaries.[1] In the case of the Shakers at North Union, this group was made up of the people who sought shelter among the Shakers from the economic hardships brought on by a combustible and unpredictable economy.[2] Once inside, this group threatened Shaker religious identity by diluting the powerful devotion to their cause that served as the lifeblood of the community and that also set it apart from the rest of the world.

Unlike the Mormons, who based their tension on cycles of crises, the Shakers sought to maintain a stable outsiderhood that eschewed crisis but that depended on strict levels of order within the community itself. The presence of a growing community of negation threatened the internal order, and thus stable outsiderhood, and induced a crisis. In response to this crisis, messages began to arrive that sought to reassert Shaker dedication, singularity, and identity through the reconstruction of stable boundaries and the expulsion of the communities of negation.

The Mormon Reformation and the Shaker Era of Manifestations were both periods of intense spiritual activity and retrenchment. In both cases, the leadership of the communities emphasized the necessity of cleansing and purging, both physically and spiritually. A close comparative study of these periods yields important clues about the significance of the specific tension models employed by the Shakers and the Mormons.

The Shaker Era of Manifestations was a response to a real crisis. The Shaker communities relied heavily on their ability to maintain a strict sense of outsiderhood that yielded a stable tension with the broader culture. Their outsiderhood model was threatened by the presence of various communities of negation within the Shaker villages. The visions and spirit messages that proliferated during the Era of Manifestations sought

to reassert stable outsiderhood by purging the villages of the communities of negation. After providing a general overview of the period, I
will enter into a detailed examination of a single Shaker village, North
Union, Ohio, during the Era of Manifestations.

In the case of the Mormon Reformation, Brigham Young and other
Mormon leaders used rhetorical and ritual vehicles to create a crisis of
deprivation in an effort to recreate the kind of tension patterns that they
had come to expect and, to a certain extent, rely upon for identity and
cohesion during the 1830s and 1840s. The Mormon Reformation came
at a time when the Mormons were enjoying a level of relative stability
in the Great Basin and before the crises driven by polygamy began in
earnest. Church leaders created a crisis to reorient and revitalize the
community and to refocus the lay members on the importance of the
hierarchy.

The Era of Manifestations

The story of the Era of Manifestations is almost as familiar as the story
of the Shakers themselves. In the late summer of 1837, a teenage girl living at the Watervliet, New York, village claimed to have communicated
with a spirit who showed her remarkable scenes from the spirit world.
Over the course of the next few months, Anna Mariah Goff experienced
multiple visionary experiences. Soon, others joined her, sometimes experiencing simultaneous visions in which the participants accompanied
one another on their transcendent journey. Goff's early visions featured
the spirits of Ann Lee and Lucy Wright and typically involved themes of
judgment. In November 1837, for example, Goff experienced a vision:

> [I] saw the family all assembled in meeting—Mother Lucy [Wright] was
> presented and soon began to preach. There seemed to be black marks on
> the arms of the brothers and sisters—some had more marks than others
> showing their different states. There seemed to be a number of Brothers
> and Sisters standing off below the ranks—Mother called them by name
> and told them they needed to repent a great deal.

Goff then reported a scene in which Jesus Christ stood before a menag-
erie of ninety strange beasts. Three groups of beasts, some with many
horns, some with many eyes, and some with "stars in their foreheads"
were being judged by Jesus. All but the starred creatures were cast out

from the room and identified as "evil spirits." A similar scene followed in which people "of the world" underwent the same process of judgment. Jesus told the people of the world whom he judged to be too evil to enjoy his presence to "depart from me all that is evil." Finally, Goff found herself in the presence of her own Shaker family, known as Watervliet's Second Family:

> The Lord Jesus was there and told them that they had come there to be judged—and they all began to tremble. He then opened the book of remembrance and leafed it over till he found the place where our family's names were written and began to read over the Sisters [*sic*] names first. He soon came to a name and stopped, and waved his hand towards the door and said "depart from me all that is evil." Then that Sister whose name he mentioned got up and walked towards the door then turned round and looked back. Mother Lucy then waved her hand towards her in a very kind manner and said "you must repent and come back."[3]

Goff's visions ushered in a new period of Shaker history that would have a lasting impact on the group. While visions had occurred sporadically throughout Shaker history, the density of the experiences that erupted in 1837 signaled that something very different was afoot. These visions multiplied and spread beyond the immediate community, first to eastern communities and eventually to Shaker villages in the West.[4] From village to village, these experiences varied in intensity and duration, but they lasted in some locations until the early 1850s.

As various scholars have correctly pointed out, this phenomenon did not represent a rupture with fundamental Shaker ideas about spiritual commerce with the (usually) unseen world. Ann Lee's experiences with the "revelatory other" were often profound, and although her death brought about certain changes in the structure and form of these experiences, "the gifts of the spirit did not disappear."[5] While most scholars agree on the basic continuity of the Era of Manifestations with previous Shaker experience, there is widespread scholarly debate about what the events of this later period meant. Edward Deming Andrews pointed out the tendency of these experiences to provide a link to the era of the founders, something especially needed during the 1830s and 1840s, by which time most of the people who had associated with Ann Lee and her immediate successors had died. Andrews thus saw the Era of Manifestations as a response to the loss of direction that accompanied the inevitable Shaker drift "beyond the inspiring personal influences of Ann and her followers."[6] Diane Sasson saw Shaker spiritualism during this period as essentially symbolic. "Such experiences, shared by the community," argued Sasson, "were a rich source of religious vocabulary."

As Sasson argued, the analogy between "the community of Believers on earth and the spiritual New Jerusalem," which allowed the Shakers to see "the Heavenly City as an image of a Shaker village," represented a prominent theme underpinning these visions and messages.[7] The power of this metaphor is plainly evident in the messages received at North Union. Priscilla Brewer made the point that the manifestations resulted primarily from the "stress of previous decades" and were co-opted and employed by Shaker leaders to "purge the communities of halfhearted members" and to "correct behavior."[8] This is fair enough, but Brewer's model does not explain the timing of the manifestations. Shaker communities had, after all, been plagued by halfhearted members from the beginning. The answer, at least in the case of North Union, lies in the complex relationship between the Shaker need for new members and their need to maintain an intentional distance between themselves and the world.

Stephen Stein argued that one of the most important legacies of this period was "a deep sense of their distinctiveness" both from the outside world and from earlier generations of Shakers.[9] Stein also made the point that the manifestations and their management provided the context for a refinement of the relationships between the hierarchy and the regular members, particularly those who became "instruments." The ministry, according to Stein, sought successfully to "support and to control the course of the revival itself, using it to reform, to discipline, and to order the members of the society."[10] Sally Promey also hinted at this when she argued that "the ministry and instruments collaborated with inhabitants of the celestial regions to consolidate, ritualize, and personalize a mythology and a tradition for young Believers."[11] Both of these general observations are borne out in the North Union context, where the youth culture was especially problematic and much of the spiritual cajoling from the other side was pointed in that direction. Aside from what these messages *meant* and the legacy they left the Shakers, considerable disagreement exists about what these messages and visions actually *were*.

The Era of Manifestations at North Union, Ohio

After the initial outbreak of spiritualistic activities at Watervliet, it did not take long for word of the spiritual manifestations to spread. By the late fall of 1837, reports began circulating of spiritual manifestations among the Shaker communities at Harvard and Shirley, Massachusetts.[12] Other eastern communities soon followed. Word of the visions reached Union Village, Ohio, the headquarters of the Shaker villages in the West, in mid-November 1837 when Elder Freegift Wells "read 2 letters from W.V.[Watervliet] N. York giving an account of an extraordinary Spiritual waking up among the youth."[13] In January 1838, two more letters arrived from unspecified villages in the East "giving extraordinary accounts of the great work of God commencing among them of late."[14] By the fall of 1838, Union Village found itself under the same spell. In November, Sally Sharp reported that "the families meet at the meeting house frequently. Mother's work[15] is now in full opperation [sic]—falling into trances, singing new songs."[16] This pattern was repeated throughout most of the Shaker villages.[17]

In June 1838, leaders at North Union wrote to their superiors at Union Village noting that letters containing details of the experiences of the eastern villages were arriving and being read with great interest. In accordance with Shaker practice, the leadership at Union Village sent out compilations of letters received from various villages reporting on the flurry of spiritualistic behavior. "These letters," the North Union elders wrote, "were very interesting to us, to hear of marvelous gifts of heavenly visions and trances with which believers have been favored in the east." The letters told of "wonderful manifestations of the good things of God" and expressed a desire for all of the villages to "see and hear the searching word of God." The results of these experiences were certainly to be envied, as they apparently had the effect of driving away "unbelief and darkness like unto a fog by a north wind." Mother Ann was heard to warn all believers to "confess their sins, one by one, and labor for the power of God to wake them up." Another letter excerpted in the composite correspondence emphasized the "spread and increase" of these manifestations, noting that the "Work" was "more or less in every Society and Family from Sodus [Bay, New York] to New Gloucester." Rufus Bishop of New Lebanon noted with astonishment that "at

Canterbury one sister continued in a trance 6 days and nights, nearly, or 139 hours!" The North Union Shakers also read with great interest of villages in the East which received "new songs by a special gift almost daily," in which "the veil between this and the spiritual world has become almost transparent to believers in general and to some altogether so."[18] The Shakers at North Union also received a letter from "Elder Jeremiah," who reported from an unidentified eastern village "the same kind of gifts and operations" taking place.

To many, it must have seemed that the Shaker world was alight with these spectacular spiritual endowments. Individuals in the community felt anxious to receive manifestations of their own. North Union resident Philander Cramer expressed such feelings in his diary: "O the gracious work of God, may my soul have a part and a lot in it, the work is moving swift; wo[e] to me if I am left behind."[19] The thought of being "left behind" was truly terrifying for the Shakers who were fully invested socially, economically, personally, and religiously in their community.

All was not well at North Union as these reports flooded in. Elder David Spinning, a former Presbyterian who had been heavily involved in the waves of revivalism that swept through Kentucky at the beginning of the Second Great Awakening, had taken over the leadership of North Union in 1832 and had presided over a period of relatively rapid population growth and economic hardship, including the Panic of 1837. Spinning expressed some of his frustrations in a series of letters to Freegift Wells and other leaders at Union Village in the spring of 1837. The economic distress in the wake of the panic had "sent prices rocketing sky-high; grain is so scarce and high priced on account of the bad weather this spring that we find it considerably difficult to procure breadstuff." To make matters worse, during the preceding spring, "it was so wet and cold in these parts that nothing would grow—especially in this stiff clay which needs draining."[20]

In addition to the economic difficulties, an even more ominous problem presented itself. Spinning wrote to Freegift Wells that "we need to have our high, proud spirits beaten down low." The problem, lamented Spinning, was that "our numbers are increasing but our peace and contentment are not increasing in proportion." Spinning was not overstating the case. The decade between 1830 and 1840 witnessed the doubling of the number of Shakers at North Union, from 100 to 200. It would never have a larger population.[21]

The reasons for this population growth are varied. Like many Shaker villages, North Union had, throughout the first decades of the nineteenth century, taken in orphans and children whose parents could ill afford to care for them. In an era when no governmental provisions existed to deal with such problems, leaving children in the care of Shakers seemed an ideal solution: the children were cared for, and the celibate Shakers collected many young charges with what the Shakers hoped would be an excellent potential for conversion. As these children matured, however, the Shakers at North Union discovered that many of them took issue with one or another of the sect's tenets, particularly, one imagines, the insistence on celibacy. This led Spinning to complain that "it is in the Youth order that we find trouble." Additionally, many younger people had been driven to the Shaker villages "due to the recent panic," and although they had "found security they do not wish to pay the price for peace."[22] Together, these two groups represented communities of negation within the walls of the Shaker community.

Looking at North Union from the outside, one would see a monolithic community. From the inside, however, at least three separate communities existed: two communities of negation that sought to exploit the benefits of the Shaker life without reciprocal investment, and the remaining Shakers, who formed the core of committed and investing believers. For purposes of clarity, the third group, defined by the willingness of its members to invest in and benefit from the Shaker order in relatively equal proportion, might be called a "community of investment." As I discussed at length in chapter 1, the Shakers derived much of their stability from their success at building communities of investment by imposing order upon exogenous influences that entered into their villages. The communities of negation at issue during the 1830s presented unique challenges to that process of ordering. This is particularly true of the youth who were deeply involved in the Shaker system and were more or less permanent fixtures.

It is thus little wonder that the Shakers at North Union keenly anticipated the arrival of the manifestations, which would, they hoped, have a similar effect as that described by the leadership at Union Village, who wrote, "nearly all of the gifts are calculated to bring down the pride and loftiness of man." Even more promising was the knowledge that "it is truly a source of much consolation to see such a work among our youth and children, that gives them new courage, life, zeal and fear of God."[23] Spinning expressed his hope that the youth could be ordered because he recognized that they could not simply be expelled.

The anxious Shakers at North Union would not have to wait long for their manifestations to begin. In late July 1838, a group of preteen girls walking near the North Union hemlock grove heard voices singing above their heads. The heavenly recital continued for ten minutes. The similarities between the opening of the era in North Union and the original experiences of Anna Mariah Goff at Watervliet are striking. It is evident that, from the beginning, these experiences followed the pattern suggested by letters proliferating through the Shaker world, usually penned by the sect's leaders. Significantly, the leadership of Union Village had that very day been in North Union "giving the most positive assurance that Mother's Work would visit and bless [them] with the miraculous and saving gifts of the Gospel such as were abundantly poured out in the east."[24] Thus, while hierarchical direction of the gifts became explicit later, even at these early stages the seeds of that control were being sown. Such hierarchical control should not be overstated, however. There is no question that the manifestations began outside of the hierarchy and continued for months outside of the total control of the Shaker leadership.

Over the next several months, various members of the community experienced gifts of tongues and repentance, and on several occasions, "young sisters were powerfully exercised in body and went into vision together." During the course of these visions, the girls reported "seeing several of the Sisters that had formerly dwelt" at North Union. They also "gathered fruits and flowers" of a spiritual nature and "spoke of seeing great numbers of spirits dressed in white with gold bands upon their heads."[25]

These manifestations continued into the fall. In October, Philander Cramer, who ran the tannery at North Union, reported that "little Rufus had a vision which lasted about ¾ of an hour." Two days earlier, Cramer had encountered "Sister Nancy," whom he observed in the midst of a vision. After her trance ended, the two "had a comfortable talk in which she told many things about the world of spirits."[26] Such experiences were typical of those that were multiplying throughout the community. Around the same time, a "powerful exercise among the boys" was reported during which the young Shakers experienced various gifts, including speaking in tongues, prophecy, discerning of spirits, and, significantly, the "gifts of exposing hidden or secret sins."[27] This theme rapidly came to dominate the visions and messages received at North Union.

One of the main functions of the various messages was to "make a separation between the clean and the unclean."[28] This obsession with spiritual cleanliness found symbolic expression in a revelation given to Elder Philemon Stewart of New Lebanon.[29] An angel named Merah visited Stewart and bestowed a "cleansing gift," a prescribed ritual for detecting and removing hidden filth, which was to be observed every twenty-third of September. On that date, the men and women were to walk through all of the village grounds and buildings, singing a sacred song while "laboring to feel . . . power and deep indignation against all filth of any nature which enters Zion!" During this process, it was incumbent upon the believers to "cleanse every spot that is dirty or neglected on the whole premises; mending all broken fences, restoring window panes, destroying weeds and putting everything in its proper place and proper order. When ye feel that any abomination hath been committed, ye shall kneel and pray silently that the filth shall be revealed."[30] The Shakers at North Union received word of this gift in time to participate in their own cleansing ceremony in September 1838. Philander Cramer spent time in his "tan house all day putting the place in shape for the Cleansing Blessing." Cramer's account offers a unique window into the form of this ceremony as well as a glimpse at the power and importance that the appointed "instruments" wielded.

> When the elders and singers came to the tannery with their procession of workers they marched up to the garret and down through the cellar; after viewing the whole shop, they proceeded in the same fashion through the tan yards. Then they suddenly returned because of a message received through our inspired one (Nancy) declaring that the tannery needed further cleansing—some hidden filth or wrong desire still lurked there. Accordingly, we took right hold of the gift and set to work in the doing of which we received a great blessing and satisfaction.[31]

The theme of the detection and exposure of hidden filth as well as the emphasis on "putting everything in its proper place and order" were central to the messages received throughout the Era of Manifestations at North Union. It is significant that these impulses were present in the earliest stages of the revival.[32] The centrality and duration of these tropes speak to the deeply held concern that evil had penetrated both the figurative and literal gates of the Shaker community in the form of disorder. The walls that set the group apart from the world served as a chief means of self-identification. The compromised status of these walls in the late 1830s served to fuel this obsession with hidden sin. Although Brewer argued that the drive to "purge the communities of halfhearted members" did not begin until after the manifestations were taken over by Shaker leaders, it appears that, at North Union at least, this theme was spontaneously present in the unregulated visions.[33] Locating the origin of the Era of Manifestations outside of the Shaker hierarchy is important evidence of the organic, rather than manufactured, nature of the Shaker crisis.

Throughout the fall and winter of 1838 and into the spring of 1839, these irregular and spontaneous visions continued. In April, however, the believers at North Union received a visit from representatives of the ministry at Union Village. Freegift Wells, John Martain, Betsy Hasting, and Sally Sharp arrived at what one believer described as a "peculiar time, soon after the manifestations of the marvelous work of God had commenced and a time when their help was greatly needed." As lead ministries were doing throughout the various villages, the representatives from Union Village had come to see that "the gifts and visionists were set in order after the manner of the Eastern Societies."[34]

The pattern set in the villages in the East consisted principally of the appointment of instruments by community leaders in an effort to "handle the tension" inherent in any hierarchical system in which adherents have direct access to godly manifestations.[35] It is noteworthy that the Union Village ministry effected this change through one Phillip Antes, an individual who "had long been distinguished as a Visionist at Union Village."[36] The use of a prominent instrument in this capacity indicates both the rising profile of such individuals throughout the Shaker world and the recognition on the part of the various ministries of the need to harness and direct this power.

At North Union, this ordering of the gifts had an immediate impact. The leading instrument of the community, a sister identified in the extant sources only as Nancy, was replaced by a young sister named Lucretia Sutton.[37] Sutton was a member of the Center Family, which was the oldest and most respected of the three families at North Union. The eighteen-year-old Sutton soon became a major player in Mother Ann's work. She is the named instrument for the vast majority of the more than 200 recorded messages received between 1841 and 1845.

The true power of these manifestations to effect change within the Shaker world was made clear when, in early 1840, David Spinning and his entire ministry packed up and moved to Union Village—all in accordance with instructions received in a gift message. No record of the message itself exists, so it is not possible to make concrete judgments about just what this turn of events signified. It could have been that Spinning wanted to leave, that the leaders at Union Village were dissatisfied with his leadership and wanted to replace him, or that the instrument wanted him gone. Whatever the reasons for their departure, Spinning's cohort was quickly replaced by Samuel Russell, Jeremiah Ingall, Rachel Russell, and Polly Torry. For the first time in its history, North Union was under the direction of members whose Shaker lives had been spent in the community.

This local leadership cadre took over during a lull in the difficulties that Spinning had lamented in the late 1830s. The next year, 1840, came to be referred to as the "fruitful" year because prices stabilized, crops flourished, and the young people appear to have settled down a bit. Perhaps in response to this relative tranquility, no heavenly messages were recorded for that year, except for the one that led to Spinning's departure. Such smooth sailing was to be short-lived, however. Late in the year, a horse was stolen from the North Union stable, and Philander Cramer's tanning house was burned, along with the cobbler's shack. The total damage was estimated at over $1,200, but the most stinging element in the affair accompanied the discovery that "a young man who had asked admission and was living in the Gathering family" had perpetrated the acts.[38]

Spinning's earlier complaint that "youth shall ever be our burden" and his deep concern over untested Shakers proved prophetic. The boundaries setting the Shakers apart from the world had been compromised as the village grew because the newer populations were resistant to order. Soon, the messages began again, and their themes were unmistakable. The visions and, especially, the messages received after 1840 warned of this breach and sought to purge the community of these evil influences and return the body of the faithful to their privileged, outsider position.

The Era of Manifestations produced many unusual and interesting artifacts. Most prominent among these were the hundreds of gift songs bestowed upon the Shakers from believers in the spirit world.[39] Gift drawings and paintings also played a major role in the manifestation of spiritual power in some villages. The beautiful and intricate pieces of art that the Shakers in some villages produced have provided scholars with a wonderful avenue into the symbolic world of mid-nineteenth-century Shaker spirituality.[40] The instruments at North Union produced few songs, and I have been able to locate none of their gift drawings, although some are mentioned in the various records kept by the believers there.[41] Earlier descriptions of visions and messages in the pre-1840 period have served to set the stage for the examination of the texts that began to be systematically recorded in 1841.

The 1841–1845 corpus of recorded messages received at North Union is remarkably consistent in terms of content. The vast majority of these documents contain the following themes: an expression of love from God (or Mother Ann, or another such figure), a reminder that tribulations and trials are the lot of the chosen people of God, an additional warning that safety from these buffetings is only to be found in a willingness to "bear the crosses" of the Shaker order, and an admonition to obey ministerial authority, usually referred to as a "visible lead." The most frequently occurring theme dealt with hidden sin that existed within the community. Particularly in the messages received between 1840 and 1842, this was often expressed in images of the presence of "wolves" among the sheep. In January 1841, the Holy Mother[42] warned the elders at North Union of "deceivers among you." The same revelation warned of "those that come in sheep's clothing to devour the flock." These people "seek their own fame and honor" and "don't believe there is a Mother."[43] Another revelation received that month, entitled "Watchfulness," again warned of "some among you who are deceitful."[44] This message linked these unsavory figures with the "many sufferings" that the believers would have to endure. The only safety from these difficulties was to be found in submission "to your visible lead" and in daily and nightly prayer.

In another communication, the Eternal Father warned that many in the community must "live nearer to what they profess" because "I will not have wolves among my people." The refuge, once again, was found in being "subject and obedient to all my holy laws."[45] Repeatedly, the Shaker heavens resounded with admonitions to return to Shaker standards, to "be obedient to what is required," and to be on guard for those who "make a fair outside show but are deceitful liars within," because those "will be purged out."[46] The messages advocated a two-pronged effort at rebuilding boundaries: increased personal commitment to the order and the expulsion of those deemed unworthy, who represented disorder.

The reestablishment of stable boundaries is clearly demonstrated in the message that reminded believers that the "wolves" "will not stand the fire, for when it begins to burn they will run—they are not such warriors as belong to that chosen number for they do not stand their ground." In that communication, the world was clearly divided between the weaklings and those "chosen warriors" who "belong." Significantly, the sign of a chosen person was a willingness to "stand their ground," a phrase evocative of boundary maintenance, to be sure.

The visit of the Eternal Father in 1845 marked the end of the most intense period of visionary activity. No messages recorded after this visit are extant at North Union. During his visit, the heavenly Father identified some believers by name and told them that they were "covering something."[47] He then informed them that they could either publicly confess their sins or leave the community. This pattern was followed in each of the three families at North Union until the heavenly Father concluded his visit.[48]

During this period, other events occurred that indicated the need to reassert the unique Shaker status as outsiders. In 1841, the leadership at North Union decided to "close our meetings to the public for the outside world does not understand the manifestations of the Holy Spirit." The community made certain that "the notice of closing our meetings has been posted at all meeting places; this notice has been sent to the Cleveland Herald, also."[49] Some scholars have pointed out that the

Shakers may have closed their meetings out of embarrassment. This is certainly possible. It seems logical, however, that closing the meetings also served to reinforce the separate nature of true believers and allowed for the unimpeded censure of wayward members. It is interesting that the leaders at North Union went to such great lengths to announce the closing of the meetings in so many venues. This may be read as a symbol of the attempted reassertion of community boundaries, a long and loud announcement to the world to "keep out."

Another telling development was precipitated by the rise to prominence of the Baptist lay minister William Miller and his apocalyptic followers. Miller developed a formula to predict the precise date of Christ's return to earth. The eponymous Millerites became an important and popular millennialist sect before the movement split into three factions after Miller failed twice to predict correctly the date of Christ's second coming.[50] In the manuscript history of North Union, Miller's influence in Ohio is recounted in detail. It is clear that some North Union Shakers had been exposed to, and perhaps intrigued by, Miller's ominous message that 1843 would bring with it the end of the world. In response,

> at a special meeting, Elder Samuel had all the trustees, deacons, peddlers and others who were in any way exposed to outside influences, stand in the center of the Meeting-hall while we labored long and hard about them in order to free them from this woeful suggestion. We must not fall under this evil spell. It is time we strengthen our faith and guard against these "wolves in sheep's clothing."[51]

Reasserting boundaries apparently also involved guarding against inroads made by "false prophets" like Miller. Miller may have represented a form of disorder inasmuch as his competing doctrines posed a threat to Shaker claims of ultimate religious truth. Some Shakers may have found Miller's strident apocalypticism appealing, especially during the stressful period of the 1840s, and Shaker leaders were wise to blunt that appeal in order to mitigate its impact on Shakerism.

It is clear that no discernible correlation existed between the contents of the messages and the instruments who received them. Three North Union instruments, all of whom were women, have been identified. They were members of the Center Family, and all were between the ages of eighteen and forty when they acted as instruments. The contents of the messages remained relatively consistent regardless of the identity of the instrument. It is telling that all of the instruments were members of the Center Family, although it is not surprising, given the well-established theory that the ministry sought to exert control over the instruments' behavior. Similarly, no immediate correlation is evident between outside influences and the messages except for the growth of population. To the extent that the North Union messages came in response to outward stimuli, they addressed the continuing problem of boundary maintenance attendant to the influx of "short-term" Shakers.

The messages remained consistent despite a variety of other external pressures. For example, no discernible change is evident in the messages received from Mother Ann in 1841, which warned of wolves among the flock, and a message received three years later from "Abraham the Patriarch." The former asked the believers to "deal more plainly" and to beware of those "wolves" who would be "purged out." She also asked her followers to "cleave to their lead." Abraham implored his hearers to "love your lead," "be honest," "fight, fight, fight," "and beware of your enemies within and prepare yourselves to fight for Mother."[52] An examination of the records of the community indicates dramatically different economic and social conditions at the time each communication was received, yet the content was remarkably similar.

As time passed, the language of the messages did change somewhat. References to wolves virtually disappeared after 1842 and were replaced by temple imagery. Most of the communications dealing with hidden sinners—and that was almost all of them—spoke in 1842 and after of a temple that "would not be defiled."[53] This language is even more suggestive of the importance of boundary maintenance than the wolves/ flock imagery. The image of the flock had been replaced by an image of a fixed building, but not just any building. Temples are, by definition, sacred space, and they only function and retain their identity if they are not defiled. Like the Shaker communities they represented, if temples were penetrated by the unworthy, they would lose their sacred, protective qualities.

There is no measurable difference in the content of messages received from various spiritual personages. Of course, differences in perspective naturally occurred. Messages from former members, for example, tended to couch their admonitions in phrases like "if you knew what I know you would behave,"[54] but such differences had no impact on the themes that figured prominently in the messages. There was a tendency toward martial language in messages from male spirits that was generally lacking in those from female spirits, although it did not substantially alter the basic message.

Some scholars have argued that the ministries were simply manipulating the instruments in order to shore up their own authority.[55] That may be true, but the more important question is why the ministries would want to do that. The continued emphasis on wolves among the flock and the exhortation for members not only to submit to their visible leads but also to purify their inner lives suggest that the Shaker leaders were concerned with both personal purity and institutional integrity. It must be kept in mind that, for the Shakers themselves, no difference existed between the religious structures that dictated their behavior and their identity as believers. Thus, in nearly every instance in which Shakers were admonished to cleave to their leads, they were also told to "purify your hearts and spirits from every carnal, vain imagination and pray." Clearly, loyalty to the immediate ministerial authority was only part of the equation. Without the hierarchically determined boundaries, their identity as Shakers became muddled. The threat posed by the breaching of boundaries was a threat not only to the hierarchy but also to the essence of Shaker identity.

Others who have studied the Era of Manifestations see in it an attempt on the part of female Shakers to assert not only their own personal authority but also the authority of women in general. One scholar has presented an argument based on psychological theories of the subconscious.[56] Drawing on the methodological rubric established at the outset, it seems plain that the majority of Shakers involved with these communications believed them to be genuine expressions of the divine mind. The records at North Union clearly indicate that issues of personal purity and religious devotion were at least as important as those concerning the strengthening of authority. The records Shakers left behind certainly provide no reason to conclude that at North Union they were pretending to believe in them. They acted, publicly and privately, as if they did believe, and that must not be ignored. However, it is also clear that the Shakers understood their community to be in danger. Reading the documents with Kanter's theory of boundary markers in mind and with knowledge of the lowered expectations placed upon entering members during the financial strife of the late 1830s leads to the conclusion that these messages functioned to rebuild the boundaries and reassert outsiderhood. The evidence suggests that the Shakers also believed this, and they believed that this was what God wanted. Of course, they would not have spoken of boundary markers and outsiderhood, but they did speak of defilers in the temple, wolves in the flock, and the impending loss of their identity as God's chosen people.

A final note should be made with regard to the success of the Era of Manifestations at North Union. Clearly, there was a vigorous reassertion of boundaries and outsiderhood through ministerial control, personal reformation, and the expulsion of "unworthy" Shakers from the community—all dominant themes in the visions and messages. In an important way, the very fact that these visions and messages were accepted among believers served to set the Shakers apart from their neighbors and to remind the Shakers themselves of their unique position regarding revelation. In the fall of 1853, Roxalana L. Grosvenor of the Shaker village at Shirley, Massachusetts, wrote to an interested spiritualist that, although open visions and revelations were common among the group's founders "insomuch that the world of spirits was as clear to their view as this mundane sphere, yet there have been seasons when Zion seemed to languish for her wonted sustenance." The Era of Manifestations, according to Grosvenor, represented the renewal of that sustenance.[57] In the end, of course, it was not enough to save the North Union community from dissolving. The manifestations did, however, allow the Shakers at North Union to reassert their identity in a time of crisis.

The Mormon Reformation

It should be evident by this point that a deep irony runs through the complex and dialectical relationships between religious communities on the margins of American society and the larger culture of which such communities are part. For such communities, outsiderhood goes far beyond a simple description of the relative position of the group vis-à-vis the religious "mainstream" and forms a central trait in their self-conception. Persecution, the quintessential sign of outsiderhood, comes to be viewed as evidence of divine favor. By the early 1850s, the Mormon sense of identity had become dependent upon the constant presence of external criticism and persecution to such an extent that church leaders had to find new crises to replace those that they had successfully managed and escaped.

Persecution and Crisis in the Early Mormon Experience

During the early years of Mormonism, from 1830 to 1847, Mormon communal identity depended heavily on a state of nearly constant crisis. More than fifty years ago, Mormon historian Leonard J. Arrington reported finding in Mormon "diaries and sermons a kind of grim satisfaction, if not outright pleasure, with the favorable disciplining effects wrought by . . . hardship, destitution, and sacrifice."[58] Lay members looked to the Mormon leadership for guidance and protection through the various wars waged on Mormons in Missouri from 1833 to 1838 and the difficulties they encountered in Kirtland, Ohio, in the mid-1830s. In the 1840s, the Mormons had to deal with the murder of their prophet/founder and their forced evacuation of Nauvoo, Illinois, a majestic city they had constructed on the Mississippi River under Joseph Smith's direction. By the time the Mormons began their settlements in the American West, they defined themselves over and against the various powers that had sought their elimination for so long.

When the first company of Mormon pioneers reached the Salt Lake Valley in the summer of 1847, they hoped that their isolation would provide a respite from the pressures they had felt from some parts of the broader American public since the early 1830s. Time proved the members of this vanguard company to be correct. However, the Mormons' success in their efforts to separate themselves from their neighbors had the unintended consequence of creating too much tranquility. In the fall of 1855, church leaders launched a campaign of harsh rhetoric and ritual that recreated the sense of crisis that had wielded such a powerful influence on Mormon development in the pre-Utah period. Contemporaries and historians labeled this effort the Mormon Reformation. Mormon leaders also used the term "reformation" frequently when referring to what they sought to accomplish during the period from 1855 to 1857, but it should not be understood as an institutional or doctrinal reformation. Rather, this episode is more accurately thought of as a period of institutional and doctrinal retrenchment designed to bring about the moral reformation of individual Mormons.

The Mormon Reformation should not be interpreted primarily as a response to an organic spiritual crisis. Rather, it was the intentional *creation* of a crisis by church leaders in an attempt to reinvigorate Mormon communal and religious identity at a time when the Mormons were between periods of major crisis with the outside world. Chronologically, the Reformation was wedged between the era of persecutions in Missouri and in Nauvoo, Illinois, that spanned the 1830s and 1840s, and the Utah War of 1857–1858, which was followed by the era of polygamy prosecutions that began in earnest around 1860 and closed out the nineteenth century. The Mormon Reformation stands as a synthetic crisis implemented by LDS leaders to reinvigorate reliance on LDS Church leaders among rank-and-file Mormons at a time when external crises were absent. Taking their cue, appropriately, from the justifications for the Reformation offered by church leaders, most scholars have viewed the Mormon Reformation as a reaction on the part of the hierarchy to what they believed was a major decline in religious fervor among Mormons in the Utah settlements, sparked by famine and food shortages in the mid-1850s.[59]

It is beyond dispute that Brigham Young engaged in a rhetoric of declension in the 1850s. It is unclear, however, how Young, or anyone else, measured that declension.[60] In other words, we need to determine how Young knew that spiritual decline was gripping the Mormons in the mid-1850s, beyond simply taking his word for it. Beyond the assertions of church leaders, there seems to be no evidence to indicate that Mormons were any less religious in the mid-1850s than they had been before. The potency of cries of spiritual decline from LDS leaders is diluted by the ubiquity of such cries in Mormon history, especially in the years after Joseph Smith's death. As historian Richard Bennett has demonstrated, Young began deploying declension rhetoric, including language of "reformation," as early as the mid-1840s, and he intensified that rhetoric during the Mormon trek from Nauvoo to Utah.[61]

According to Thomas Alexander, "Church leaders promoted spiritual reform hoping to restore the spirituality that the Saints had enjoyed during the hardships of Kirtland, Missouri, Nauvoo, and during the exodus and the early settlement in Utah."[62] Alexander is exactly correct that church leaders perceived some degree of loss when they compared life in the isolated environs of Utah to the turbulent cycle of settlement and eviction that dominated Mormon life in the 1830s and 1840s. In my judgment, however, the lack of outside pressures, the very pressures that the Mormons sought so desperately to flee, resulted in a diluted sense of religious identity, rather than in a diminution of religious devotion. There is, after all, no firm evidence to suggest that the Mormons were any more "spiritual" during previous years, but they *were* driven together by constant crisis. Mormon identity and community dynamics had come to depend on an episodic, crisis-driven cultural tension. When they successfully escaped their persecutions, they eventually and temporarily found themselves without a crisis. The result was a sense of disorientation, especially on the part of church leaders. Unlike the most commonly cited causes of the Reformation—spiritual declension and food shortages—the absence of a major external crisis was something relatively new for the Mormons, and external crisis had never been absent from the Mormon world for so long as it had been by 1855.

The Irony of Isolation and Control

By the spring of 1855, the Mormons, under Young's powerful and effective leadership, had created their own world. Apostle George Albert Smith had noted ironically that in Utah, a vast "American desert," the Mormons had "been permitted to accomplish the very thing we desired; we had to flee into these valleys to establish the institution which our enemies in driving us here thought to annihilate."[63] Indeed, the Mormons managed to put themselves temporarily beyond the reach of their erstwhile foes. As Young wrote on behalf of the First Presidency in April 1855, "these distant vales have thus far proved a safe retreat, wherein the Saints have found quiet, health, prosperity and peace." He noted that, although "much damage was done by grasshoppers" during the preceding summer, the Mormons had for the first time produced a "surplus of grain." They had come to terms with the indigenous populations in Utah, and Young noted with pride that he had concluded a treaty with Chief Walker of the Black Hawk nation in May 1854. Public works and "county and city improvements" also moved forward at what he described as an "astonishing pace."[64]

Furthermore, the Mormons had taken great strides toward mastering the essential art of irrigation farming in the desert, which allowed them to harness the streams and creeks flowing out of the mountains and to redirect the moisture to areas designated for agriculture.[65] Young occupied the governor's chair in the territory, and the Mormons controlled all elements of government from the town to the territorial levels. The Mormon proselytizing enterprise continued to bear fruit, particularly in Great Britain and Scandinavia, and each summer and fall witnessed a new wave of immigration to the Salt Lake Valley as the new converts "gathered" with the main body of Mormons. Students of this era in Mormon history agree that the new phase of relative isolation enjoyed by the Mormons was important to the advent of the Reformation. Disagreements arise, however, when scholars try to define that significance. Peterson argued that, for the first time, "controversial doctrines could be aired and practiced publicly," and this opened the door for fiery rhetoric and increased plural marriages.[66]

Rumblings of Reformation

In May 1855, Jedediah M. Grant, the newly appointed second counselor in the church's governing First Presidency, blasted the Mormons with rhetorical sunshine. Speaking in Salt Lake City's Social Hall, Grant told the group:

> [I want] the Saints to be impressed with the motto of being happy all the time; if you cannot be happy to-day, how can you be happy to-morrow? I speak this from what I have learned myself; though it has given me much of trouble, and a great amount of perseverance, to be happy under all circumstances. I have learned not to fret myself. I have learned the secret of happiness.[67]

Under ordinary circumstances, such a discourse would be seen as nothing more than good-natured self-help advice. What makes this address so significant, however, is that its author, Grant, would soon emerge as the leading zealot of the Mormon Reformation. Those who observed Grant in full frenzy in 1856 would have been hard-pressed to locate the happy-go-lucky fellow who had learned "not to fret." Grant would be dead eighteen months after giving this address, his demise a result of his insistence on rebaptizing members of the church outdoors in the dead of a Utah winter.

One should not entertain the opinion that Grant was usually a minister of light and airy advice. In February 1855, for example, he had given a spirited address which "commenced the tug of war" and in which "strong and large guns were fired with red hot balls." Grant's anger was directed at outsiders, "gentiles," who were attempting to "traduce and corrupt the daughters and wives of the Latter-day Saints." Heber C. Kimball followed by stating that he, and any righteous man, should kill both his wife and her lover if they were caught in flagrante delicto.[68] Some scholars have been tempted to view this particular series of addresses as foreshadowing the advent of the Mormon Reformation some months later.[69] As scandalous as such rhetoric sounds to modern ears, however, it was relatively common in nineteenth-century Utah, and it should be carefully compared and contrasted with the words and deeds of church leaders during the Reformation period. The crucial differences between this type of heated discourse and the sort spewed forth during the Mormon Reformation were threefold. First, the earlier material was directed, for the most part, at outsiders. Second, the words were rarely coupled with actions. Finally, the charges in the earlier rhetoric were specific and easily solved, e.g., people are committing adultery so they should stop. The Mormon Reformation was qualitatively different from earlier screeds on all of these counts.

Obviously, something changed between the time of Grant's buoyant 1855 address and his death from pneumonia in December 1856. In July 1855, Grant offered a sneak preview of the themes that would come to dominate the Mormon Reformation. Speaking at a meeting in Provo, he crankily decried the "poor pussyism" he detected among the Mormons. Without external pressure and energizing crises, the Mormons were becoming weak and tolerating wickedness around them, springing up like weeds that choked their fields. Grant castigated those who would allow persons of questionable character into their homes, where they were permitted to swear, "trample," and "ridicule" the laws of God. Invoking for the first time the language that would come to define Mormon discourse for the next two years, he called for "a reformation" among the Mormons.

Although Grant paid casual attention to the general category of the "Law of God," which deserved greater adherence, he focused intensely on the idea of filth. In an unusual turn of thought, he pointed out that "one doctrine which you need is to make your families, your streets, and every thing about you clean, and to prepare proper outhouses. Purify yourselves, your houses, lots, farms, and every thing around you on the right and on the left, then the Spirit of the Lord can dwell with you."[70] This theme of purification would become central later, but at the time it seemed to garner little attention.

The substantive changes began in the fall of 1855. Brigham Young stood to address the church's semi-annual conference and offered more than his usual hard-nosed admonitions. His address, as the beginning of the Mormon Reformation, deserves careful scrutiny. He offered a nuanced and, for the faithful at least, quietly terrifying evaluation of the Mormons' situation. Young argued that, despite all outward appearances, a dark force was at work in the valley. Satan, he suggested, was blinding the Mormons, who were "liable in many ways to be led astray by the power of the adversary, for they do not fully understand that it is a hard matter for them to always distinguish the things of God from the things of the devil."[71]

The people of God had lost their spiritual depth perception; everything was flat and out of focus. Mormon efforts were mixed when it came to adherence to God's commandments, he suggested, and while some of them had a sufficient measure of the "Spirit of the Lord" to discern good from evil, too many were "inclined to do wickedly and seem to love wickedness; there are some who are filled with idolatry, and it seems as though it were impossible for them to overcome the spirit of the world, to keep from loving it and from cleaving to it and to the things of the world."[72] Young was setting the stage for a crisis. Brilliantly, he provided no guidance as to which Mormons fell into the camp of the righteous and which were wicked. In fact, he had undercut all traditional Mormon epistemological approaches by explicitly stating that the wicked could not know if they were under the influence of Satan because they had been cut off from the wellspring of truth, the Holy Spirit. As a result, the wicked were likely to think that they were righteous. The only conclusion that Mormons listening to Young could reach was that safety could be found only in an assumption of their own wickedness. In subsequent sermons, Young and others suggested that certain severe, but unnamed, calamities would befall the Mormons if they did not refocus themselves.

Esaias Edwards, a Mormon sawmill operator and farmer in Utah, recorded in his journal in early 1857:

> [T]here has been a great reformation during the last fall and winter such
> as has not been since we have [been] in the valleys of the mountains.
> And the first Presidency is urging us to sanctify and purify ourselves
> against the day of trial which is just at hand which they say will try every
> Saint both man and woman. I do not know what we will have to pass
> through.[73]

Young thus managed to establish among his followers the notion that
wickedness had penetrated the cordon of purity that was supposed
to protect the Mormons, and he made it impossible for individual
Mormons to locate that hidden wickedness with their own powers of
discernment.

As late as 1857, Young was warning of an *impending* calamity. Because it was impossible to identify the wicked, the process of purging
the evil elements in their midst was nebulous. It would need to involve
the purification of every Mormon. Therein lay the crisis. The solution,
of course, would have to come from Young himself. He asked, "If your
faults are not made known to you, how can you refrain from them and
overcome them? You cannot. But if your faults are made manifest, you
have the privilege of forsaking them and cleaving unto that which is
good. The design of the Gospel is to reveal the secrets of the hearts of
the children of men."[74] Perhaps he really was simply trying to correct
the moral laxity that he said he perceived among the Mormons. On the
other hand, by presenting a crisis that only church leaders could quell,
Young had deployed a sophisticated strategy to recapture the loyalty
and devotion of his followers, which had waned as the crises of the early
decades of Mormonism faded.

During the Mormon Reformation, Young and his fellow Mormon
leaders inflicted the crisis and claimed sole proprietorship of the salve
to heal it. Simultaneously, Young's manufactured crisis served the same
function that all previous Mormon crises had: it drove the community
together to fight a common enemy and focused the attention and loyalty
of church members on the church hierarchy. The difference, of course,
was that this time the enemy was invisible and hiding inside the Mormon stronghold.

Young used his October 1855 address to introduce the first of several institutionally based solutions to the new crisis. The Mormons, of course, had always been deeply involved in proselytizing. Throughout the church's history, new converts frequently found themselves on proselytizing missions while still dripping with their own baptismal water. So Young spoke in a language everyone in the audience understood when he introduced the concept of "home missionaries." Rather than going into the world to preach the Mormon gospel, these home missionaries would visit the homes of every member of the church, examining Mormons about their adherence to church practices and reporting their findings to their ecclesiastical superiors.[75] Wilford Woodruff recorded in his journal that Young called Orson Pratt, Woodruff, and "many others" to serve "Home missions."[76] At a meeting held in October, the Utah territory was divided into six missionary districts, and twenty-eight home missionaries were assigned.[77]

Institutional Surveillance

The introduction of the home missionaries in the fall of 1855[78] represents a major development in the history of the Mormon Reformation.[79] The home missionary program began a system of hierarchical or institutional surveillance. Directed by the leadership in Salt Lake City, the surveillance reached to individual Mormons throughout the settlements in Utah. In Michel Foucault's work on the cultural development of discipline in modernity, he argued that a tactic of surveillance typically evolves when cultures reach a certain level of maturity. Surveillance becomes "a specific mechanism in the disciplinary power" wielded by a social hierarchy.[80] Such observational techniques, having grown into "special functions," are performed by "specialized personnel" who act at the behest of agents occupying the top strata of power.[81] During the Mormon Reformation, the LDS Church hierarchy deployed an increasingly sophisticated example of what Foucault described as a "mutual type" of surveillance. In this model, "three procedures are integrated into a single mechanism: teaching proper, the acquisition of knowledge by the very practice of pedagogical activity and a reciprocal, hierarchized observation."[82] Foucault described a system of "control" and "domination" disguised as something simpler, usually an educational or devotional "examination." The examination combined "hierarchical surveillance and normalizing judgment."[83] As one Mormon reported it, home missionaries were "appointed for evry [sic] ward in the City [of Salt Lake]" and ordered to "live in the ward until they [had] prepared the inhabitants thereof for baptism."[84] Over the course of the Reformation, this plan evolved, and the Mormon leadership deputized home missionaries who then sent members of local LDS wards to observe and examine church members in ways that resembled Foucault's model of surveillance.

During the period between October 1855 and the fall of 1856, the home missionaries carried with them a general charge to encourage the Mormons to better their spiritual lives. They also apparently reported any problems or unresolved sins to local leaders. Initially, these examinations were informal. At the first quarterly conference of home missionaries, held in late October 1855, the theme of examination was raised more than once. Gilbert Clements, one of the recently assigned home missionaries, told the assembled group that all Mormons should "examine yourselves and see if ye be in the faith," arguing that only through thorough examination could they "know, not think merely, that they were in the faith."[85]

The leaders of the home missionaries held meetings in the six mission districts in the fall and winter of 1855–1856. In all of the meetings, the themes were substantially the same. Speakers, drawn from the ranks of the home missionaries, placed heavy emphasis on the perceived weakening of the Mormons in Utah, and they frequently offered anecdotal evidence to demonstrate this declension. The speakers often touched on the dangers that the Mormons faced from within, especially the threats emanating from apostates. The general devotion of the Mormons was questioned, and the home missionaries were told to urge the Mormons they visited to pray frequently and to keep their homes and persons clean.

On 10 November, John Lyon said that he had "seen many that had enjoyed the gifts of God, that have apostatized, and said it was all a delusion." Brigham Young suggested that Mormons were eating and drinking too much, which exerted a "clogging" and "stupefying" effect on the intellectual and spiritual faculties.[86] He also indicated that Mormons should avoid physicians, claiming that those who enjoyed a full measure of the Holy Spirit would know how to heal their "tabernacles" without recourse to doctors. Thomas Grover warned that the progress of the "kingdom of God" relied entirely upon the personal worthiness of individual Mormons, which he called into question. Zera Pulsipher wistfully recalled the days of his youth when a single instance of thievery would "generate more talk than it would in these valleys if a thousand things were stolen." His goal, and the goal of the home missionaries in general, was to assure that "confidence is restored among this people." Wilford Woodruff decried the multitude of hidden sins concealed among the Mormons and encouraged the home missionaries to be aware of anyone "lying, swearing, stealing, profaning the name of God, committing adultery, [or] worshipping things except the God of heaven." Woodruff also added that anyone who would "permit evil to dwell in Zion" also jeopardized the community.[87]

One week later, the scene was repeated. Among the topics discussed at the meeting were the "dangers attending prosperity," the "increasing rage of the adversary [Satan]," the tendency of the Mormons to "set their hearts upon the things of this life," and the failure of saints to engage in sufficiently frequent family prayers.[88] In December, the traveling conference of home mission leaders visited Kaysville, a small settlement north of Salt Lake City. Thomas Grover made it clear that the home missionaries bore the responsibility of "visiting the saints, and rooting out all iniquity from the church." The ever-nostalgic Zera Pulsipher recalled the "past trials and persecution of the church," noting that only if the Mormons could become "humble before the Lord" would they find the "future glory" promised them. Pulsipher suggested that, without the constant crises that had followed the Mormons during their time in the East and the Midwest, they seemed to have trouble maintaining a common purpose and sense of community.[89]

As the Reformation grew in intensity in the fall of 1856, church leaders took an important new step in the institutionalized surveillance that had begun with the home missionaries. In November, they developed a formal "catechism," which the home missionaries were instructed to use in their visits to Mormon homes. Although originally containing thirteen questions, the catechism soon grew to include a total of twenty-seven. The most basic function of the catechism was to allow the home missionaries to gauge the level of devotion of the church members they visited. Historian Davis Bitton suggested that these catechisms were devices of "self-assessment leading to repentance." Surely, the fact that human representatives mediated between the catechism and the catechized indicates that more than simple "self-assessment" was involved.[90] Brigham Young sent a copy of the catechism to the stake president in Sanpete County, Utah, explaining that the questions were necessary because many Mormons were "guilty of the most heinous crimes in the sight of both God and man." The catechism was intended to induce Mormons to "confess their sins and repent of their wickedness,"[91] and it performed other functions as well. It suggested both to those asking the questions and to those answering them the types of behaviors that were acceptable and those that were not. In this sense, the catechism worked as a teaching device. It was also, however, a reminder that the community was in crisis. Why else, the Mormons might have wondered, would these questions be asked unless many, perhaps even most, Mormons were in violation of the community's religious standards?

The catechism was designed to be comprehensive—to ensure, in other words, that no one could pass the test. Beginning with a broad question about whether the Mormon being catechized had committed murder, the catechism narrowed in focus until it reached the most personal of issues, including the care of one's own body. "Do you wash your body," the home missionaries were instructed to ask their neighbors, "as often as health and cleanliness require?"[92] The questions also focused on filth in homes and yards. The catechism was an important tool of surveillance that served to inflict guilt and induce confession—a cathartic act that bound the individual Mormons to their leaders. Heightening the drama of the catechizing visit was the formality with which the home missionaries staged the event. Homer Brown, a Mormon living in Salt Lake City, was instructed that when the home missionaries

> come to visit us we ought to place the first wife at our left hand with her little ones around her, and the second at her left hand and so on. We should then place our oldest son at our right hand and the next oldest next to him and our oldest daughters to the left of our wives and the hired women to the left of the daughters and the hired men to the right of the sons. Then place the teacher in front, and receive his instructions.[93]

The hierarchical design described by Brown served to accentuate both the ritualized feeling of the catechetical experience as well as the feeling of dependence upon church leaders for assistance during the time of spiritual crisis.

Anthropologist Mary Douglas's groundbreaking work on the relationship between social structures and cosmological organization may help us to better understand the intense, inward-looking element of the Mormon Reformation that found clear expression in the institutionalized surveillance described above. Douglas devised a graph that measured the relative strength of two social variables: along the horizontal axis, the degree to which individual egos are controlled by other people ("group") and along the vertical axis, the degree to which persons share public, as opposed to private, classifications of the world in which they live ("grid"). During the early Utah period, Mormons clearly belonged to the upper-right quadrant of Douglas's diagram. They evinced "piety and sacralized institutions" and insisted on "strong boundaries between purity and impurity." Furthermore, they believed that "all moral failings [were] at once sins against religion and the community."[94] They believed in a "punishing moral universe" and insisted upon "routinized piety toward authority and its symbols" that was made possible through a clear delineation of hierarchical and social roles.[95]

The ritual and rhetorical activities of the Mormon Reformation, however, more closely fit another of Douglas's categories, witch hunting. According to Douglas, the tendency to seek out and punish witchcraft is found in small, tightly knit communities located relatively high on the grid axis but low on the group axis, that is, they share a world view and maintain clear boundaries with the outside world, but have little formal structure within their group. Lest the terminology mislead us, we should note that, for Douglas, "accusations of witchcraft" simply boil down to the notion that certain individuals within the group are bringing evil upon the whole group and must therefore be discovered and expelled.[96] By that definition, the sifting process of the Mormon Reformation could appropriately be classified as a period of witch hunting, simply because it was an effort to locate and expel evil that was believed to reside within the confines, physical and spiritual, of their religious community. It was an unprecedented time of introspection, a period in which Mormons, following the path marked by their leaders, "put immense pressure on one another and [strove] incessantly to define and close the circle of their friends."[97] To a certain extent, of course, the Mormons had always done this, but the focus had usually been on the evil that lurked beyond their boundaries and that sought their physical and spiritual destruction at every turn. In the 1850s, Brigham Young and other Mormon leaders, sensing a paucity of immediate external evil and recognizing the centrality of crisis to Mormon communal identity, turned the searching eye of God inward. Douglas argued that the "witch doctrine is used as the idiom of control, since it pins blame for misfortune on trouble-makers and deviants."[98] Young seized upon the most convenient misfortune at hand, famine and pestilence, and then launched a crusade to identify those evildoers responsible for bringing the judgments of God upon the community.

While it is difficult to understand why a high grid/high group community would resort to a witch doctrine, Douglas provided a clue in her argument that communities that hunt for internal evil do so in an effort to "shore up the weak internal organization of the group."[99] One of the themes that emerged prominently during the Mormon Reformation was the sense among Mormon leaders that the rank-and-file believers had grown slack in their attentiveness to church leadership. Because the church hierarchy was the cornerstone of Mormon social organization and because the external threats that had always served to focus Mormon attention on church leaders had temporarily vanished, one could argue that the internal organization of Mormonism was weakening in the years preceding the Mormon Reformation. With no external threat looming, the Mormon leadership sought to convince their followers that the crisis was internal, and hence a sort of witch doctrine emerged. Through the innovative disruption and redeployment of Mormon ritual as well as through the performance of specially choreographed rhetorical dynamics, Young and other church leaders proceeded to deepen their created crisis under the aegis of a hunt for occult wickedness.

Ritual and the Mormon Reformation: Crisis of Deprivation

The first change in Mormon ritual to emerge during the Mormon Reformation was a renewed emphasis on the practice of rebaptism. From at least 1830, Mormons had engaged in the ecclesiastically unusual practice of rebaptism in which persons who had already received baptism into the church would do so again. Rebaptisms were occasionally performed as a symbol of renewed commitment to the church. D. Michael Quinn documented rebaptisms for the purpose of such personal renewal in the 1840s, including when the church underwent what might be termed a "mini reformation" in 1841.[100] Thus, most Mormons living in Utah at the time of the Reformation had probably already been baptized more than once.[101] The rebaptisms practiced during the Mormon Reformation differed from the baptismal ritual as it surfaced at other times chiefly in terms of scale. On two levels the rebaptisms performed during the Reformation dwarfed previous and subsequent instances of the ritual. First, rebaptisms in 1856–1857 were usually group events at which dozens, and sometimes hundreds, of persons received the ordinance. Even during the small-scale reformation that occurred in Nauvoo in 1841, the rebaptisms appear to have been informal and not centrally directed, as they were during the Mormon Reformation. Second, the overall scope of the practice meant the rebaptism of a sizable portion of the members of the church in Utah over the course of the Mormon Reformation. Indeed, during the Reformation it became the ritual centerpiece of Mormon life.

The standard procedure for mass rebaptism during this time was unique in Mormon history. Typically, a sermon would be delivered, emphasizing the sorry state of spiritual affairs among the Mormons. Following the sermon, all those who desired to recommit themselves to their faith would be rebaptized. The first such mass rebaptism occurred on Sunday, 14 September 1856. Jedediah M. Grant mounted the stand on the second day of a two-day conference of home missionaries in Davis County. Grant "called upon the people to repent and be baptized for the remission of their sins." Such a request must have struck the audience as somewhat strange, given the fact that most, if not all, of the people in attendance had already undergone Mormon baptism. Rebaptisms, when they had occurred previously, typically preceded a significant event, such as a marriage or the reception of the endowment ordinances, and symbolized a recommitment to the basic tenets of the church preparatory to entering into more serious covenants. One Salt Lake City resident, for example, reported in his journal that his father rebaptized him the day before he received his temple endowment in October 1855.[102] Grant's call for a general rebaptism presented a familiar ritual in an unfamiliar context.

It is likely that the importance of the ritual of rebaptism was further impressed upon Grant when, on 2 October 1856, eleven church leaders, including the First Presidency and several of the apostles, gathered to dedicate the baptismal font in the newly constructed endowment house.[103] At that meeting, Heber C. Kimball of the First Presidency offered a dedicatory prayer in which he explicitly linked rebaptism and the Reformation. "Now O Lord except [sic] of this dedication at our hands and as we go into this water may our sins be forgiven & not be remembered against us any more. May we feel the power of God and have power to work a great Refermation [sic] among this people."[104] After the dedication ceremony concluded, the entire First Presidency and the others present were rebaptized and reconfirmed as members of the LDS Church. It is important to note that these leaders were baptized in a private ceremony, not publicly as was the case with all other church members. Immediately after the rebaptisms, Woodruff and Grant went to a meeting of home missionaries in Salt Lake City's seventeenth ward.[105]

For five hours, the assembled Mormons at the conference were bombarded with a variety of sermons relating to the need for purification of their personal lives and also of "their lands and their houses." Finally, Grant asked for a show of hands to indicate how many in the audience were willing to enter the waters of baptism to "renew their covenants." Not surprisingly, a unanimous vote was recorded. The next morning, the conference reconvened in preparation for the rebaptism rituals. Grant carefully orchestrated the proceedings, demanding that the Mormons "observe the utmost decorum and reverence while the sacred ordinance of baptism was being attended to." Over the course of the next eight hours, some 500 Mormons underwent rebaptism by immersion. Grant directed that the highest ecclesiastical officers present be baptized first. A sustained spate of rebaptism rituals throughout the territory followed. The next day, in fact, 93 persons underwent rebaptism following a church conference in West Jordan, Utah. After a day-long conference, the attendees were instructed to assemble the following morning to be rebaptized. At the baptismal assembly, "President D. D. Hunt explained [church members'] duties in relation to the renewal of our covenants."[106]

News of the new emphasis on rebaptism spread rapidly throughout the Mormon settlements. In November 1856, Helen Smith wrote to her brother Joseph, then serving as a missionary in Hawaii, that "there is a reformation a goin [sic] on and we have all got to repent of our sinss [sic] and be baptized and do even the first work over again."[107] Helen Smith's letter portrays the widely held view that this ritual signified nothing less than a total obliteration of the past and a literal renewing of one's relationship to the LDS Church. By early 1857, mass rebaptisms were being conducted in the Mormon settlement at San Bernardino, California, at "times appointed" by local church leaders. In January, San Bernardino resident Louisa Barnes Pratt and her daughters experienced rebaptism along with about "fifty others at the same time."[108]

The ritual element of the Mormon Reformation was laced with irony. On the one hand, church leaders required rebaptism as a sign of renewed commitment to church principles and leaders while simultaneously suspending the weekly ritual of the sacrament of the Lord's Supper. The Mormon version of the common Protestant and Catholic rituals of "communion" originated with a revelation recorded by Joseph Smith in April 1830 that enjoined the Mormons to "meet together often to partake of the bread and wine in remembrance of the Lord Jesus."[109] This revelation translated into the practice of weekly "sacrament meetings." By 1856, most Mormon settlements held meetings during which the faithful consumed bread and water and ritually covenanted to remember the sacrifice of Jesus Christ and to take Christ's name upon them while securing the promise that "His Spirit will always be with them."[110] In a sermon delivered in 1865, Brigham Young explained that Mormons "partake of bread and water to witness that we remember Jesus Christ, who gave his life a ransom for us, and that we are willing to keep His commandments."[111] Although clearly related to the family of Protestant and Roman Catholic rituals involving the symbolic consumption of Christ's flesh and blood, the Mormon ritual differed both in terms of the substances consumed (usually, after August 1830, bread and water instead of bread and wine) and in terms of the particular symbolism of the act itself. The Mormon ritual, simply referred to as "the sacrament" among church members, allowed participants to renew the covenants they made when they originally entered the waters of baptism and to secure anew the promised "remission of sins" attendant to baptism. Heber C. Kimball, for example, taught, "In partaking of this ordinance [of the sacrament], we renew our covenants, and we have a promise that we shall receive a renewal of the Holy Spirit, to enable us to be humble and to perform the duties that are enjoined upon us as Saints."[112] In other words, the sacrament functioned in basically the same way as rebaptism but in a less dramatic fashion.

In November 1856, Heber C. Kimball and Jedediah M. Grant spoke at a meeting at which local leaders were preparing to administer the sacramental ritual. Kimball interrupted the proceedings with a scathing indictment of the "unworthy" Mormons who dared to "trifle with this ordinance" by partaking of the bread and water with unrepentant hearts. In accordance with Mormon scriptural dictates, LDS bishops had always withheld the sacrament from individuals known to be guilty of serious sin. Kimball's effort to "forbid all unworthy persons [from] partaking of this sacrament" was equivalent to forbidding it to everyone. "This ordinance is administered on condition of your living in righteousness, and of your hearts being true to your God and to your brethren."[113] Grant followed Kimball's lead and instructed that all the "unrighteous" should "leave the bread in the salvers and the water in the cups, and not partake of the sacrament unless they are right."[114] A central theme of the Reformation, of course, was that no one could trust his or her heart or soul to be right. Within the Reformation context, few if any Mormons felt completely free from sin. Kimball and Grant seemed to be daring Mormons to partake of the sacrament, thus declaring their total worthiness and inviting inspection. Homer Brown attended the meeting and recorded in his journal that many Mormons "did not partake, myself among the number."[115] Apparently few, if any, Mormons at the meeting decided to court such inspection, and the sacrament was withdrawn from the church generally soon thereafter. In January 1857, Young wrote to Apostle George A. Smith explaining that "the bread and cup we have withheld from the Saints for some months, to afford them space and time for repentance, restitution, and when ready, for a renewal of their covenants."[116]

Young's statement is complicated by the fact that rebaptisms, which allowed Mormons to renew their covenants, continued to be performed even when the sacrament was not administered. If the rituals were functionally equivalent, why would Young suspend a traditional practice and reemphasize a less common one? The answer lies in the very different *kinds* of rituals represented in the sacrament and rebaptism. The sacrament, although administered in congregational settings, was a very personal ritual. Mormons sat quietly pondering their individual relationships with God and Jesus Christ. Every week, they had the opportunity to begin anew. Rebaptism, like the public confessions that characterized the early phases of the Reformation, was an exercise in communal, ritual humiliation and reconciliation—a public admission on the part of most Mormons in any given community that they were deeply unworthy of their place in God's kingdom. Previously, only excommunicated Mormons required rebaptism for reintegration into the Mormon community, but during the Mormon Reformation it was apparently required of those who had not been subject to church discipline. Rituals of public humiliation have been part of Christianity since antiquity and, as Mary C. Mansfield perceptively noted, the "public humiliation of sinners is perhaps the most powerful means of instilling conformity in a community."[117]

By abrogating the weekly ritual of cleansing and renewal, Young cut Mormons off from what they believed to be a major source of personal communion with God. Young understood that Mormonism had formed and developed against the backdrop of chronic crises of deprivation. The history of Mormonism in the 1830s and 1840s rested on a foundation of deprivation; Mormons were deprived of land, peace, and their lives. They were deprived of their temples and of their founding prophet. Ultimately, they were deprived of their country. At least, that is how the Mormons interpreted their experiences and that is how they shaped their discourse and their communal identity. After the initial struggles to build their western settlements, the Mormons found that religious deprivations and crises had not followed them.

An editorial in the *Deseret News* expressed anxiety over the prosperity the Mormons enjoyed in Utah. The Mormons were beginning to falter because "commodious buildings are multiplied, numerous fields are enclosed and the comforts and luxuries of life accumulate around us." In Mormon rhetoric of the period, the necessity for reformation was linked to prosperity.[118] The cure for prosperity, of course, is deprivation. Lacking a viable external source of deprivation, Brigham Young apparently undertook a program of ritual deprivation during the Mormon Reformation in order to correct the laxity that he claimed had developed during the "years of comparative uninterruption [*sic*] in our mountain homes."[119]

Brigham Young had unsuccessfully attempted to correct this laxity once before. In 1854, he had attempted to institute the practice of consecration and stewardship that Joseph Smith had originally introduced in the 1830s. According to this system, members of the church were to consecrate all of their possessions to the church's agent, who would give the individuals back what was required for their "needs" and then redistribute the surplus to needy people within the church. Unlike many contemporary communitarian experiments, the Mormon effort "was designed in such a way as to retain a large measure of freedom of enterprise."[120] But Young's attempt to implement the law of consecration never really took hold. According to Leonard Arrington and his colleagues, "The first step in the plan, that of consecration, was taken only by a minority of Latter-day Saints and the second, the assignment of stewardship, was not taken at all."[121] It is unclear why Young did not press more forcefully to bring about compliance with the law of consecration.[122] It is plain that, in the wake of this failure, Young sought to find a less drastic and more efficient way of ritually refocusing the Mormons, and he found it in the suspension of the weekly ritual of the sacrament.

By interrupting the most basic and frequent ritual of Mormon life, the ritual by which Mormons measured their lives week by week, Brigham Young created a crisis of spiritual deprivation. This was a completely novel exercise for the Mormon community. During Joseph Smith's fourteen-year tenure as church president, he had added many rituals, but he had never denied access to any rituals on such a wide scale. Because church authorities abrogated the ordinance, the crisis became communal. Young did not cut the Mormons off completely from ritual life. Rather, he made use of the existing, but infrequently deployed, ritual of rebaptism to provide a renewed sense of community.

The unusual nature of rebaptism, coupled with its public performance as part of special conferences, functioned as a reminder of the crisis and contributed to a general sense of ritual disorientation. Young also allowed other rituals to continue, most notably those associated with the temple. Marriages, especially plural marriages, were encouraged during this period.[123] The ritual of the sacrament, however, was the only one that could be withdrawn to effect a crisis of deprivation that would be felt by the entire culture. Religious historian Edward Muir pointed out that "sacred time is cyclical, a continuous return to the same place, a sameness guaranteed by the rituals repeated on the sabbath."[124] For the Mormons, the only ritual performed on the sabbath was the sacrament of bread and water, and that rite had been revoked. Brigham Young's removal of that ritual dispossessed Mormons of an important act designed to demarcate sacred and profane time. Young created a crisis and exacerbated the severity of that crisis among the Mormons by removing their accustomed moral support.

The Performance of Reformation Rhetoric

Every study of the Mormon Reformation undertaken to date leans heavily on the movement's rhetorical dimension. This is understandable given the exaggerated and inflammatory discourse that was the order of the day. Scholars of the period are obliged to include in their narratives several particularly memorable sermons, such as Jedediah Grant's promise to "rain pitchforks" down on the Latter-day Saints. A significant debate has emerged over the so-called blood atonement rhetoric that figured prominently during the Reformation, and many scholars feel the need to take a side on that issue. *Blood atonement* is the act of shedding the blood of someone guilty of sins so heinous that Christ's atonement would not alone suffice. Brigham Young and others claimed that for some sins, such as murder and adultery, the blood of the violator would be required as part of a complete act of repentance. There is some evidence to suggest that isolated incidents of violence motivated by the blood atonement rhetoric occurred. Some scholars, such as D. Michael Quinn and Will Bagley, have spun these incidents into narratives of the Mormon Reformation that portray Young as condoning these violent acts. Other scholars, most notably Paul Peterson, have argued that Young was speaking symbolically and that he never intended for anyone to take him literally. As evidence, the latter group offers letters written to Young in which persons asked to be killed as part of the repentance process, with Young's responses saying in essence that "this one time" he would let the sinner live.[125] Although the present study is not centrally concerned with the issues attendant on the blood atonement debate, certain discernible themes inscribed both in the rhetoric of that period and in the performance of that rhetoric have significant implications.

Beginning with Young's October 1855 sermon discussed above, Mormon leaders sculpted a discourse that heightened the sense of crisis among the Latter-day Saints. The key element of the crisis rhetoric involved the idea of infiltration. The Mormons, the rhetoric suggested, were laboring under the false belief that the relatively secure physical boundaries and stable religious system they enjoyed in the Great Basin meant that all was well. The rhetoric of the Mormon Reformation suggested that, on the contrary, the boundaries had been infiltrated on all levels. Evil spirits and devils surrounded the Mormons, looking for any crack in the spiritual foundations. Wilford Woodruff wrote of his belief that "there was a Legion of Devils in the valley congregated against [us] trying to destroy [us]."[126] From what the church leaders saw, the demons had improved their opportunities, and their evil work was bearing bitter fruit among the Mormons. The homes and bodies of the Latter-day Saints had also been infiltrated; filth and "stink" festered in the dooryards and bodies of Mormondom.

Beyond the specific content of the sermons, however, the issue of performance has received little attention. During the Mormon Reformation, unusually frequent interactions between speaker and audience were enlivening the meetings. Church authorities employed spiritual powers to search the crowd for hidden sins and to elicit public confessions. Most of the sermons appeared in full or in part in the church's newspaper, the *Deseret News*. But church leaders also went on extensive tours of Utah to spread the Reformation message. The psychological impact of being called a filthy, demon-harboring hypocrite was much higher when the message was delivered in person than when the words were read in the relative comfort of a Mormon's home.

John Smith preserved a vivid account of a typical Reformation meeting in a letter he wrote to his teenage brother, future church president Joseph F. Smith.

> There were some hard questions asked about committing sins of every description and any man that was guilty of adultery, theft, lying, murder, and many others to[o] numerous to mention had to confess there and agree to do so no more and a curse was put upon any one that lied there to cover his sins. Now Joseph one word to you be careful of what you do and do nothing but wright [sic] and do not go to sleep on your mission for fear of the displeasure of our Beloved President Brigham Young and your god.[127]

Smith's letter opens a window on the performance of the Reformation rhetoric that is missing from most published accounts of the sermons. As with the catechism, the questions posed to the men, and to the women in meetings with mixed-gender audiences, were so broad that scarcely anyone could escape guilt. At the very least, one would find many "liars" in any group, and one suspects that the litany of wrongs "to[o] numerous to mention" consisted chiefly of pedestrian or mundane acts. Furthermore, the performance called for public confessions from those present. Anyone who covered his sins, which in practice meant anyone who did not participate in the public confession of sin, left the meeting with a very public curse on his head. Such a curse, of course, carried with it the fear of isolation and ostracism, particularly because the Mormons were being told that any unresolved wickedness in the community could bring grave problems for all.

Although John Smith did not specifically mention it in his account of the meeting, church leaders had developed a dramatic and, for those present, probably terrifying technique of supernatural surveillance. Through the instrumentality of the "candle of the Lord," which was apparently a special spiritual power rather than an object, certain leaders would gaze upon each individual in the meeting and "the whole body was searched with a scrutinizing Eye and all sins rebuked by the power of God."[128] Devout Mormons would have found this process deeply disconcerting and a strong inducement to rebaptism. Benjamin F. Johnson recalled that, in December 1856, he underwent examination "by the candle of the Lord," and it revealed "more evil than [he] wished to carry." Deeply moved by the experience, Johnson immediately "laid all down at the feet of the Lord and his servants" and reentered the "waters of baptism and repentance and sought to live a higher, more perfect life."[129] Although Johnson did not specify that he made confession in connection with this event, his reference to laying his burdens at the feet of God's "servants" strongly suggests that confession to LDS leaders was part of his personal reformation.[130]

The public confessions elicited during the Mormon Reformation served several purposes. First, they acted as a means of reinforcing group identity because everyone seemed to be in the same difficult circumstance. Second, witnessing mass confessions by one's friends, neighbors, and family cultivated a sense of crisis. As the tone of Smith's letter indicates, those leaving such meetings were more convinced than ever of the declension that threatened their spiritual lives. The sense of declension was manufactured simply by casting the widest possible net to catch every possible sin, and it was amplified by the effect of large groups of friends and neighbors confessing in front of one another. Manufactured or not, it must have seemed all too real for Mormons who observed, and unwittingly participated in, the performances of Reformation rhetoric. Third, these meetings directed group loyalty toward church leaders, the only individuals who could offer safety from the crisis at hand. It is of no little significance that Smith warned his brother to do all in his power to avoid the wrath of Young and "god" in that order.

There is no reason to believe that Mormons during the Reformation carried more hidden sins than they had at any other time, but the public confessions made it seem so because they reversed what sociologists refer to as a state of pluralistic ignorance. *Pluralistic ignorance* is a "psychological state characterized by the belief that one's private thoughts, attitudes, and feelings, are different from those of others, even though one's public behavior is identical."[131] In a religious context, such as that in pioneer era Utah, persons tended to be acutely aware of their own perceived moral flaws and their failure to live up to their public façade of piety, while assuming that the righteous public appearance of their neighbors was genuine. While in some contexts this might be a source of personal dismay, in a community that was based on an ideal of communal covenants in which everyone's prosperity was linked to the community's general righteousness, believing that everyone else besides oneself was righteous tended to bolster confidence in the general standing of the group before God. Leonard J. Arrington, perhaps the most distinguished historian of Mormonism, correctly observed that Young's "overriding vision was the literal establishment of the Kingdom of God in the valley of the mountains [Utah]. The Mormon village was a covenant community . . . [and its] citizens must yield personal desires to the whole," and to the degree that they did so their communities would find favor with God.[132] Catherine L. Albanese stated the fact even more plainly when she wrote that nineteenth-century "Mormons did religion in community."[133] Pluralistic ignorance thus served to increase the confidence of each individual Mormon in his or her own failure, but it also boosted confidence in the righteousness of the community as a whole.

Public confessions of the sort described by Mormons during the period of the Reformation served as "informational cascades"—the formal name for the processes of rupturing the membrane of pluralistic ignorance.[134] Informational cascades "shift collective behavior in a direction opposite of the status quo." In the case of the Mormon Reformation, the informational cascades moved Mormons away from the belief that they had achieved safety in their western isolation and instead created a sense of deep unease about the spiritual state of their communities.[135] It bears repeating that, if public confessions had been required of Mormons at any point in their history, they would have had the same effect. It is not that there were more sins to be confessed during the mid-1850s; it was simply that an average level of sin was amplified through scorching injunctions followed by public confessions.

Jonathan Z. Smith perceptively suggested that, throughout time, mythical, rhetorical, and ritual innovations have sprung up in response to "difficult and incongruous" circumstances—periods in which the expected and anticipated futures of religious communities have emerged in an "unexpected or 'wrong' way."[136] On the surface, the Mormon flight from persecution and tension held the tantalizing possibility of separation and peace. The Mormon Reformation might be read as an innovative response to an unexpected discovery that only became obvious once relative peace had been achieved, namely, that Mormon self-definition was fundamentally grounded in a dialectical relationship with tension and crisis. The Mormon Reformation was thus an exercise in crisis creation and crisis management, an attempt to recapture the crisis-driven tension upon which the Mormons had come to rely for a sense of communal identity and religious zeal. Having removed themselves from the sources of those crises, they found themselves without the energy that the crises provided. The Mormon ship had begun to languish in the doldrums of isolation, and it needed a hearty crisis to push it along until the external winds of "persecution" revived again. In an effort to remedy the situation, the Mormon leadership created crises.

The Mormons did not have to wait long for external crises to emerge once again. In 1857, the U.S. Army invaded Utah. Following the Utah War, and the Civil War which immediately followed, the polygamy prosecutions began in earnest, and, as we have seen, that crisis provided tension for the rest of the nineteenth century. On the heels of the Utah War, the polygamy prosecutions began in earnest, and, as we have seen, that crisis provided tension for the rest of the nineteenth century. In 1858, a Mormon who was called by Brigham Young to leave Salt Lake City and scout locations for a possible removal of the Mormons in the face of the incoming U.S. Army wrote the following poem in his journal:

> Long we've been driven and oppressed,
> On Earth we've scarcely found a rest:
> Our leaders have been basely slain
> Their blood still smokes upon the plain!
> We fled to Utah's distant vale
> That they no more might us assail;
> We left our houses and our lands
> Which fell into their greedy hands.
> But we increased in wealth and power
> And blessings on our head did shower,
> But now again we're forced to roam
> And in the desert find a home.[137]

The poem situates the period of the Mormon Reformation, associated with wealth and power, squarely between the earlier periods of near-constant crisis and persecution and the new impending external crisis coming in the form of the U.S. Army. In the eyes of this diarist, at least, the time in which the Mormons were free from external persecution was anomalous, and the coming Utah War signaled a return to religion as usual.

Conclusion

In the mid-nineteenth century, both the Shakers and the Mormons underwent revivalistic periods in which each group attempted to remedy problems with their boundary maintenance structures. While the two periods demonstrated some superficial similarities, especially in the unusual level of spiritual intensity they generated, they performed very different cultural work. The Mormon Reformation represented an attempt to recapture the crisis-driven tension upon which the Mormons had come to rely for a sense of communal identity and religious zeal. Having removed themselves from the sources of those crises, they found themselves without the energy that the crises provided.

The Shaker Era of Manifestations represented a response to an actual crisis. Unlike the Mormons, the Shakers drew maximum benefit from stable, non-crisis-driven tension that was based upon their own notions of cultural outsiderhood. Shaker villages, including the one profiled in detail in this chapter, were experiencing a genuine crisis that stemmed from the presence of communities of negation within the Shaker system. The various spiritualistic messages received during this period began organically among rank-and-file Shakers. These visions were designed to purge the community of intrusive elements and to reassert the stable outsiderhood that had come to define Shaker communal identity. Mormon leaders employed a rhetoric of declension and infiltration, one that began at the top and was always directly controlled by the hierarchy. In all likelihood, the Mormon Reformation was really about refocusing the attention of rank-and-file Mormons on their need for prophetic leadership. For the Shakers, however, there was a clear shift in the delicate balance that existed within each individual village between Shakers and non-Shakers.

Thus, the episodes of crisis differed in their specific goals. The Mormons sought to create a crisis in order to energize their polity while the Shakers sought to blunt a crisis that was enervating their community and diluting their sense of outsiderhood. However, each period represented an attempt to return each group to the ideal tension models upon which they had come to rely.

CONCLUSION

Today, thirty-five miles northwest of Portland, Maine, the three remaining Shakers make their home. In key respects, these Shakers believe and live as their nineteenth-century forebears did. They are celibate, they own all property in common, and they live quietly in their immaculately groomed village. Salt Lake City is a bustling semi-metropolis, the headquarters of a church that claims more than 13 million members of record worldwide. More than half of those live outside of the United States. Gone are the episodes of crisis. Mormons are discouraged from speculating unduly about an eventual return to Jackson County, Missouri; they faithfully tithe 10 percent of their income, but they do not live lives of full economic consecration; they marry eternally, mostly monogamously, in LDS temples and are rankled by media reports of Mormon fundamentalists who practice plural marriage.

Arnold Hadd, fully one-third of the world's remaining Shakers, told a newspaper reporter that "the reason we're celibate is Christ was celibate."[1] The reporter's question would have elicited precisely the same answer from Calvin Green in 1819. In 1998, LDS Church president Gordon B. Hinckley was asked about the church's stand on plural marriage. "These people who practice polygamy are not members of this Church," Hinckley replied, adding, "Any man or woman who becomes involved in it is excommunicated."[2] One wonders what Brigham Young would have said.

The point of this book has been, in part, to explain the historical roots of these divergent approaches to the past manifested among the Shakers and Mormons in the twenty-first century.

The Shaker boundary markers provided outsiderhood and stability, but they did not burn brightly enough to ignite growth. Those markers still exist today. It is important to note that stability is not synonymous with changelessness. The Shakers have been the victims of romanticization far too often, and any suggestion that they existed in some sort of utopian eternal "now" would simply add to the dubious pile of romantic notions. The Shaker world underwent significant social changes during the nineteenth century. Their charismatic movement was formalized, they expanded into the West and receded again, individual villages experienced cycles of apostasy and stagnation as well as periods of growth and dynamic leadership. Nineteenth-century Shakerism shifted from a society with a basically equal gender division to one predominantly female. As a result, Shakers had to bring in large numbers of outside laborers.

It is not incongruous to suggest that, although Shakerism changed over the course of the nineteenth century, the boundary markers that the group employed and the general position of the group vis-à-vis the broader culture remained basically stable. The fact that the signature boundary markers of Shakerism, celibacy and village life under the principle of joint interest, remained relatively stable against a backdrop of immense changes in Shaker fortunes only serves to render that stability more remarkable. By contrast, nineteenth-century Mormonism glowed red-hot with crisis-driven tension that served to make Mormonism into a cause and helped to propel it to international success. The cost, of course, was that the nineteenth-century Mormon boundary markers burned out, one by one, and were reformulated, spiritualized, and relegated to what appears to be an increasingly distant future. Today, Mormons' physical boundaries are worn beneath their clothes, and the boundary markers of plural marriage and Zion are also hidden, but not gone.

The church-sect continuum model that I discussed at the beginning of this volume is helpful but incomplete. The histories of nineteenth-century Shakerism and Mormonism tell us a great deal about the variety of potential tension models within the high-tension category. Other religious groups that occupy similar positions relative to American culture may display even greater diversity. No satisfactory model has yet been produced to explain high-tension groups that seem to go even further than the nineteenth-century Mormons did in seeking crisis. Consider the Branch Davidians under the leadership of David Koresh, who endured a grueling standoff with FBI agents only to die en masse during the government's raid on their Waco, Texas, compound in April 1993. Clearly, the Branch Davidians were a high-tension group, but they had little in common with, for instance, Jehovah's Witnesses or the Old Order Amish. All three groups fit the criteria for high-tension sects, but the traditional church-sect typology does not provide sufficient depth for understanding the kinds of tension that exist between these groups and the broader culture.

There is a more pressing reason than simple academic curiosity for looking carefully at the tension dynamics of particular groups. A great deal of misunderstanding exists between certain segments of American culture, particularly the news media and law enforcement, and groups that are likely to garner media attention or cross paths with law-enforcement officers. An inability to grapple with the complexities of and differences among high-tension religious groups carries tremendous potential for poor decision making. The assumption, for example, that all high-tension groups (which are frequently and incoherently labeled "cults" by the news media) have the potential to commit mass suicide dominated many of the decisions made by the U.S. government during the standoff at Waco. The infamous mass suicide of the members of the Peoples Temple at Jonestown, Guyana, in November 1978 became the generic template by means of which many people crafted expectations for all high-tension groups.[3] As a result, this incorrect template was applied when gauging the temperament and potential for self-inflicted violence of the Davidians, which in turn may have led to an escalation of the confrontation in an effort to save lives that probably were not initially in danger.

Beginning from the premise that both Shakers and Mormons were high-tension groups, I have, in this study, sought to evaluate the quality of that tension and to answer some key questions. Was the tension constant or cyclical? What types of resistance did the tension-generating boundary markers of each group elicit, and from which elements of the broader culture did that resistance come? Was there consistency demonstrated within each group in both physical boundary creation and doctrinal/ritualistic boundary creation? Although I have described at considerable length the answers I found to these questions, it may be helpful at this stage to state succinctly the formal models that developed out of my research.

During the formative period of Mormonism, the group came to rely heavily on what I call an *episodic crisis-driven tension model*. The Mormons employed boundary markers that elicited highly negative responses and that drew large-scale official, legal, and vigilante responses from the host culture. The Mormons developed a tendency to assert themselves aggressively in their relationship with the broader culture and responded to negative reactions from that culture with increased aggression. At the final possible moment, when faced with the choice of continuing with their tension-generating activities or continuing to survive as a movement, the Mormons chose to reduce the tension, reformulate their boundary markers, and begin the process again. Thus, the history of nineteenth-century Mormonism may be understood in terms of these episodic cycles of mounting tension followed by capitulation and the reformulation of boundaries.

An essential element that contributed to the flexibility of Mormon boundaries, both physical and doctrinal/ritualistic, is that the rhetoric usually far outstripped the lived reality.[4] The two major areas of Mormon boundary maintenance with which I dealt both illustrate this point. In the case of the physical boundaries, the Mormons engaged in aggressive and belligerent rhetoric, particularly during the Missouri period, dealing with their plans for the land on which they were going to build their holy city. Such rhetoric generated intense and violent opposition from their neighbors even though little was ever accomplished in the way of settlement building. Similarly, relatively few Mormons practiced polygamy, but the broader public acted as if all Mormons were in the grip of this vice. The reason is that the Mormons themselves employed a rhetoric in which polygamy became the idealized form of marriage.

In each of these cases, the Mormons used the opposition they evoked to great effect in energizing their religious community and increasing the loyalty that rank-and-file Mormons demonstrated to the Mormon hierarchy. When the Mormons were faced with annihilation, however, they could more easily reverse course and adjust their boundary markers because the rhetoric outstripped the practice. In other words, in the early stages of their tension model, the Mormons typically magnified the appearance of their boundary markers to maximize the impact those markers had on the broader culture. In reality, the boundary markers were not practiced by most Mormons at any given time. Nineteenth-century Mormon history is thus strewn with suspended practices and ideas, including full economic consecration, plans for the construction of cities in Missouri and Illinois, and plural marriage. All of these boundary markers outlived their usefulness and had to be adjusted and reworked.

The Shakers, by contrast, adopted boundary markers that clearly identified them as outsiders. For the Shakers, the ideal type of tension existed in what I call a *stable high-intensity moderate-risk tension model.* This involved the selection of boundary markers that drew moderately negative reactions: little if any official or legal response but substantial, and occasionally violent, social response from the broader public.

The most common signs sent by the outside culture to the Shakers came in the form of negative publications. Like the Mormons, the Shakers encoded the responses generated by these signs into a narrative of persecution that reinforced their self-understanding as the chosen people of God.[5] Unlike the Mormons, the Shakers did not draw substantial legal or physical reprisals with their sign-laden boundary markers. Of course, the Shakers were not spared the effects of physical brutality. They did suffer, in some cases substantially, as in the case of the community at Busro, Indiana, at the hands of vigilantes. However, such activity was not the norm for the Shakers and paled in comparison to the cultural demonization that the group endured. Such violence never resulted, for instance, in major shifts in Shaker practices or geographic location. All of this allowed the Shakers to maintain a high level of cultural outsiderhood while usually avoiding the cycles of crisis that the Mormons experienced.

Shaker boundary markers were high intensity in the level of involvement they demanded from all insiders, and of moderate risk in terms of the level of response that the boundary markers tended to draw from the larger culture. For the Shakers, rhetoric usually matched reality, at least in terms of celibacy and joint interest. All Shakers lived in villages and practiced celibacy, which meant that any adjustments to these boundary markers would be much more disruptive than similar changes made to Mormon boundary markers.

This extended look at the tremendous differences that existed in terms of the structures and motivations that guided interactions with the broader culture, even among groups as apparently similar as the nineteenth-century Shakers and Mormons, suggests the necessity of care in evaluating such high-tension groups in the contemporary age.

NOTES

Introduction

1. I use the term *boundary marker* in reference to practices in which Shakers and Mormons engaged that set them apart from the broader culture. Technically, beliefs are not boundary markers, but discourse that explains or voices those beliefs may be boundary markers.

2. Although the notion of a church-sect continuum has been around since the 1920s, the earliest exposition of the current understanding of church-sect typology is found in Johnson, "On Church and Sect," 539–549.

1. The Shakers in the World

1. Geertz, "Religion as a Cultural System," 91.

2. The idea of "cultural postulation" is derived from the work of anthropologist Melford E. Spiro. Spiro explained that the elements of a culturally postulated view, when "cross-culturally viewed, [appear] obscure and/or arbitrary . . . [and are] not susceptible of ordinary scientific proof." See Spiro, "Religion: Problems of Definition and Explanation," 96–98.

3. Stein, *The Shaker Experience,* 23–24.

4. Green and Wells, *Summary View,* 58.

5. Watson Andrews, "Communism," *Shaker* 2:10 (1872): 76.

6. Dunlavy, *The Manifesto,* 305. For a discussion of Dunlavy's work as a response to Reformed theology and as a major step in the systematization of Shaker theology, see Stein, *The Shaker Experience,* 74–75.

7. "Covenant at Sodus Bay, 1828," MS, WRHSSC I: B-10.

8. "Covenant of the East Family, New Lebanon, 1826," MS, WRHSSC, I: B-41.

9. "The Covenant of the South Family in the United Society in Enfield, Conn., 1827," MS, LCSC, box 2, item 3.

10. "A Record of the Covenant or Constitution of the Church at Tyringham, 1841," MS, LCSC, box 9, item 21.

11. "The Covenant of the South Family in the United Society in Enfield, Conn., 1827," MS, LCSC, box 2, item 3.

12. "A Record of the Covenant or Constitution of the Church at Tyringham, 1841," MS, LCSC, box 9, item 21.

13. Letter from Elisha Allen to Enoch Pease, 22 Jan. 1833, MS, LCSC, box 2, item 1; emphasis added.

14. See, for example, Thurman, *"O Sisters Ain't You Happy?"* 39; and Brewer, *Shaker Communities, Shaker Lives,* 37.

15. "To Our Friends of the Household of Faith," 1848, New Lebanon, MS, WRHSSC, VII: B-100.

16. "Church Record, Including Biographical Register of the Shaker Community at Pleasant Hill, Mercer County, Kentucky, 1806–1879," LCSC, MS, box 2, item 27.

17. "Mother Ann—Vision of Her by a Girl, 1847," LCSC, MS, box 9, item 138.

18. Four of the remaining, non-active Shaker villages have become tourist attractions and are probably the major public sources of information on Shakerism. William D. Moore points out that the opening of these villages as historic sites represented significant "milestones in the reevaluation of Shaker life and culture," and the major goal of these sites is "not [to serve] the needs of the sect, but those of the American touring public." Moore, "Interpreting the Shakers," 2.

19. Kanter, *Commitment and Community,* 83–84.

20. Ham, "Shakerism in the Old West," 163.

21. Nordhoff, *Communistic Societies,* 198, 193.

22. Stein, *The Shaker Experience,* 135.

23. In an important, but largely overlooked, study, Carol Weisbrod demonstrated how several utopian groups, including the Shakers, maintained almost total integration with American culture in terms of the legal system. Weisbrod argued that the Shakers designed their membership covenants as contracts that could be honored by U.S. courts. As a result, the Shakers won almost every challenge brought by apostates regarding consecrated property and funds. Weisbrod's work suggested that, at least in the legal arena, the antipathy between the Shakers and the U.S. government was not as intense as either side portrayed it. Weisbrod, *Boundaries of Utopia.*

24. "A Dialogue Between Jacob and Esau," reproduced in Patterson, *Shaker Spiritual,* 140–141.

25. Stein, *The Shaker Experience,* 142.

26. Journal of Elder Peter Pease, 1806–1813, 8 Aug. 1806, LCSC, MS, box 17, item 232.

27. Rufus Bishop, "Daily Journal of Passing Events," 15 Feb. 1830; 15 Aug. 1830, MS, NYPLSMC, item 1.

28. Ibid., 8 and 10 Apr. 1830.

29. Ibid., 8 Mar. 1835.

30. Betsy Bates, "A Journal of Events, Beginning April 7th 1833," New Lebanon, 18 Aug. 1833, MS, WRHSSC, V: B-128.

31. For a discussion of this phenomenon in a broader theoretical context, see Scott, *Domination,* 10.

32. Rufus Bishop, "A Daily Journal of Passing Events," 9 July 1832, NYPLSMC, item 1.

33. Ibid., 16 July 1832.

34. Ibid., 12 July 1832.

35. Rosenberg, *The Cholera Years*, 42. Rosenberg points out that many otherwise religiously lukewarm Americans turned to religion in the face of the 1832 pandemic, noting that "at least eleven states eventually proclaimed fast days in an effort to avert cholera," 52–53. It is thus not surprising to see persons turning to the Shakers as well.

36. Brewer, *Shaker Communities, Shaker Lives*, 37.

37. Thurman, *"O Sisters Ain't You Happy?"* 39.

38. For a theoretical discussion of the role of the "experienced world" among religious peoples, see Geertz, "Religion as a Cultural System," 119–120.

39. Prudence Morrill, "Account of a Journey of Prudence Morrill and Elizabeth Sharp, 1847," Emma B. King Library, Shaker Museum, Old Chatham, N.Y. Quoted in Filley, *Recapturing Wisdom's Valley*, 12.

40. Stein, too, made the case that Shaker villages were governed by order and fear of contamination, and he noted the various methods by which the Shakers imposed order upon new members. I am arguing that the imposition of order upon less-permanent visitors and objects from the world, in addition to new members, helps us to understand the apparent contradiction between the Shakers' rhetoric of separation and the permeability of their physical boundaries in practice. See Stein, *The Shaker Experience*, 96.

41. Smith, *Map Is Not Territory*, 97.

42. Ibid., 112.

43. Ibid., 98.

44. "Diary of Richard McNemar," 28 Apr. 1827, LCSC, MS, box 21, item 253.

45. Johnson, "Millennial Laws," 36.

46. "Young believers" were those Shakers who converted in the West, while eastern Shakers were referred to as "old believers."

47. Wright [McNemar], *Memorial of the Labors*, 12. The first meeting occurred on 6 December 1825.

48. Ibid., 13–14. This meeting took place on 1 January 1826, and the book burning followed shortly thereafter, although Wright [McNemar] does not provide a specific date.

49. Betsy Bates, "A Journal of Events, Beginning April 7th 1833," New Lebanon, 3 Jan. 1834, MS, WRHSSC, V: B-128.

50. "Journal of Aaron D. Bill, New Lebanon," 16 Jan. 1834, MS, WRHSSC, V: B-132. In their book-burning activities, the Shakers closely followed the pattern of other instances of "libricide" as described by archivist Rebecca Knuth. Knuth wrote that, in tightly controlled hierarchies, "those in power seek to ensure conformity and transformation through control of information and ideas." Knuth further commented, "When books come to be seen as capable of threatening ideological orthodoxy or policies, then book burning is adopted as a measure to eliminate challenges to the collective good (as defined by a regime) and purge alternatives." Knuth, "Systemic Book Burning as Evil?" 5–6.

51. For a discussion on the relationship between purity and book burning, see Hillerbrand, "On Book Burnings," 604–605.

52. This broadside probably dates to the 1840s. In the twentieth century, it found a second incarnation as a piece of mass-produced Shaker kitsch available at the gift shops of various Shaker museums and restored villages. See, for example, http://shakermuseumandlibrary.org/home.htm (accessed 1 Dec. 2008).

53. Robinson, *Concise History,* 117–118. The historian must handle this source with care. Robinson was a sympathetic outsider, and his "history" was little more than a glowing endorsement of the Shakers as virtuous people. The book is useful in the instance cited in the text because it contains the entire "Table Monitor" poem.

54. Johnson, "Millennial Laws," 47.

55. Dunlavy, *The Manifesto,* 267.

56. Evans, "Autobiography of a Shaker," 422.

57. Turner, *Ritual Process,* 131–132.

58. Ibid., 132. For the Shakers, this process involved the creation of social personae such as elders, eldresses, deacons, deaconesses, trustees, old believers, and young believers.

59. Ibid., 154–155.

60. "Records of the Church at Watervliet, N.Y. Comprising the Principal Events Relative to the Said Church, in Connection with Other Families and Societies, since the Year 1788," n.d., MS, WRHSSC, V: B-29.

61. Ibid.

62. "Covenant or Constitution of the Church at Harvard, Massachusetts," MS, WRHSSC, I: B-18.

63. "Journal Kept by Seth Y. Wells of New Lebanon, New York, on a Journey to Sodus Bay, New York, 1832," MS, WRHSSC, V: B-101, 14–15.

64. "Rules and Orders for the Church of Christ's Second Appearing, Established by the Ministry and Elders of the Church, New Lebanon, NY, 1860," MS, LCSC, box 3, item 33.

65. "Records of the Church at Watervliet, N.Y. Comprising the Principal Events Relative to the Said Church, in Connection with Other Families and Societies, since the Year 1788," entry for 24 June 1801, MS, WRHSSC, V: B-29.

66. "Journal Kept by Seth Y. Wells of New Lebanon, New York, on a Journey to Sodus Bay, New York, 1832," MS, WRHSSC, V: B-101, 14–15.

67. Altschuler and Blumin, *Rude Republic,* 16.

68. Green and Wells, *Summary View,* 61.

69. For a helpful discussion of the effects of free-riders on the overall level of commitment within religious communities, see Stark, *Rise of Christianity,* 175.

70. "A Revision and Confirmation of the Social Compact of the United Society (called Shakers) at Pleasant Hill, 1830," MS, LCSC, box 2, item 28.

71. "The Covenant of the Church at Union Village, in the Country of Warren and the State of Ohio, to Which Is Prefixed a Concise Statement of the Nature and Foundation Principles of Church Union, 1812," MS, LCSC, box 22, item 261.

72. Rachel Spencer to Ruth Farrington, July 1819, MS, WRHSSC, IV: A-33.

73. Murray, "Human Capital in Religious Communes," 219.

74. Ibid., 224.

75. David Darrow and John Meacham to Central Ministry at New Lebanon, LCSC, MS, box 20, item 245.

76. Diary of Richard McNemar, 28 Apr. 1827, LCSC, MS, box 21, item 253.

77. Letter from Elder William Deming to Elder Benjamin S. Youngs, 8 June 1832, LCSC, MS, box 2, item 5.

78. The Shakers apparently made sure that such unproven individuals as Ellen never spent much time out of range of Shaker eyes.

79. Letter from leaders at Enfield, Connecticut, to the Eldership at Harvard, Mass., 10 Aug. 1848, LCSC, MS, box 2, item 5.

80. Nordhoff, *Communistic Societies,* 192.

81. "Records of the Church at Watervliet, N.Y. Comprising the Principal Events Relative to the Said Church, in Connection with Other Families and Societies, since the Year 1788," n.d., MS, WRHSSC, V: B-29.

82. Rohrbough, *Trans-Appalachian Frontier,* 89.

83. Cooper, *Notions of the Americans,* 2:248.

84. Thomas Hunt, "Autobiographical Sketches," 1850, MS, LCSC, box 14, item 186, 25.

85. Eleazar Wright [Richard McNemar], *A Review of the Most Important Events Relating to the Rise and Progress of the United Society of Believers in the West* (Union Village, Ohio, 1831), 23.

86. Ibid., 22.

87. Ibid., 11.

88. Ibid., 22.

89. Ruth Farrington to Lucy Wright, 16 Aug. 1806, MS, Ohio State Historical Society Shaker Collection, box 1. Published in Humez, *Mother's First-born Daughters,* 146–150. Although I have consulted the manuscripts themselves, many of the letters from Shakers in the West quoted in this section can also be found in Humez's work, particularly in chapter 3, 133–208.

90. Cassandra Goodrich to Molly Goodrich, 8 Aug. 1812, MS, WRHSSC, IV: B-35.

91. Ham, "Shakerism in the Old West," 173.

92. In 1803–1804, Shaker missionaries, including some who would later become prominent in the Shaker move west, undertook itinerant missionary journeys in New York and New England. Stein, *The Shaker Experience,* 56.

93. "Records of the Church at Watervliet, N.Y. Comprising the Principal Events Relative to the Said Church, in Connection with Other Families and Societies, since the Year 1788," n.d., MS, WRHSSC, V: B-29.

94. Ibid.

95. Nicholas Summerbell, *A True History of the Christians and the Christian Church, A.M. 4004–A.D. 1870: Origin and Character of Popery; Origin of the Popes; Origin of the Temporal Power,* 3rd ed. (Cincinnati, Ohio: Office of the Christian Pulpit, 1873), 533.

96. Levi Purviance, *The Biography of Elder David Purviance, with His Memoirs, Containing His Views on Baptism, the Divinity of Christ, and the Atonement, Written by Himself* (Dayton, Ohio: Ellis, 1848), 237.

97. Letter signed by David Meacham, Amos Hammond, and Ebenezer Cooley, "In Behalf of the Church at New Lebanon, 30 December 1805, to a People in Kentucky and the Adjacent States." A copy of the letter is found in the "Daily Record of Events of the Church Family, Union Village, Ohio," MS, WRHSSC, V: B-230.

98. Stein discusses the feeling among some Shaker missionaries that they were being asked to hide their true beliefs concerning Lee, a move they felt exerted a deleterious influence on Shaker missionary work. See Stein, *The Shaker Experience,* 68.

99. Wright [McNemar], *Review of the Most Important Events,* 11.

100. Ibid., 4.

101. Stein, *The Shaker Experience,* 58–60.

102. Purviance, *Biography of Elder David Purviance*, 147–148, 199, 238.

103. Conkin, *Cane Ridge*, 126.

104. "Journal of Constant Mosely's Journeys with the Brethren and Sisters, 1808–1809," MS, LCSC, box 9, item 119.

105. Stein, *The Shaker Experience*, 58.

106. Ruth Farrington, Martha Sanford, Lucy Smith, Prudence Farrington, Molly Goodrich, and Ruth Darrow to the Elder Sisters of the First Family, New Lebanon, N.Y., 16 Aug. 1806, MS, WRHSSC, IV: A-66.

107. Rachel Johnson to Deborah and Susanna, 12 Sept. 1807, MS, WRHSSC, IV: A-67.

108. Molly Goodrich to Calvin Green, 22 Nov. 1818, MS, WRHSSC, IV: A-60.

109. Ruth Farrington to Rachel Spencer, New Lebanon Church Family, 21 Apr. 1819, MS, WRHSSC, IV: A-69.

110. Ruth Farrington to Rachel Spencer, 7 Dec. 1813, MS, LCSC, box 20, item 245.

111. Wright [McNemar], *Review of the Most Important Events*, 5, 13.

112. This version of the story was reported by a visitor to the Shakers named William Cargilll. Quoted in Glendyne R. Wergland, ed., *Visiting Shakers: Watervliet, Hancock, Tyringham, New Lebanon, 1778–1849* (Hamilton, N.Y.: Couper Press, Hamilton College Library), 128.

113. "Journal of Constant Mosely's Journeys with the Brethren and Sisters, 1808–1809," MS, LCSC, box 9, item 119.

114. Ibid.

2. Imagination and Reality in the Mormon Zion

1. Revelation received at Kirtland, Ohio, 18 Sept. 1831. Typescript of original manuscript in Marquart, *Joseph Smith Revelations*, 83–84.

2. Enoch is mentioned in Genesis 5 in the Hebrew Bible and three times in the New Testament, in Luke 3, Hebrews 11, and Jude 1. One historian of ancient Christianity noted that Enoch literature emphasizing the "renovation of Jerusalem and the coming judgment of the Son of Man" figured prominently in Jewish apocalyptic thought between 100 BCE and 100 CE. Fredriksen, *From Jesus to Christ*, 81–82.

3. The Enoch material produced by Smith is now found in Moses 7 in the Pearl of Great Price. Smith's work on Enoch was produced in late 1830, around the same time that he began recording revelations about the new city of Zion.

4. Smith was undoubtedly also influenced by the Zionic themes in the Hebrew Bible, especially material in Isaiah. As John H. Hayes argued, the author of Isaiah melded "pre-Israelite traditional thought concerning Zion as a holy place protected by the divine" with the belief that faith in Yahweh was a condition of "salvation and protection" and with the notion that God could destroy Zion as an act of punishment. Mormon notions of Zion in the period between 1830 and 1846 closely adhere to the pattern Hayes identified in the Hebrew Bible. Hayes, "The Tradition of Zion's Inviolability," 421, 425–426.

5. My use of the terms *mapping, building,* and *inhabiting* is drawn from Tweed, *Crossing and Dwelling*, 67–100.

6. For scholars who rely on the idea of Utah as ultimate boundary, see Arrington, *Great Basin Kingdom*; Hill, *Quest for Refuge*; and Erickson, *Thief in the Night*.

7. I have chosen not to discuss Mormon community building in Kirtland, Ohio, and that decision requires an explanation. The Mormons discovered Kirtland in the fall of 1830 on the way to the "West," where they hoped to meet and convert indigenous peoples. On the way, the Mormon missionaries met Sidney Rigdon, a disaffected Campbellite preacher, who enthusiastically embraced the new faith. Rigdon brought a good number of his congregants with him, and in December 1830 Smith received a revelation commanding the church to "assemble together at the Ohio." The next month, another revelation informed the Mormons that they must go to Ohio in order to "escape the power of the enemy, and be gathered unto me [God] a righteous people, without spot and blameless." Smith and his followers moved en masse to Kirtland beginning in early 1831. In Ohio, Smith received nearly one-third of all the revelations that make up the Doctrine and Covenants, built a temple, and practiced a limited and unsuccessful type of communal consecration. Smith fled Kirtland in 1838 after a series of scandals resulted in the apostasy of one-third of the church's general authorities. Kirtland is important in Mormon history, but it is less important in the history of Mormon physical boundaries. This is largely due to the fact that Kirtland was rapidly eclipsed by Missouri as the revealed location of the city of Zion. In 1830, Smith received a revelation that stated, "[N]o man knoweth where the city Zion shall be built, but it shall be given hereafter." The revelation did drop a hint, however: Zion would be in the "borders by the Lamanites," generally believed to be west of Ohio. Smith never believed that Kirtland was Zion, and it is the one place of Mormon settlement in the period between 1830 and 1847 that the Mormons did not intend to be either permanent or semi-permanent. In fact, a revelation received on 11 September 1831 specifically stated that Kirtland would be a "strong hold" for "five years." Although Smith spent most of his time in Kirtland between 1831 and 1838, Kirtland was never truly viewed as a physically separated community in the way that communities in Missouri and Illinois were. For these reasons and others that will be spelled out below, my discussion of Mormon physical boundary maintenance focuses on developments in Missouri and Illinois.

8. Revelation received at Fayette, N.Y., 5 Sept. 1830; typescript of original manuscript in Marquart, *Joseph Smith Revelations*, 83–84. In the original document, the word *Zion* is never mentioned. The reference is to "the city." In the 1835 edition of the Doctrine and Covenants, the term *Zion* is added.

9. Book of Mormon, introduction.

10. Book of Mormon, 3 Nephi 21:23.

11. Gunn, *Oliver Cowdery*, 77.

12. "A Revelation Received on 6 June 1831 for the Elders of the Church," MS, Newell K. Whitney Collection, Special Collections, BYU Archives; currently, section 52 of the Doctrine and Covenants.

13. Revelation received 20 July 1831, MS 4583, Kirtland Revelations Book, Revelations Collection, LDS Archives, box 1, folder 1, 89.

14. *Times and Seasons* 5:5 (1 Mar. 1844): 450.

15. Revelation received 8 Mar. 1833, MS, Newell K. Whitney Collection, LTPSC.

16. Revelation received 30–31 Aug. 1831, MS, Newell K. Whitney Collection, LTPSC.

17. Joseph Smith to N. E. Seaton, 4 Jan. 1833, MS 155, box 2, folder 1, Joseph Smith Collection, LDS Archives.

18. *Independent Messenger* (7 June 1832).

19. *Evening and Morning Star* 1:10 (Mar. 1833).

20. Westergren, *From Historian to Dissident,* 85–86.

21. Manuscript History of the Church, MS, CR 100 102, vol. 1, 139, LDS Archives.

22. The only significant study to address the issue of the sacred center in Mormon history is Olsen, *Mormon Ideology of Place.* As I argue below, I disagree with Olsen's reading of important sources regarding the uses of the sacred center imagery during the Nauvoo period.

23. Apostle Wilford Woodruff noted in his journal, "Jackson County is the garden of Eden Joseph has declaired [*sic*] this & I am as much bound to believe it as much as I am to believe Joseph is a prophet of God." Kenney, *Wilford Woodruff's Journal,* entry for 15 Mar. 1857, 5:33. Brigham Young claimed that Smith had taught him that "Jackson County was the place where the Garden of Eden was." Brigham Young's Office Journal, 2 Feb. 1861, LDS Archives, also on *New Mormon Studies* CD-ROM (Salt Lake City, Utah: Signature, 1998).

24. Arrington, *Great Basin Kingdom,* 7.

25. "Mormonism," *Western Monitor* (2 Aug. 1833). This newspaper and several others from the period have been scanned and preserved on the internet at http://www.sidneyrigdon.com/dbroadhu/MO/Misr1833.htm.

26. Manuscript History of the Church, MS, CR 100 102, vol. 8, 215, LDS Archives.

27. Allen and Leonard, *Story of the Latter-day Saints,* 95.

28. See Ahlstrom, *A Religious History,* 422–423, for a discussion of voluntary associations as a major legacy of the Second Great Awakening.

29. The date of the meeting was 25 July 1833. The meeting is mentioned in several places, including the diary of Mormon Newel Knight.

30. "To His Excellency, Daniel Dunklin, Governor of the State of Missouri." The note bears the date of 2 September 1833, although the letter was clearly written before 20 July because the writers threatened to meet to discuss "ulterior movements" on 20 July 1833. There is evidence that this letter was circulated among many Mormons shortly after it was written in early July. "Journal History of the Church," 2 Sept. 1833, CR 100 137, vol. 4, LDS Archives.

31. Allen and Leonard, *Story of the Latter-day Saints,* 95.

32. *Evening and Morning Star* 2:14 (July 1833).

33. Manuscript History of the Church, MS, CR 100 102, vol. 8, 204, LDS Archives.

34. Allen and Leonard, *Story of the Latter-day Saints,* 96–98.

35. Sidney Rigdon, F. G. Williams, and Joseph Smith Jr. to "Beloved Brethren" in Missouri, 6 Aug. 1833, MS 4583, Kirtland Revelations Book, Revelations Collection, box 1, folder 1, 62.

36. The new sketch of the city of Zion "Drawn by F. G. Williams" is housed in the LDS Archives. See Romig and Siebert, "Jackson County, 1831–1833," 286–304. Page 297 contains a photo of the revised plat of the city of Zion (Aug. 1833).

37. In the language of semiotics, the Mormons assigned an interpretant of annihilation to the violence they faced in late 1833.

38. Revelation received 7 Aug. 1831. Originally published in *Evening and Morning Star* (July 1833).

39. Letter from Joseph Smith to the "Exiled Saints in Missouri," 10 Dec. 1833, at Kirtland, Ohio, MS 4583, Kirtland Revelations Book, Revelations Collection, box 1, folder 1. Published in *Times and Seasons* 6 (15 June 1845): 928–929.

40. Joseph Smith to Lyman Wight, Edward Partridge, John Corrill, Isaac Morley, "and other of the High Council of Zion," 16 Aug. 1834, MS, LDS Archives, reprinted in Smith, *History of the Church*, 2:145.

41. In reality, the Mormons were basically neutral on the issue of slavery and, although they never condoned it during Smith's lifetime, they were pragmatic and flexible in the degree to which they backed abolitionism. Brigham Young continued this tradition of pragmatism when he legalized slavery in the Utah territory in 1852. See Mauss, *All Abraham's Children*, 214–215.

42. "Minutes of a Public Meeting at Liberty, Missouri," 29 June 1836, Manuscript History of the Church, MS, CR 100 102, vol. 9, 656, LDS Archives.

43. "Minutes of a Public Meeting of the Saints in Clay County, Missouri, Held to Consider the Proposition of the Citizens of Clay County That the Latter-day Saints Move into Another Part of the State," 1 July 1836, Manuscript History of the Church, MS, CR 100 102, vol. 9, 658, LDS Archives.

44. Joseph Smith, Sidney Rigdon, Oliver Cowdery, Frederick G. Williams, and Hyrum Smith to John Thornton, Peter Rogers, Andrew Robertson, James V. T. Thompson, Colonel William T. Wood, Doctor Woodson, I. Moss, James H. Hughes, David R. Atchison, and A. W. Doniphan, 25 July 1836, Manuscript History of the Church, MS, CR 100 102, vol. 9, 667, LDS Archives.

45. Revelation received 24 Feb. 1834, Kirtland, Ohio, MS 4583, Kirtland Revelations Book, Revelations Collection, box 1, folder 1.

46. Ibid.

47. Ibid.

48. Ibid.; and "Letter of the Presidency of the Church of Jesus Christ of Latter-day Saints to Elder Orson Hyde," 7 Apr. 1834, Manuscript History of the Church, MS, CR 100 102, vol. 8, 288, LDS Archives.

49. Revelation received 24 Feb. 1834, Kirtland, Ohio, MS 4583, Kirtland Revelations Book, Revelations Collection, box 1, folder 1.

50. "President Joseph Smith's Journal, Kept by Willard Richards," vol. 4, entry for 8 Apr. 1844, MS 155, box 1, folder 8, Joseph Smith Collection, LDS Archives.

51. "A Proclamation of the First Presidency of the Church to the Saints Scattered Abroad," 15 Jan. 1841, Manuscript History of the Church, MS, CR 100 102, vol. 10, 274, LDS Archives.

52. Originally published in the *Nauvoo Neighbor* (20 Dec. 1843). Republished in Gregg, *The Prophet of Palmyra*, 475; emphases in original.

53. Kenney, *Wilford Woodruff's Journal*, entry for 8 Apr. 1844, 2:388.

54. "President Joseph Smith's Journal, Kept by Willard Richards," vol. 4, entry for 8 Apr. 1844, MS 155, box 1, folder 8, Joseph Smith Collection, LDS Archives.

55. The first account comes from the speech as recorded by one of Smith's clerks, William Clayton, in his journal; the second comes from Wilford Woodruff's account of the same speech. See Cook and Ehat, *Words of Joseph Smith*, 363–364.

56. John Taylor, "Patriarchal," *Times and Seasons* 6:1 (1 June 1845): 921.

57. Smith, *History of the Church*, 6:318–319.

58. Kenney, *Wilford Woodruff's Journal*, entry for 8 Apr. 1844, 2:388.

59. The interpretation of the Nauvoo period as one that witnessed the complete decentralization of the Zionic ideal is as dominant as it is erroneous. From the earliest historical works on Mormonism to the present, this schema has been repeated. One example is found in Campbell, *Images of the New Jerusalem*. Campbell recognized that references to the city of Zion in Jackson County practically disappeared during the Nauvoo period, something that he attributed to the decentralization thesis. He was unable, however, to explain why the Jackson County rhetoric returned strongly during the Utah period. My theory accounts for both phenomena.

60. "A Proclamation of the First Presidency of the Church to the Saints Scattered Abroad," 15 Jan. 1841, Manuscript History of the Church, MS, CR 100 102, vol. 10, 273, LDS Archives.

61. Ibid.; emphasis mine.

62. Smith had planned to build a temple at least since October 1840, when he proposed that church members give one day out of every ten to construct a temple. See Leonard, *Nauvoo*, 235. The revelation of 19 January, while often seen as "commanding" the Mormons to build a temple, actually gave divine sanction to something that was already well under way. The proclamation of 15 January, for example, stated that the temple "is in the process of erection here."

63. Revelation received 19 Jan. 1841; first published in *Times and Seasons* 5:11 (June 1841).

64. Manuscript History of the Church, 2 Aug. 1831, MS, CR 100 102, vol. 1, 139, LDS Archives.

65. For an effort to downplay the powers granted by this charter, see Leonard, *Nauvoo*, 91–92.

66. Smith, *Intimate Chronicle*, entry for 30 June 1843, 109.

67. Kenney, *Wilford Woodruff's Journal*, entry for 30 June 1843, 2:250.

68. Ibid.

69. Ibid.

70. "Matters and Things at Nauvoo," *Warsaw Signal* (8 May 1844): 2.

71. Joseph Smith Journal, entry for 16 July 1843, MS 155, box 1, folder 7, LDS Archives.

72. William Law to the "Editors of the Upper Mississippian," *Rock Island Upper Mississippian* (1 Sept. 1844): 1; published in Hallwas and Launius, *Cultures in Conflict*, 164–165.

73. "President Joseph Smith's Journal, Kept by Willard Richards," vol. 4, entry for 7 May 1844, MS 155, box 1, folder 8, Joseph Smith Collection, LDS Archives.

74. "Matters and Things at Nauvoo," 2.

75. "President Joseph Smith's Journal, Kept by Willard Richards," vol. 4, entry for 7 June 1844, MS 155, box 1, folder 8, Joseph Smith Collection, LDS Archives.

76. Joseph Smith, "Proclamation," Nauvoo, Ill., 11 June 1844, published in the *Nauvoo Neighbor* (22 June 1844).

77. Smith, *Intimate Chronicle*, entry for 10 June 1844, 132.

78. "President Joseph Smith's Journal, Kept by Willard Richards," vol. 4, entry for 10 June 1844, MS 155, box 1, folder 8, Joseph Smith Collection, LDS Archives.

79. Knuth, "Systemic Book Burning as Evil?" 8.

80. Foster, "Tremendous Excitement—Unparalleled Outrage," 2; published in Hallwas and Launius, *Cultures in Conflict*, 157–159.

81. Willard Richards wrote his account of the event in his journal on 27 June 1844. Willard Richards Journal, Willard Richards Papers, MS 1490, box 1, vol. 10, LDS Archives.

82. For a more detailed account of the murders, see Bushman, *Rough Stone Rolling*, 544–550.

83. Taylor, *Last Pioneer*, 93. More recently, scholars have called into question the bullet and watch story, suggesting that the watch may have been broken as Taylor fell to the floor. Letter from Professor David J. Whittaker to the author, 25 Nov. 2006. Taylor survived his wounds and eventually became the third president of the LDS Church.

84. Willard Richards Journal, Willard Richards Papers, MS 1490, box 1, vol. 10, LDS Archives.

85. Roberts, *Life of John Taylor*, 144–145.

86. Amasa Lyman Journal, entries for 3–6 July 1844, Amasa Lyman Collection, MS 829, box 1, vol. 6, LDS Archives.

87. Charles C. Rich Journal, entries for 6–11 July 1844, MS 1215, box 1, vol. 1, Charles C. Rich Collection, LDS Archives.

88. George A. Smith, "Memoirs of George A. Smith," MS 1322, box 1, folder 2, 252–253, LDS Archives. Smith's memoir is a handwritten document in journal style. The quotes in the text come from Smith's entries for 13 and 14 July 1844.

89. Vilate Kimball to Heber C. Kimball, 30 June 1844, MS, Kimball Family Collection, LDS Archives; published in Ronald K. Esplin, ed., "Life in Nauvoo, June 1844: Vilate Kimball's Martyrdom Letters," *BYU Studies* 19:2 (Winter 1979): 240.

90. Wilford Woodruff, untitled article, *Deseret Weekly*, 14 Nov. 1891, 658–659.

91. "A Series of Instructions and Remarks by President Brigham Young, at a Special Council," 21 Mar. 1858, published in Eugene E. Campbell, ed., *The Essential Brigham Young* (Salt Lake City, Utah: Signature, 1992), 113.

92. Brigham Young to Wilford Woodruff, 11 Feb. 1845; published in Clark, *Messages*, 1:250.

93. "The Nauvoo Diary of Zina Diantha Huntington Jacobs," MS, LDS Archives; published in *BYU Studies* 19:3 (Spring 1979): 311.

94. Brigham Young to Parley P. Pratt, 26 May 1845, Brigham Young Letterpress Copybooks, MS, CR 1234, box 1, LDS Archives.

95. Brigham Young to Wilford Woodruff, 27 June 1845; published in Clark, *Messages*, 1:272.

96. At this point, three important groups functioned at the highest echelons of church leadership. Whitney and Miller are probably referring to the Quorum of the Twelve, the Anointed Quorum, and the Council of Fifty. Newell K. Whitney and George D. Miller to Parley P. Pratt, 22 July 1845, Brigham Young Letterpress Copybooks, MS, CR 1234, box 1, LDS Archives.

97. Ibid.

98. Allen and Leonard, *Story of the Latter-day Saints*, 230.

99. "John Taylor to Several Governors," 14 Mar. 1845, MS, LDS Archives; reproduced in Hallwas and Launius, *Cultures in Conflict*, 268–270.

100. Charles C. Rich Journal, 11 Sept. 1845, MS 889, box 1, vol. 7, LDS Archives.

101. Solomon Hancock to "Dear Brother," 13 Sept. 1845, in Jessee, *John Taylor's Nauvoo Journal*, 90.

102. Charles C. Rich Journal, 13 Sept. 1845, MS 889, box 1, vol. 7, LDS Archives.

103. Brigham Young to Solomon Hancock, 12 Sept. 1845, "Journal History of the Church," CR 100 137, vol. 19, LDS Archives.

104. Jessee, *John Taylor's Nauvoo Journal*, entry for 14 Sept. 1845, 89.

105. "Journal History of the Church," 14 Sept. 1845, CR 100 137, vol. 19, LDS Archives.

106. Brigham Young to Levi Williams, in Smith, *Intimate Chronicle*, entry for 16 Sept. 1845, 183.

107. A. B. Chambers to Brigham Young, 18 Sept. 1845, "Journal History of the Church," CR 100 137, vol. 19, LDS Archives. Chambers was sincerely attempting to broker a peace deal, and he had been sent to Nauvoo to tell the Mormons of the objections that the "anti-Mormons" had to the language in the proclamation. Chambers and those he represented undercut their denials of involvement with the violence, however, by promising that, if the offensive language was excised from the proclamation's preamble, they would ensure that the violence against the Mormons would cease.

108. Robert Bruce Flanders, *Nauvoo: Kingdom on the Mississippi* (Urbana: University of Illinois Press, 1965), 330.

109. Consider, for example, the case of the Branch Davidians led by David Koresh. During the siege of their Waco, Texas, compound in the spring of 1993, the Davidians refused to surrender to the FBI, a scenario that matched Koresh's teachings about the end times. For a detailed discussion, see Tabor, "Religious Discourse and Failed Negotiations," 263–281.

110. Brigham Young to the Quincy Committee, 24 Sept. 1845; published in Josiah B. Conyers, *A Brief History of the Leading Causes of the Hancock Mob in the Year 1846* (St. Louis, Mo.: n.p., 1846), 17. The visit to the Carthage jail is mentioned in Heber C. Kimball's journal. According to Kimball, a group of apostles traveled to Carthage and then met at John Taylor's home to draft the statement to the committee, which they finished at about 1 AM. Stanley B. Kimball, *On the Potter's Wheel*, diary 2, part 3, 136.

111. Minutes of the Meeting of the Quincy Committee at Carthage, Illinois, 1–2 Oct. 1846; published in Conyers, *A Brief History,* 19.

112. Brooks, *On the Mormon Frontier,* 1:73, 26 Sept. 1845. Young made good on his promise not to return; after 1848, he never left the Great Basin and died in Salt Lake City in 1877.

113. Amasa Lyman, Sermon, Church Historians Office, General Church Minutes, CR 100 318, box 1, folder 39, 1, LDS Archives.

114. Heber C. Kimball, Sermon, 7 Oct. 1845, Nauvoo, Ill., Church Historians Office, General Church Minutes, CR 100 318, box 1, folder 39, LDS Archives.

115. Parley P. Pratt, Sermon, 7 Oct. 1845, Nauvoo, Ill., Church Historians Office, General Church Minutes, CR 100 318, box 1, folder 39, LDS Archives

116. LDS Church Circular, *Times and Seasons* 6:16 (1 Nov. 1845): 1017.

117. Erastus Snow Journal, MS 1329, box 1, 3:58, LDS Archives. Snow did not internally date his journals, but they are written in a memoir style within certain date ranges. The material quoted above comes from his journal labeled April 1845–May 1846. Snow was a member of the second Quorum of Seventy from 1836 until his call as an apostle in 1849.

118. Kenney, *Wilford Woodruff's Journal*, entry for 1 Nov. 1845, 2:610.

119. Ibid.

120. On this point, I am indebted to the work of two theoreticians, Daniele Hervieu-Leger and Bruce Lincoln, who, in strikingly divergent ways, artfully explore the tendency of religious communities to recast collective memory in the face of communal trauma. See, for example, Hervieu-Leger, *Religion as a Chain of Memory*, 87; and Bruce Lincoln, *Discourse and the Construction of Society: Comparative Studies of Myth, Ritual, and Classification* (New York: Oxford University Press, 1989), 27–37.

121. Thomas Bullock Minutes, LDS Archives, 8 Apr. 1846; quoted in Esplin, "A Place Prepared," 93.

122. Church Historian's Office Journal, CR 1001, 2 Dec. 1847, LDS Archives.

123. Sermon delivered in Salt Lake Valley by Orson Pratt, 1 Aug. 1847, in Smith, *Intimate Chronicle*, 373–374.

124. Thomas Bullock Minutes, LDS Archives, 24 Sept. 1848; quoted in Esplin, "A Place Prepared," 85.

125. Jonathan Duke Oldham Autobiography, 1:10, Vault MS 227, LTPSC.

126. "A Series of Instructions and Remarks by President Brigham Young, at a Special Council," 21 Mar. 1858; published in Campbell, *Essential Brigham Young*, 112.

127. Smith dictated his official history, which was copied by hand by scribes; after Smith approved, the history was preserved. When Smith died, however, he had not yet finished dictating the history, so later editors took manifold liberties in their work. His version, along with the journals and writings of Smith's contemporaries, was used to produce the seven-volume *History of the Church* after Smith's death. The published version of that history contains the following passage, which has been used by many to justify their claims of Smith's knowledge of the Mormons' eventual destination in the West: "I prophesied that the Saints would continue to suffer much affliction and would be driven to the Rocky Mountains. Some of you will live to go and assist in making settlements and build cities and see the Saints become a mighty people in the midst of the Rocky Mountains." Smith, *History of the Church*, 5:85. The published version says nothing about the irregularities of the manuscript. An examination of the original manuscript, however, reveals that the entire passage relating to the Rocky Mountains was added, in a different hand, to the interlinear space of the entry for 6 August 1842. Manuscript History of the Church, MS, CR 100 102, vol. 10, 473, LDS Archives. As Davis Bitton and others have argued, it is extremely likely that the prophecy found its way into the manuscript history after the move to Utah. Bitton, "Joseph Smith in Mormon Folk Memory." For an interesting discussion of the impact of similar manipulations of manuscripts in religious communities in antiquity, see Ehrman, *Orthodox Corruption of Scripture*.

128. This story has been circulating in various versions for years and has been published frequently. The original is in the Oliver B. Huntington Journal, 27 Sept. 1897, typescript, LTPSC. It was reprinted in McConkie, *Remembering Joseph*, 138–139; and also cited in Christian, "Mormon Foreknowledge of the West," 405–406.

129. McConkie, *Remembering Joseph*, 189.

130. Published ibid., 150–151.

131. Wilford Woodruff, Conference Report, 1898, 57; published in McConkie, *Remembering Joseph*, 167–168.

132. The sheer number of these historically dubious accounts has led many scholars to conclude that Joseph Smith did, in fact, have detailed and specific foreknowledge of the Mormons' move to the Salt Lake Valley as early as 1831. Typically, these scholars reproduce the accounts cited above, along with many others like them, without paying due attention to the paucity of contemporary accounts. See, for example, Esplin, "A Place Prepared." Lewis Clark Christian, in his unpublished M.A. thesis, his Ph.D. dissertation, and his 1981 *BYU Studies* article, also argued that Mormon foreknowledge of the western migration was early and specific. To make his case, Christian uses many of the documents that I have cited here, none of which were produced in the pre-Utah period. Christian, "A Study of Mormon Knowledge," esp. 53–59; Christian, "Mormon Foreknowledge of the West," 403–415.

133. Kenney, *Wilford Woodruff's Journal*, entry for 27 Apr. 1834, 1:9.

134. Levi Jackman Journal, 29 Mar. 1847, Vault MS 79, LTPSC; also available in digitized form through the Brigham Young University digital texts database.

135. Wilford Woodruff records Joseph Smith as calling for "an exploring expedition to California" in February 1844. The group met and "confirmed" the decision to send an expedition to California. Kenney, *Wilford Woodruff's Journal*, entries for 21 and 24 Feb. 1844, 2:351. Joseph Smith's journal differs on the destination and records that the expedition was to head for Oregon. "President Joseph Smith's Journal, Kept by Willard Richards," vol. 4, entry for 23 Feb. 1844, MS 155, box 1, folder 8, Joseph Smith Collection, LDS Archives. Earlier that month, Smith had received word from a group of Mormons who had been sent to Texas that the region was suitable for a "place of gathering for all of the South." Lyman Wight and George Miller to the First Presidency, 15 Feb. 1844; published in Smith, *History of the Church*, 6:255–257.

136. Heber C. Kimball to Parley P. Pratt, 17 June 1842; quoted in Buerger, *Mysteries of Godliness*, 46. Buerger offered a detailed comparison of Nauvoo era temple rituals and contemporary Masonic ceremonies. Other works dealing with this topic include Homer, "Similarity of Priesthood in Masonry"; Forsberg, *Equal Rites*; and Brooke, *Refiner's Fire*.

137. Manuscript History of the Church, MS, CR 100 102, vol. 10, 473, LDS Archives.

138. Brigham Young, as quoted in L. John Nuttall Journal, 7 Feb. 1877, typescript, LTPSC.

139. Anderson and Bergera, *Joseph Smith's Quorum*, xxxiii. Beginning in 1843, Smith admitted women into the quorum, contingent upon their acceptance of the doctrine of plural marriage.

140. These accounts come from the Manuscript History of the Church and Manuscript History of Brigham Young. Both accounts are published in Anderson and Bergera, *Joseph Smith's Quorum*, 39–40.

141. Smith, *Intimate Chronicle*, entry for 22 Jan. 1844, 125.

142. Manuscript History of the Church, MS, CR 100 102, vol. 10, 473, LDS Archives.

143. Anderson and Bergera, *Nauvoo Endowment Companies*, xxvii.

144. See Bathsheba W. Smith's various affidavits given in the 1892 Temple Lot Case, published in Anderson and Bergera, *Joseph Smith's Quorum*, 45–47. Today,

the endowment is presented as a motion picture in every temple in the world except for those at Salt Lake City and Manti, Utah, where live casts are employed.

145. Smith, *Intimate Chronicle*, entry for 12 Dec. 1845, 209.

146. George A. Smith, "Memoirs of George A. Smith," MS 1322, box 1, folder 2, 337, LDS Archives.

147. Bushman, *Rough Stone Rolling*, 451.

148. Alexander, "A New and Everlasting Covenant," 57.

149. Shipps, *Mormonism*, 129; Flake, "Not to be Riten," 12.

150. Smith, *Intimate Chronicle*, entry for 2 Jan. 1846, 251.

151. Some may argue that Smith's plan for the city of Zion in Jackson County, which called for a complex of twenty-four temples, indicates that Smith advocated the idea of multiple temples as early as 1833. Although the temple complex in Jackson County was to house multiple temples, the fact remains that they all remained focused on one geographic point and did not represent a diffusion of temples throughout space.

152. Brigham Young, untitled discourse, 2 Mar. 1862, *Journal of Discourses*, 9:239.

153. Evelyn T. Marshall, "Garments," in *Encyclopedia of Mormonism*, ed. Daniel H. Ludlow (New York: Macmillan, 1992), 2:534. Technically, these marks are what make the garments sacred. From the time of Joseph Smith until the present, endowed persons have been required to cut the marks from the fabric and destroy them before disposing of the garments. Once this has been accomplished, the garments are no longer considered sacred.

154. See Genesis 3:21.

155. Once endowed, Mormons must periodically renew their certifications, or "recommends," to enter the temple. To do this, they must answer a series of questions about their beliefs and behavior, one of which is "Do you wear the authorized garments as underclothing night and day?"

156. Smith, *Intimate Chronicle*, entry for 21 Dec. 1845, 221.

157. At the same meeting, Heber C. Kimball told the assembled group that although "Joseph and Hyrum and Elder Taylor were shot to pieces," Richards, "having on his robe," was protected from harm. Ibid., 223.

158. Brigham Young, "The Wilderness Was Kinder to Us than Man," *New York Herald* (Sept. 1877); republished in Campbell, *Essential Brigham Young*, 239–240.

159. "Journal History of the Church," 18 July 1846, CR 100 137, vol. 20, LDS Archives.

160. Joseph F. Smith, "Testimony," *Improvement Era* 9:10 (Aug. 1906): 813. Also quoted in Carlos E. Asay, "The Temple Garment: An Outward Expression of an Inward Commitment," *Ensign* (Aug. 1997): 20.

161. William H. Smart, Diary no. 24, William H. Smart Papers, box 4, folder 7, entry for 5 June 1912, MS, University of Utah, Marriott Library Special Collections. For Smart's biography, see Smart, *Mormonism's Last Colonizer*.

162. William H. Smart, Diary no. 24, William H. Smart Papers, box 4, folder 7, entry for 1 Sept. 1924, MS, University of Utah, Marriott Library Special Collections.

163. Charles W. Penrose, sermon delivered 29 Nov. 1879, published in *Journal of Discourses*, 21:49–50.

164. L. John Nuttall to Gregory Teasdale, 15 Nov. 1879, L. John Nuttall Letterbooks, book 1, letter 32, LTPSC.

165. Brigham Young, untitled discourse, 16 Jan. 1853, *Journal of Discourses,* 1:3.
166. Ibid.; emphasis added.
167. Brigham Young, untitled discourse, 23 Oct. 1853, *Journal of Discourses,* 2:5.
168. Cannon and Cook, *Far West Record,* 14.
169. Catherine L. Albanese, *America: Religions and Religion,* 4th ed. (Belmont, Calif.: Wadsworth Thomson, 2007), 158. This use of the idea of Zion is graphically illustrated in a drawing produced circa 1900 which showed "Deseret" and "The Promised Land" of "Canaan" from the Hebrew Bible side by side. This drawing is published on the same page in Albanese as the quote cited above.
170. Hamilton, *Nineteenth-Century Mormon Architecture,* 43.
171. For an architectural history of these temples, see Andrew, *Early Temples of the Mormons.*

3. Godly Marriage and Divine Androgyny

1. In 2006, the LDS Church issued a statement objecting to the portrayal of polygamists as Mormons in the popular HBO television series *Big Love.* According to the press release:

> The central characters of *Big Love* are not "Mormons," or, more properly termed, Latter-day Saints. HBO has said the script makes it clear that members of The Church of Jesus Christ of Latter-day Saints do not practice polygamy. Still, placing the series in Salt Lake City, the international headquarters of The Church of Jesus Christ of Latter-day Saints, is enough to blur the line between the modern Church and the program's subject matter and to reinforce old and long-outdated stereotypes. (http://www.lds.org/newsroom/mistakes/0,15331,3885-1-22339,00.html)

2. D'Andrade, "Schemas and Motivations," 31. The suitability of applying this theoretical approach to the problem of sexuality and religion was first brought to my attention in de Munck, "Cultural Schemas of Celibacy," 214–228.
3. Green and Wells, *Summary View,* 99.
4. Dahl and Cannon, *The Teachings of Joseph Smith,* 232.
5. See, for example, Joseph Smith's revelation on plural marriage, now section 132 of the Doctrine and Covenants, which states that those who faithfully live the law of plural marriage "shall be gods, because they have all power, and the angels are subject unto them." Doctrine and Covenants 132:20. While post-1890 Mormon exegesis has interpreted this passage to refer to monogamous marriages in Mormon temples, it is clear that the revelation originally was interpreted as referring to plural marriage. See Taysom, "A Uniform and Common Recollection."
6. Smith made these statements at a meeting of the apostles on 5 January 1841, and they were recorded by William Clayton and published in Smith, *Intimate Chronicle,* appendix A, 516.
7. Sometimes, very different master-motive schemas result in identical performances, in which two systems seem to be deceptively, and superficially, similar. In the early Christian world, for example, communities based on the teachings of Tatian and Marcion both practiced celibacy, but "the meaning of this [practice] was not the same for each group." For a full discussion, see Brown, *The Body and Society,* 88.

8. I should emphasize at this point that neither the Shakers nor the Mormons viewed celibacy or polygamy as functioning chiefly as boundary markers or as signs to the broader culture. I am arguing, however, that these practices did serve, among other functions, as boundary markers. My discussion of signs and counter-signs is informed by semiotic theory, particularly the work of Morris, *Writings on the General Theory of Signs*.

9. The close tie between the standard of monogamy and the health of America as viewed in the nineteenth century is explored at length in Cott, *Public Vows*.

10. Whittaker, "The Bone in the Throat," 294. Whittaker's article is valuable for its detailed discussion of the basis and parameters of formal Mormon defenses of plural marriage. Whittaker identifies three major categories used by the Mormons to defend plural marriage systematically: scriptural, historical/social, and constitutional. In order to carry out these defenses, the Mormons established several periodicals edited by Mormon apostles throughout the United States that were dedicated primarily to the defense of polygamy. These periodicals were the *St. Louis Observer*, edited by Erastus Snow and Orson Spencer; the *Mormon* (New York City) edited by John Taylor; the *Seer* (Washington, D.C.), edited by Orson Pratt; and the *Western Standard* (San Francisco), edited by George Q. Cannon.

11. Smith, *Imagining Religion*, 63.

12. Bell, *Ritual*, 115.

13. Green and Wells, *Summary View*, 141.

14. Muir, *Ritual in Early Modern Europe*, 6.

15. Gold, "Celibacy," 1:144.

16. Ibid., 145.

17. See, for example, the work of Stephen A. Marini, who presented material from the testimonies without qualification as having come from Ann Lee. Marini did not cite the published book, *Testimonies*, but rather depended for his quotations upon a methodologically weak biography of Ann Lee published in 1976 (Nardi Reeder Campion, *Ann the Word: The Life of Ann Lee, Mother of the Shakers* [Boston: Little, Brown, 1976]). See Marini, *Radical Sects*, 76–77, 185n35. Richard D. Francis's *Ann the Word* is presented as history but might as well be fiction, given the author's stated reliance on Youngs et al., *Testimonies*, which he acknowledges as "the most important source" for his biography of Lee. Francis, *Ann the Word*, xii.

18. Youngs, Bishop, and Wells, *Testimonies*, 38–39.

19. Stein, *The Shaker Experience*, 78.

20. Rathbun, *Some Brief Hints*, 6. Rathbun was sufficiently impressed by his experience that he joined the Shakers, but he soon left the sect and published his account as a former member. While apostate writings must be carefully scrutinized, Rathbun's work serves a very limited purpose here—as a simple witness to the early Shaker ideas about celibacy. For an account of Rathbun's dealings with the Shakers, see Stein, *The Shaker Experience*, 15–18.

21. "Testimony of Thomas Stebbins," 18 Dec. 1843, LCSC, MS, box 1, item 2.

22. Meacham, *A Concise Statement*, 9–10.

23. Green and Wells, *Summary View*, 169.

24. Ibid., 152; emphases in original.

25. Calvin Green, "A Virgin Life, Composed and Written by Calvin Green," n.d., MS, WRHSSC, VII: A-7. In an 1830 address, Green pointed out that persons

who had engaged in sexual intercourse before taking up the Shaker cross of celibacy became "virgins in the spirit" upon joining the Shaker order. Calvin Green, "Atheism, Deism, Universalism, and Fatalism Refuted: A Discourse Delivered in the Meeting House of the United Society at Harvard, Massachusetts, September 19, 1830," MS, WRHSSC, VII: B-255.

26. Green did not provide a reference to a specific scriptural text, but the language he used is found in Mark 12:25 and Matthew 22:30.

27. "The Church of Christ—Today and in the Future," 17.

28. Bowers, *Concise Statements*, 5.

29. John Lyon, "A Brief Exposition of the Great Mystery of What Is Commonly Called Shakerism, Showing the Propriety of a Life of Celibacy or Continence as Believed and Practiced by Every True Shaker," 1854, MS, WRHSSC, VII: B-9, 22.

30. Ibid., 23.

31. Ibid., 33.

32. Giles B. Avery, "Divine Judgments: Law to the Children of the New Creation of God in Every Branch of Zion on the Earth, 1859," MS, WRHSSC, VII: A-5.

33. Oliver C. Hampton, "Right Feelings," 1866, hymn, LCSC, MS, box 13, item 183.

34. Oliver C. Hampton, untitled hymn, 1866, LCSC, MS, box 13, item 183.

35. "Mother Lucy's Sayings, Spoken at Different Times and under Various Circumstances," n.d., LCSC, MS, box 6, item 88; emphasis in original.

36. Harvey L. Eads, "Questions, Answers, and Problems Concerning Shakerism," 1873, MS, WRHSSC, VII: A-18; emphasis in original.

37. Alonzo G. Hollister, "Marriage, Shakers, and the End of the World," 1879, MS, WRHSSC, VII: A-9.

38. "Fifteen Years a Shakeress," *Galaxy: An Illustrated Magazine of Entertaining Reading* 13:1 (Jan. 1872): 33.

39. Henry R. Bears, "Split Zephyr," *Century: A Popular Quarterly* 26:2 (June 1883): 276.

40. "Mysticism," *New Englander and Yale Review* 5:19 (July 1847): 355.

41. Nicholas Summerbell, *A True History of the Christians and the Christian Church, A.M. 4004–A.D. 1870: Origin and Character of Popery; Origin of the Popes; Origin of the Temporal Power,* 3rd ed. (Cincinnati, Ohio: Office of the Christian Pulpit, 1873), 533.

42. "Narrative of Four Months' Residence among Shakers at Watervliet," typescript, E. D. Andrews Collection, Winterthur Library; reprinted in Glendyne R. Wergland, ed., *Visiting Shakers: Watervliet, Hancock, Tyringham, New Lebanon, 1778–1849* (Hamilton, N.Y.: Couper Press, Hamilton College Library), 94.

43. "On Somnambulism," *Living Age* 63:801 (10 Oct. 1859): 3.

44. W. L. Stone, "Matthias and His Impostures," *North American Review* 41:89 (Oct. 1835): 325. For a scholarly discussion of Matthias's prophetic career, see Wilentz and Johnson, *Kingdom of Matthias.*

45. Elizabeth A. DeWolfe has gone so far as to argue that the "belief that Shakers would cause their own extinction [through celibacy] had lessened public fear of the sect." This was certainly true for some Americans, but on the whole the reaction was significantly more complex. DeWolfe, *Shaking the Faith,* 163.

46. Charles W. Shields, "The Social Problem of Church Unity," *Century: A Popular Quarterly* 40:5 (Sept. 1890): 688.

47. "Shakers," *Niles' Weekly Register* (19 Sept. 1829): 17.

48. O. A. Bierstadt, "Sister Agnes: A Story of Shakers," *New England Magazine* 5:26 (Dec. 1886): all quotes from 181.

49. "Editor's Easy Chair," *Harper's New Monthly Magazine* 20:19 (Apr. 1860): 701.

50. "Shakerism," *Scribner's Monthly: An Illustrated Magazine for the People* 3:3 (Jan. 1872): 359.

51. "Marriage as a Test," *Scribner's Monthly: An Illustrated Magazine for the People* 18:4 (Aug. 1879): 620.

52. Ibid., 621.

53. Ibid., 620.

54. Ibid., 621.

55. "Romanists and the Roman Catholic Controversy," *New Englander and Yale Review* 2:6 (Apr. 1844): 246.

56. Carl Benson [Charles Astor Bristed], "The Things of the Day," *Galaxy: An Illustrated Magazine of Entertaining Reading* 9:6 (June 1870): 842.

57. "Egyptian Dervishes," *Littell's Living Age* 155 (16 Dec. 1882): 670.

58. "Communism in America," *Scribner's Monthly: An Illustrated Magazine for the People* 9:6 (Apr. 1875): 769.

59. Ibid., 770.

60. "French Republicanism and American Democracy," *United States Democratic Review* 34:3 (Sept. 1854): 276.

61. Minot J. Savage, "The Inevitable Surrender of Orthodoxy," *North American Review* 148:391 (June 1889): 721.

62. "To Our Friends of the Household of Faith," 1848, Mount Lebanon, N.Y., MS, WRHSSC, VII: B-100.

63. "Testimony of Mary S. Russell, Enfield, Connecticut," 13 Dec. 1843, LCSC, MS, box 1, item 2.

64. Ibid.

65. Several members of the North Family at Enfield, Connecticut, wrote testimonies in December 1843, but only that of Richard A. Willcox discloses the fact that the family's leaders had requested and approved the documents. "Testimony of Richard A. Willcox, Enfield, Connecticut," 22 Dec. 1843, LCSC, MS, box 1, item 2.

66. Samuel Rollins to "Beloved Elders," 26 Apr. 1812, LCSC, MS, box 35, item 351b.

67. Flood, *The Ascetic Self,* 6. Flood here employed the term *interpretant,* which is a technical term from semiotics. It simply means the sense made of the sign by the interpreter.

68. Ibid., 222.

69. Ibid., 225.

70. "Some of the Words of Daniel Goodrich That He Spake on September 23rd 1792," LCSC, MS, box 14, item 185.

71. Lyon, "A Brief Exposition of the Great Mystery," 1854, MS, WRHSSC, VII: B-9, 33.

72. Ibid., 35.

73. "Discourses on the Gospel by Calvin Green, Copied by John Wood, 1833," LCSC, MS, box 5, item 75.

74. Samuel Rollins to "Beloved Elders," 26 Apr. 1812, LCSC, MS, box 35, item 351b.

75. Brown, *The Body and Society*, 77.

76. Girard, *Violence and the Sacred*, 13.

77. Bainbridge, "Decline of the Shakers," 22; Stein, *The Shaker Experience*, 243, table 4.

78. In 1850, for example, the infant mortality rate in the United States was 216.8 per 1,000 births per annum. To place this number in context, by 1900 it had been cut by more than 50 percent, to 100.8, and in 1990 the rate stood at 7.6 percent. Haines and Steckel, *A Population History of North America*, 308.

79. Giles B. Avery, "Shakers," n.d. (the context suggests the 1870s), MS, WRHSSC, VII: A-5, 4.

80. Stein, *The Shaker Experience*, 160.

81. For a formal argument supporting this observation, see Berger, *Sacred Canopy*, 45.

82. By 1870, most Shaker villages had a composition of about two-thirds women and one-third men. Thurman, *"O Sisters Ain't You Happy?"* 28–29.

83. Stein, *The Shaker Experience*, 182.

84. Stewart, *A Holy, Sacred, and Divine Roll and Book*, 127. As Paul C. Gutjahr pointed out, with the exception of one major scholarly article, this document has "gone almost entirely unstudied." This is especially striking when it is compared to the Book of Mormon, a document with many similarities to Stewart's *Holy, Sacred, and Divine Roll and Book*, which has garnered much more attention. Gutjahr, "The State of the Discipline," 375. The exception to this is Stephen J. Stein, "Inspiration, Revelation, and Scripture: The Story of a Shaker Bible," *Proceedings of the American Antiquarian Society* 105:2 (1996): 347–376.

85. Unless otherwise noted, all quotes come from Seth Y. Wells to Rufus Bishop, 7 Oct. 1843, LCSC, MS, box 1, item 14.

86. Richard Bushnell, "Considerations Relative to Certain Sentiments in the Sacred Roll," 1844, MS, WRHSSC, VII: B-64.

87. John Lyon, "An Answer, by Way of Investigation, to the Foregoing Suggestions," 1844, MS, WRHSSC, VII: B-64. By 1854, Lyon had reversed his position on this issue as evidenced by his essay "A Brief Exposition of the Great Mystery," WRHSSC, VII: B-9.

88. For a history of the earliest plural marriages, see Compton, *In Sacred Loneliness*. Historian Danel W. Bachman has argued that polygamy developed in three distinct phases, beginning with Smith's revisions of the Old Testament in 1831, continuing with the dedication of the Kirtland temple in 1835–1836, and culminating in the commitment of the principle to writing in the summer of 1843. Bachman, "A Study of the Mormon Practice of Plural Marriage before the Death of Joseph Smith," unpublished master's thesis, Purdue University, 1975.

89. Revelation received 12 July 1843; published currently as Doctrine and Covenants 132.

90. Smith, *Intimate Chronicle*, entry for 12 July 1843, 110.

91. The work of sociologist Kimball Young suggests that one major and recurring theme in non-Mormon portrayals of polygamy during this period was the supposedly frequent "early deaths" of polygamous wives due to the "combination of heavy childbearing and undue physical labor." Young, *Isn't One Wife Enough?* 19.

92. Frederick Loba, "Utah and the Mormons," *New York Times* 7:2069 (7 May 1858): 8.

93. George Q. Cannon, "The Improvement of Our Species," *Western Standard*, 7 Aug. 1857, 2. The link between monogamy and prostitution of which the Mormons frequently spoke was raised elsewhere. German philosopher Arthur Schopenhauer argued that "polygamy provides for all women, while monogamy leaves many women without husbands and creates the hypocritical proliferation of prostitutes." His view is summarized in Ruether, *Goddesses and the Divine Feminine*, 254.

94. Cannon, "Improvement of Our Species," 2.

95. Joseph F. Smith, untitled sermon, 29 Oct. 1882, *Journal of Discourses*, 24:8.

96. Kirk H. Porter, ed., *National Party Platforms* (New York: Macmillan, 1924), 48.

97. Rudger Clawson to Lydia Clawson, 24 July 1885, published in *Prisoner for Polygamy: The Memoirs and Letters of Rudger Clawson at the Utah Territorial Penitentiary, 1884–1887*, ed. Stan Larson (Urbana: University of Illinois Press, 1993), 172.

98. Kenney, *Wilford Woodruff's Journal*, entry for 9 Oct. 1875, 7:251.

99. Ibid., entry for 27 Nov. 1882, 8:133–144.

100. Brigham Young, Manuscript History of Brigham Young, 14 Mar. 1863, Church Historian's Office, CR 100, vol. 33, LDS Archives.

101. *Journal of Discourses*, 20:24.

102. *Journal of Discourses*, 11:268–269.

103. John Taylor and George Q. Cannon, "An Epistle from the First Presidency to the Officers and Members of the Church of Jesus Christ of Latter-day Saints," 6 Oct. 1885, published in *Woman's Exponent* 14 (15 Oct. 1885): 67; Clark, *Messages*, 3:23–41.

104. Daynes, *More Wives than One*, 72–73.

105. A major exception to this general rule is, of course, Shaker celibacy, which was an absolute requirement for membership in Shaker communities.

106. Horace Greeley, "Overland Journey. XXI. Two Hours with Brigham Young," *New York Daily Tribune*, 20 Aug. 1859, published in *Doing the Works of Abraham: Mormon Polygamy, Its Origin, Practice, and Demise*, ed. B. Carmon Hardy (Norman, Okla.: Clark, 2007), 192.

107. Ivins, "Notes on Mormon Polygamy," 231. Richard S. Van Wagoner synthesized all of the relevant demographic studies of Utah towns in his history of Mormon polygamy, paying special attention to a survey of polygamous marriages in 1880. His findings: "Almost 40 percent of St. George households were polygamous compared to 11 percent in nearby Harrisburg/Leeds. In Rockville only 10 percent was polygamous, while 67 percent of Orderville was. In South Weber, north of Salt Lake City, 5 percent practiced polygamy, compared to nearly 30 percent in Bountiful." Van Wagoner, *Mormon Polygamy*, 91.

108. Franklin D. Richards Journal, MS 1215, box 3, vol. 30, 14 Oct. 1882, LDS Archives.

109. LDS Church genealogy records indicate that Seymour Young married his first wife, Ann Elizabeth Riter, in 1867 and took his first plural wife, Abby C. Wells, on 28 April 1884. LDS Family History Library, Salt Lake City, Utah, Ancestral File nos. 2133–2172.

110. Remarks of John Taylor, recorded by Wilford Woodruff. Kenney, *Wilford Woodruff's Journal*, entry for 13 Nov. 1882, 8:126.

111. Kenney, *Wilford Woodruff's Journal*, entry for 26 Jan.. 1880, 7:617.:

112. Franklin D. Richards Journal, MS 1215, box 4, vol. 37, 28 Nov. 1889, LDS Archives.

113. For an excellent and detailed study of the legal elements of Mormon polygamy and its relationship to the First Amendment, see Gordon, *The Mormon Question*.

114. *Congressional Globe*, 36th Cong., 1st sess., 1860, 1514.

115. Allen and Leonard, *Story of the Latter-day Saints*, 320.

116. Firmage and Mangrum, *Zion in the Courts*, 132.

117. Unnamed federal official quoted in "Why Polygamy Cannot Be Suppressed," *American Socialist* 14 (Sept. 1876): 7.

118. "The Inauguration," *Oakland Daily Times* (5 Mar. 1881).

119. Ray Jay Davis, "Anti-Polygamy Legislation," in *Encyclopedia of Mormonism*, ed. Daniel Ludlow (New York: Macmillan, 1992), 1:115.

120. Discourse delivered by Brigham Young, Bowery, Salt Lake City, Utah, 31 Aug. 1856, *Journal of Discourses*, 4:39.

121. Erastus Snow, sermon, 26 Feb. 1882, recorded in Charles Ora Card Journal, 26 Feb. 1882, LTPSC, MS 1543.

122. W. W. Phelps, "Persecution," *Evening and Morning Star* 1:1 (June 1832).

123. George Q. Cannon, address in Tabernacle, 24 Sept. 1882, *Journal of Discourses*, 24:107–108.

124. L. John Nuttall to Leonard Nuttall, 15 Sept. 1885, L. John Nuttall Letterbooks, book 3, letter 398, LTPSC.

125. L. John Nuttall to Daniel H. Wells, 19 May 1885, L. John Nuttall Letterbooks, book 3, letter 328, LTPSC.

126. Kenney, *Wilford Woodruff's Journal*, entry for 9 Oct. 1875, 7:250.

127. John Taylor, Discourse, 30 November 1879, *Journal of Discourses*, 20:356.

128. Heber J. Grant, "Draft on Polygamy," 12 Feb. 1876, Grant Papers, LDS Archives; quoted in Walker, *Qualities That Count*, 55.

129. John Taylor and George Q. Cannon to John Irvine, 1 Jan. 1887, MS, LDS First Presidency Letterpress Copy Books, LDS Archives; archived at http://jfs.saints withouthalos.com/pri/fp_87_01.htm.

130. Alexander, *Things in Heaven and Earth*, 248.

131. Van Wagoner, *Mormon Polygamy*, 136.

132. Franklin D. Richards Journal, MS 1215, box 4, vol. 37, 20 Dec. 1888, LDS Archives; emphasis added.

133. Heber J. Grant Journal, entry for 20 Dec. 1888, LDS Archives. The Grant journals are not currently open to researchers, but excerpts are available on the *New Mormon Studies* CD-ROM (Salt Lake City, Utah: Signature, 1998). All quotations in the following paragraphs come from this source.

134. This revelation rescinded the commandment to build the temple in Missouri and contained a statement of a general principle which held that, when God gives "a commandment unto any of the sons of men to do a work and those sons go with all their might and with all they have to perform that work, and their enemies come upon them and hinder them from performing that work, it behooveth me to require that work no more at their hands." Doctrine and Covenants 124:49.

135. Kenney, *Wilford Woodruff's Journal*, entry for 19 May 1890, 9:94.

136. Brigham Young Jr. Journal, entry for 24 Nov. 1889, MS, LDS Archives. Also available on *New Mormon Studies* CD-ROM (Salt Lake City, Utah: Signature, 1998).

137. Kenney, *Wilford Woodruff's Journal*, entry for 24 Nov. 1889, 9:68.

138. William H. Smart, Diary no. 6A, William H. Smart Papers, box 1, folder 6, entry for 18 Dec. 1889, MS, University of Utah, Marriott Library Special Collections. These comments are set in the broader context of Smart's life and relationship with the church in Smart, *Mormonism's Last Colonizer*, 71–72.

139. Joseph F. Smith to Charles W. Nibley, 18 July 1890, Joseph F. Smith Letterpress Copybooks, MS 1325, box 32, folder 1, letter 197, LDS Archives.

140. On Smith's personality, see Kenney, "Before the Beard," 20–42.

141. Joseph F. Smith to Charles W. Nibley, 18 July 1890, Joseph F. Smith Letterpress Copybooks, MS 1325, box 32, folder 1, letter 197, LDS Archives.

142. The Manifesto was first published in the *Deseret News* on 25 September 1890 and has been included as part of the Doctrine and Covenants since 1908. The text of the Manifesto is currently published in the Doctrine and Covenants as "Official Declaration—1." For the publication history of the document, see Cook, *Revelations*, 352. There is disagreement among scholars as to how radical the Manifesto really was. Thomas G. Alexander, for example, pointed out that since 1882 "church leaders had encouraged men to arrange their families so they lived under the same roof with only one wife," and during the unsuccessful fight for Utah statehood in 1887–1888 "statements prepared under the direction of Joseph F. Smith had begun to move the church in the direction of making plural marriages optional rather than mandatory." Smart's comments quoted above were probably made in response to some of these small-scale moves. Given the shock produced by the Manifesto among most Mormons, it seems that such efforts as Alexander described had only limited success in penetrating Mormon collective attitudes about plural marriage before 1890. Alexander, *Things in Heaven and Earth*, 265. While most unauthorized plural marriages had ceased by 1910, as late as 1919 U.S. senator and LDS apostle Reed Smoot confided in his journal that he was "fearful [that] more drastic measures will have to be taken before these sporatic [*sic*] cases of plural marriage are stopped." See Heath, *In the World*, 411–412, entry for 21 Mar. 1919.

143. Franklin D. Richards Journal, MS 1215, box 4, vol. 39, 24 Sept. 1890, LDS Archives.

144. Joseph F. Smith Journal, MS 1325, box 5, folder 13, 17 Aug. 1890, LDS Archives. Smith recorded parts of Woodruff's sermon in a small notebook, which is kept as part of the Joseph F. Smith Collection but which is separate from his formal journals. Woodruff made no mention of his remarks in his journal, simply noting the names of the speakers and the length of time of their addresses. See Kenney, *Wilford Woodruff's Journals*, entry for 17 Aug. 1890, 9:106.

145. Franklin D. Richards Journal, MS 1215, box 4, vol. 39, 10 Oct. 1890, LDS Archives.

146. George Q. Cannon, "The History of the Manifesto," discourse delivered at Salt Lake City, Utah, 6 Oct. 1890; published in Stuy, *Collected Discourses*, 2:129.

147. Ibid., 2:131.

148. Ibid., 2:134; emphasis added.

149. "They Will Never Be Satisfied," *Deseret News* (6 Oct. 1890).

150. Quoted in Sillito, *History's Apprentice*, 226–227. Davis Bitton noted that George Q. Cannon anticipated this shift from practice to belief as early as 1880, just

after the Reynolds decision was handed down, but his was a lonely voice and he was suggesting the *possibility* of such a move in the future, rather than advocating an immediate shift. Bitton, *George Q. Cannon*, 236.

151. Hatch, *Danish Apostle*, 69.

152. Ibid., 71–72.

153. Larson, *A Ministry of Meetings*, 130. The second quote is from Hatch, *Danish Apostle*, 69. Both Rudger Clawson and Anthon Lund kept detailed notes of this meeting in their diaries.

154. Hatch, *Danish Apostle*, 73.

155. Larson, *A Ministry of Meetings*, 379; quote of apostolic charge, ibid., 342.

156. Ibid., 386.

157. Ibid., 567.

158. Quoted in Hoopes and Hoopes, *Mormon Apostle*, 292.

159. William H. Smart, Diary no. 9, William H. Smart Papers, box 3, folder 1, entry for 21 Aug. 1901, MS, University of Utah, Marriott Library Special Collections.

160. Heber J. Grant to William H. Smart, 23 Aug. 1901, William H. Smart Papers, MS, University of Utah, Marriott Library Special Collections; published in *The Journal of William H. Smart, 11 April 1898–24 October 1937*, ed. William B. Smart (Logan: Utah State University Press, 2008), 2,519.

161. *Salt Lake Tribune*, 26 July 1937, quoted in Van Wagoner, *Mormon Polygamy*, 185.

162. Sessions, *Mormon Democrat*, 67. Moyle was an attorney and an influential Mormon who served as special assistant to Secretary of the Treasury Henry Morgenthau. Moyle's son Henry D. Moyle served as an LDS apostle.

163. It should be noted that both Cowley and Clawson entered plural marriages well after the Manifesto was issued. Clawson, for example, married Pearl Udall in 1903 in Mexico. Despite their post-Manifesto marriages, it is clear that Clawson and Cowley were not openly encouraging rank-and-file members of the church to practice plural marriage but only to believe in it. On 26 February 1901, for example, Clawson noted in his journal that, if the Mormons attempted to pass a law in Utah mandating that only an aggrieved wife could bring charges of adultery, "our enemies would claim that we were taking steps to revive the practice of plural marriage, which is not true." Larson, *A Ministry of Meetings*, 249. Clawson apparently believed that the practice of limited post-Manifesto plural marriage did not constitute a "revival" of the practice among the Latter-day Saints. Some have seen these later polygamous marriages (between 100 and 300 between 1890 and 1906) as evidence that Woodruff was using the Manifesto as a disingenuous ploy to buy time for the Mormons. I find this argument less than convincing. I agree with Davis Bitton's judgment that the 1890 Manifesto represented an "official statement of intent," which signaled "the beginning of the end of polygamy." Bitton, *Historical Dictionary of Mormonism*, 110. It seems appropriate to view the persistence of plural marriages into the early twentieth century as a necessary period of adjustment to the reversal of a deeply entrenched practice, one that involved the gradual replacement of the practice of plural marriage with the idealization and spiritualization of the doctrine. In my view, what is surprising is not that post-Manifesto polygamy existed but, given the centrality of the practice in Mormon theology for the better part of fifty years, that it was relatively circumscribed and did not lead to larger schisms

within the community. For information on Clawson's 1903 marriage to Udall, see Hoopes and Hoopes, *Mormon Apostle*, 215–220. For the argument that the 1890 Manifesto was a "tactical retreat," see Hardy, *Solemn Covenant*, 127–153. Kenneth L. Cannon does a masterful job of linking the oscillating intensity of post-Manifesto marriages to the particular views of church presidents Woodruff, Snow, and Smith in "After the Manifesto." For an extended discussion of post-Manifesto plural marriages, including a list of the members of the hierarchy participating, see Quinn, "LDS Church Authority and New Plural Marriages."

164. McConkie, *Mormon Doctrine*, 578.

4. Boundaries in Crisis

1. Kanter, *Commitment and Community*, 178.

2. Two major panics occurred in the period before the Era of Manifestations, in 1819 and 1837. These panics were economy-wide events in which "everyone committed to the money economy was in peril, as bank notes depreciated in their pockets." Sellers, *The Market Revolution*, 137. The 1837 crisis was especially difficult and was brought on by "rising prosperity, wild speculations, and inflation." This panic soon evolved into a "major depression lasting until the mid-1840s." Ellis, "The Market Revolution," 171–172.

3. "Anna Mariah Goff's Vision, 16 Nov. 1837," MS, WRHSSC, VIII: B-234.

4. For detailed accounts of this process, see Stein, *The Shaker Experience*, 168ff.; Thurman, *"O Sisters Ain't You Happy?"* 94; Brewer, *Shaker Communities, Shaker Lives*, 116; Andrews, *People Called Shakers*, 152ff.

5. Garrett, *Spirit Possession and Popular Religion*, 213.

6. Andrews, *People Called Shakers*, 155.

7. Sasson, *Shaker Spiritual Narrative*, 18, 207.

8. Brewer, *Shaker Communities, Shaker Lives*, 122–123.

9. Stein, *The Shaker Experience*, 199.

10. Stein, "Shaker Gift and Shaker Order," 112.

11. Promey, *Spiritual Spectacles*, 7.

12. Thurman, *"O Sisters Ain't You Happy?"* 94–95.

13. Sally Sharp Journal, 16 Nov. 1837, LCSC, MS, box 26, item 298.

14. Ibid., 15 Jan. 1838.

15. Shakers frequently referred to the Era of Manifestations as "Mother's work."

16. Sally Sharp Journal, 21 Nov. 1838, LCSC, MS, box 26, item 298.

17. In the 1840s, many villages compiled various vision accounts into books that sometimes included the history of the revival in each individual village. See, for example, "Record of Visions, Messages and Communications, Which Were Given by Divine Power, 1838–1842," Enfield, Conn., MS, WRHSSC, VIII: B-5–8. This collection consists of eight volumes, some of which were compiled for, and sent to, the Central Ministry at New Lebanon.

18. Composite Letter from the Ministry at Union Village to the Elders at North Union, 15 June 1838, MS, WRHSSC, IV: B-27.

19. Philander C. Cramer Diary, 14 Oct. 1838, MS, WRHSSC, VII: B-218.

20. Elder David Spinning to Union Village, 30 Mar. 1837, MS, WRHSSC, IV: A-51.

21. Berry, *America's Utopian Experiments*, 31. North Union steadily decreased in numbers after 1840 until, at its demise in 1880, it was approximately the same size it had been in 1830.

22. Elder David Spinning to Freegift Wells at Union Village, Summer 1837, MS, WRHSSC, IV: A-51.

23. Elder Freegift Wells to North Union, 12 June 1838, MS, WRHSSC, IV: B-27.

24. Manuscript History of James Prescott, MS, WRHSSC, V: B-176.

25. Ibid. Shakers described receiving various "gifts" that were invisible to the natural eyes but could apparently be discerned spiritually.

26. Philander C. Cramer Diary, 15 and 17 Oct. 1838, MS, WRHSSC, VII: B-218. This mention of a "comfortable talk" occasioned by a vision may have represented one of the reasons that the ministry would seek to take some control of the manifestations.

27. Manuscript History of James Prescott, MS, WRHSSC, V: B-176.

28. From Union Village to Pleasant Hill, Ky., 3 Apr. 1837, WRHSSC, IV: B-24.

29. Stewart eventually became a leading visionist of the New Lebanon community and one of the most prominent instruments throughout the entire Shaker network, although not without causing considerable controversy. See Stein, *The Shaker Experience*, 174–183.

30. Message from Angel Merah to Philemon Stewart, MS, WRHSSC, VIII: B-112.

31. Philander C. Cramer Diary, 24 Sept. 1838, MS, WRHSSC, VII: B-218.

32. Although the cleansing gift took on an unusual intensity during the Era of Manifestations, it had surfaced occasionally during earlier years. In 1833, for example, in the village at New Lebanon, "a gift [was] spoken of to clean up our shops, barns, sheds, shoes, boots, socks, etc." "A Journal of Events, Kept by Betsy Bates, Beginning April 7th, 1833," entry for 3 Dec. 1833, MS, WRHSSC, V: B-128.

33. Brewer, *Shaker Communities, Shaker Lives*, 122.

34. "A Brief Record of the Rise and Progress of the Church at North Union, 1855," MS, WRHSSC, V: B-176.

35. Stein, "Shaker Gift and Shaker Order," 103.

36. "A Brief Record of the Rise and Progress of the Church at North Union, 1855," MS, WRHSSC, V: B-176.

37. Information on Lucretia Sutton is derived from Shaker Membership Card File, MS, WRHSSC, reel 123.

38. "A Brief Record of the Rise and Progress of the Church at North Union, 1855," MS, WRHSSC, V: B-176. The fear of fires was widespread in Shaker villages, and this fear manifested itself in spirit messages. In 1847, a vision was received at New Lebanon in which Ann Lee's spirit warned Shakers to "not let sin enter your dwellings in no wise for surely if you do your buildings will be burnt." "Mother Ann: Vision of Her by a Girl, 1847," LCSC, MS, box 9, item 133.

39. The two major treatments of Shaker gift songs are Andrews, *The Gift to Be Simple*; and Patterson, *Shaker Spiritual*. Patterson's massive tome stands in sharp contrast to Andrews's slim volume, both in terms of size and the sophistication of the analysis.

40. For more on Shaker gift drawings and paintings, see Promey, *Spiritual Spectacles*; and Morin, *Heavenly Visions*.

41. I am concerned chiefly with visions and written messages recorded at North Union between 1840 and 1843 (few occurred as late as 1845). The reasons for this are essentially practical. North Union was a small community, and it did not last as long as many of its sister villages. Documents from this community were not as carefully preserved as they might have been had the village been better known. Only five revelation books remain intact, although it is apparent that at least three others were once kept. In the five books that exist, over 200 messages were recorded, although a good number are duplicated.

42. This being should not be confused with Ann Lee. Holy Mother, or Holy Mother Wisdom, and Eternal Father were the female and male incarnations of the deity. Although, as I have pointed out elsewhere, Shakers maintained a view of God as manifesting both male and female characteristics from the beginning, during the Era of Manifestations this idea was refined, and anthropomorphic representations of the mother and father sides of God were revealed as separate personages. Stein points out that the introduction of Holy Mother Wisdom and Eternal Father was one of the major theological legacies of the Era of Manifestations. Stein, *The Shaker Experience*, 195.

43. MS, WRHSSC, VIII: B-205, no. 32.

44. Ibid., no. 37.

45. Ibid., B-210.

46. Ibid., B-205.

47. "A Brief Record of the Rise and Progress of the Church at North Union, 1855," MS, WRHSSC, V: B-176.

48. I will argue later in this chapter that public confessions served to deepen the sense of crisis among the Mormons during their Reformation. Very early in their development, however, Shakers had engrained the ritual of confession into their liturgical lives. The process of public confession was thus much less disruptive in a Shaker context than it was in a Mormon context and served to soothe the crisis rather than exacerbate it.

49. Manuscript History of James Prescott, MS, WRHSSC, V: B-176.

50. Numbers and Butler, *The Disappointed*, xv. The second failed attempt, which predicted that Christ would return on 22 October 1844, came to be known as the Great Disappointment. After Miller failed the second time to predict the parousia correctly, many of his flock sought religious communion elsewhere, including with the Shakers. Hundreds of Millerites joined Shaker villages in the late 1840s, but few remained more than a few years. See Stein, *The Shaker Experience*, 209–210; and Lawrence Foster, "Had Prophecy Failed? Contrasting Perspectives of the Millerites and Shakers," in Numbers and Butler, *The Disappointed*, 173–188. For a broader treatment of Miller and his eschatological context, see David L. Rowe, *God's Strange Work: William Miller and the End of All Things* (Grand Rapids, Mich.: Eerdmans, 2008).

51. Manuscript History of James Prescott, MS, WRHSSC, V: B-176.

52. MS, WRHSSC, VIII: B-210.

53. Ibid., B-207.

54. Ibid., B-206. Some of the early visions at Watervliet contained frightening images of sinners in hell; one instrument

saw one man and one woman standing close by the side of each other, whose arms were chained around each other, and would scream with torment. The woman said to the man, "it is your fault that I have to suffer here, for you coaxed and flattered me till you got me away." He said "it is not my fault any more than yours for you had no business to be coaxed or flattered by me." ("Anna Mariah Goff's Vision, 16 November 1837," MS, WRHSSC, VIII: B-234)

55. Other scholars have offered a variety of interpretations of this period in Shaker history. Priscilla Brewer emphasized the power issue repeatedly in her book. Although she acknowledged that the revival began spontaneously outside of the hierarchy, she claimed that by 1838 the leadership had seized control over the entire situation. Her view of the Era of Manifestations as a power play runs so deep that it leads her to declare, without evidence, that Philemon Stewart and other instruments were "corrupted by the power newly bestowed upon" them. Brewer, *Shaker Communities, Shaker Lives*, 126. Diane Sasson emphasized the role of gender in her article "Individual Experience, Community Control, and Gender." For a psycho-historical take on the subject, see Foster, *Women, Family and Utopia*.

56. Foster, *Women, Family, and Utopia*, 43–56.

57. Roxalana L. Grosvenor to Henry Spicer, 21 Oct. 1853; published in Spicer, *Sights and Sounds*, 195.

58. Arrington, *Great Basin Kingdom*, 161. This argument is made at length in Stephen C. Taysom, "There Is Always a Way of Escape: Continuity and Reconstitution in Nineteenth-Century Mormon Boundary Maintenance Strategies," *Western Historical Quarterly* 37 (Summer 2006): 183–206.

59. Archival evidence suggests that there are serious problems with the posited causal link between famine and the onset of the Mormon Reformation. Paul H. Peterson viewed the Mormon Reformation as a reaction on the part of LDS leaders to genuine spiritual decline occasioned in large part by the dilution of "old stock" Mormon pioneers by the large influx of new, mostly European converts into Utah in the early 1850s. The isolation of the Mormons, according to Peterson, allowed them to speak more openly than they ever had before, which led to the rhetorical excesses and increases in plural marriage during the Reformation. He also argued that agricultural hardships led Brigham Young and other leaders to conclude that "the only cure for pestilence and vexation lay in more strict compliance with divine commandments." Peterson, "Mormon Reformation," 33, 45. Similarly, historian Thomas G. Alexander argued that "some of the General Authorities came to believe that many Church members and leaders had fallen spiritually asleep" and that "the Saints seemed unable to maintain spirituality in the face of increasing prosperity." Alexander, "Wilford Woodruff and the Mormon Reformation," 25–36. Gustive O. Larson argued that the Reformation was chiefly a "reaction to the crop destructions of 1855–1856 which were interpreted as a divine rebuke for wastefulness and moral laxity." Larson, "The Mormon Reformation," 46. Howard Searle viewed the Mormon Reformation as a necessary "call to repentance" that brought about a much-needed "spiritual awakening." Howard C. Searle, "The Mormon Reformation of 1856–1857," master's thesis, Brigham Young University, 1956, 10.

60. In an article on Brigham Young's role in the Mormon Reformation, Paul Peterson took an agnostic approach about spiritual declension, stating, "whether

there had been progression or retrogression in keeping the commandments was hardly the point." He was content with the knowledge that church leaders "deemed insufficient" the level of obedience in the early 1850s. The question still remains, however, as to how the church leaders came to that conclusion. Paul H. Peterson, "Brigham Young and the Mormon Reformation," in *Lion of the Lord: Essays on the Life and Service of Brigham Young,* ed. Susan Easton Black and Larry C. Porter (Salt Lake City, Utah: Deseret, 1995), 246.

61. Richard E. Bennett, "'My Idea Is to Go Right Through Right Side Up with Care': The Exodus as Reformation," in *The Collected Leonard J. Arrington Mormon History Lectures* (Logan: Utah State University Special Collections and Archives, 2005), 55–70. Historian Eugene E. Campbell argued that "calls to repentance were persistent during the first decade in the Great Basin." Campbell further held that the Reformation rhetoric differed in degree but not in kind from typical rhetoric of the period. Campbell, *Establishing Zion,* 182.

62. Alexander, "Wilford Woodruff and the Mormon Reformation," 28.

63. George A. Smith, untitled address, delivered 10 Sept. 1854, published in *Deseret News* 4:45 (18 Jan. 1855): 168.

64. All quotes are from Brigham Young, Heber C. Kimball, and Jedediah M. Grant, "Twelfth General Epistle of the Presidency of the Church of Jesus Christ of Latter-day Saints, to the Saints in the Valleys of the Mountains, and Those Saints Scattered Abroad Throughout the Earth," *Deseret News* 5:7 (25 Apr. 1855): 52.

65. By the 1850s, the Mormons had made great strides in the fields of irrigation and agronomic watering. In 1856, they had made sufficient progress to establish the Deseret Agricultural and Manufacturing Society, which "experimented with novel varieties of field crops, distributed the seeds of those which proved promising to farmers throughout the Mormon settlements, and made an effort to educate farmers in better farming methods, including irrigation techniques." Leonard J. Arrington, "A Different Mode of Life: Irrigation and Society in Nineteenth-Century Utah," *Agricultural History* 49:1 (Jan. 1975): 11.

66. Peterson, "Mormon Reformation," 205.

67. Jedediah M. Grant, "The Holy Spirit, Learning, and Science," lecture given 31 May 1855, published in *Journal of Discourses,* 3:7.

68. Kenney, *Wilford Woodruff's Journal,* entry for 4 Feb. 1855, 4:303.

69. Paul Peterson cited the speeches of 4 February 1855 as one component of a strong brew consisting of irritation with outsiders, the failure of the reinstitution of the law of consecration, and severe economic hardship, which ultimately created the environment necessary for the Reformation to commence. See Peterson, "Mormon Reformation," 33.

70. Jedediah M. Grant, untitled address, 13 July 1855, *Journal of Discourses,* 3:55.

71. Brigham Young, untitled address, 6 Oct. 1855, *Journal of Discourses,* 3:43.

72. Ibid., 47.

73. Esaias Edwards Diary, 8 Feb. 1857, MS 184, LTPSC. Young had employed the same tactic a decade earlier during the pioneer trek from Nauvoo to Utah. On 29 May 1847, Young called "the camp together [and] he reproved them sharply for their conduct and warned them of the distress that would come on them without repentance and reformation." Levi Jackman Journal, 29 May 1847, Vault MS 79, LTPSC.

74. Esaias Edwards Diary, 8 Feb. 1857, MS 184, LTPSC, 46.

75. Alexander, "Wilford Woodruff and the Mormon Reformation," 26.

76. Kenney, *Wilford Woodruff's Journal*, entry for 6 Oct. 1855, 4:338.

77. Woodruff refers briefly to the meeting in his journal: Kenney, *Wilford Woodruff's Journal*, entry for 10 Oct. 1855, 4:339; the names of the missionaries were published in *Deseret News* 5:32 (17 Oct. 1855): 256. The names of the first cohort of home missionaries were published as follows: P. Pratt, O. Pratt, G. A. Smith, E. Snow, J. Young, L. D. Young, H. S. Eldredge, J. Gates, H. Herriman, J. G. Hovey, J. L. Heywood, Wm. Snow, A. Farr, J. F. Hutchinson, D. Carter, D. D. Hunt, T. D. Brown, J. B. Nobles, G. B. Wallace, Z. Pulsipher, G. Clements, J. W. Johnson, R. Cook, Wm. Gibson, J. Lyon, L. Richards, T. Grover, and G. Woodard.

78. The dating of the onset of the Reformation is problematic, and there is some contention among scholars. Few historians have chosen to date the beginning of the Reformation at 1855. Thomas G. Alexander did so in his 1992 article, and he also cited the introduction of the home missionary program as signaling the birth of the Reformation. Alexander divided the Reformation into three distinct phases with differing methods and goals. Alexander, "Wilford Woodruff and the Mormon Reformation," 25–38. Most scholars cite 13 September 1856, the date of Jedediah M. Grant's sermons in Davis County, as the inauguration of the movement. Peterson argued that the Reformation began on 6 September 1856. Peterson rejected any earlier dates on the grounds that he could find no evidence of specific Reformation rhetoric in the letters of Brigham Young during the first half of 1856. Based on that measure alone, it is reasonable to conclude that dating the Reformation earlier than the fall of 1856 would be in error. However, a variety of factors beyond Young's own preserved letters suggests that an earlier date may be appropriate. There is some evidence, for example, that talk of the necessity of a "reformation" of morals and standards was circulating through the settlements in late 1855. On the first day of 1856, Charles Rich wrote from San Bernardino, California, to Brigham Young. He noted the presence of what he called the "floating class of Saints," by which he meant lukewarm Mormons who had left Utah for California. Rich reported that he had engaged in a program to encourage these individuals to "reform and do the works of righteousness." In November 1855, Apostle Ezra T. Benson spoke in Tooele, a city just west of the main settlement at Salt Lake City. In his address, Benson flatly called for "a reformation in Tooele City and throughout this territory" ("Minutes of a Quarterly Meeting Held in Tooele City, November 10–11, 1855," *Deseret News* 5: 36 [14 Nov. 1855], 282). Clearly, under Brigham Young's orders, rhetorical and institutional apparatuses were deployed in an effort to effect a religious retrenchment in late 1855. See Charles C. Rich to Brigham Young, 1 Jan. 1856, MS 889, box 2, folder 1, Charles C. Rich Collection, LDS Archives.

79. For a discussion of home missionaries in the broader context of internal Mormon missiology, see Humphreys, "Missionaries to the Saints," 76–77.

80. Foucault, *Discipline and Punish*, 175.

81. Ibid., 174.

82. Ibid., 176.

83. Ibid., 191–192.

84. "Journal of Homer Brown," entry for 9 Nov. 1856, MS 2181, LDS Archives. Typescript in author's possession.

85. Wilford Woodruff, "Report of Quarterly Conference of Home Missions," *Deseret News* 5:33 (24 Oct. 1855): 258.

86. Young did not attempt to reconcile his cautions against overindulging in food and drink with the widespread food shortages in the territory.

87. "Minutes of a Quarterly Meeting Held in Tooele City, November 10–11, 1855," *Deseret News* 5:36 (14 Nov. 1855): 282.

88. "Minutes of a Quarterly Meeting Held in the City Bountiful," *Deseret News* 5:37 (17–18 Nov. 1855): 290.

89. "Minutes of a Quarterly Meeting Held in Kaysville," *Deseret News* 5:41 (19 Dec. 1855): 322.

90. Bitton, "Mormon Catechisms," 419.

91. Brigham Young to Welcome Chapman, 13 Nov. 1856, MS, CR 1234 1, box 3, Brigham Young Letterpress Copybook, LDS Archives, 186.

92. The full list of questions may be found in the LDS Archives and, more conveniently, in Peterson's dissertation. See Peterson, "Mormon Reformation," 74–75.

93. "Journal of Homer Brown," entry for 24 Jan. 1857, MS 2181, LDS Archives.

94. Mary Douglas, *Natural Symbols: Explorations in Cosmology* (1970; reprint, London: Routledge, 2003), 70.

95. Ibid., 66.

96. Ibid., 67.

97. Ibid.

98. Ibid., 118.

99. Ibid., 126.

100. Quinn, "The Practice of Rebaptism at Nauvoo."

101. LDS historian James Allen pointed out that, in addition to their original baptism into the church, Mormons were rebaptized at least one additional time upon their entrance into the Salt Lake Valley. Allen, *"No Toil nor Labor Fear,"* 270.

102. "Journal of Homer Brown," entry for 24 Oct. 1855, MS 2181, LDS Archives.

103. No temples were dedicated by the Mormons between 1845 (Nauvoo, Ill.) and 1877 (St. George, Utah). In the interim period, the Mormons performed temple ordinances in the Council House (1851–1854) and the Endowment House (1855–1889), which stood in downtown Salt Lake City near what is now Temple Square. The baptismal font in the Endowment House was designed chiefly for the performance of the ordinance of baptism for the dead.

104. Kenney, *Wilford Woodruff's Journal,* entry for 2 Oct. 1856, 4:458.

105. Ibid., 461.

106. All quotes relating to the 13–15 September conference are from "Great Reformation," *Deseret News* 7:29 (24 Sept. 1856): 229.

107. John Smith to Joseph F. Smith, 4 Nov. 1856, MS 1325, box 8, folder 26, Joseph F. Smith Collection, LDS Archives. The quote cited in the text was from a postscript that Helen added to a letter composed primarily by John Smith.

108. Louisa Barnes Pratt, *The History of Louisa Barnes Pratt: Being the Autobiography of a Mormon Missionary Widow and Pioneer,* ed. S. George Ellsworth (Logan: Utah State University Press, 1998), 240.

109. This revelation is part of a larger document called "Articles and Covenants of the Church of Jesus Christ," which was drafted over the course of several days in April 1830 and the manuscript of which is in the LDS Archives. The entire docu-

ment was first published in the *Evening and Morning Star* in June 1832. The portion of that document quoted in the text is published currently as Doctrine and Covenants 20:75.

110. William G. Hartley, "Common People: Church Activity during the Brigham Young Period," in *Nearly Everything Imaginable: The Everyday Life of Utah's Mormon Pioneers,* ed. Ronald W. Walker and Doris R. Dant (Provo, Utah: Brigham Young University Press, 1999), 268. For an interesting look at ecclesiastical and social life in one pioneer era Mormon congregation, see Ronald W. Walker, "Going to Meeting in Salt Lake City's Thirteenth Ward, a Microanalysis, 1849–1882," in *New Views of Mormon History: Essays in Honor of Leonard J. Arrington,* ed. Davis Bitton and Maureen Ursenbach Beecher (Salt Lake City: University of Utah Press, 1987), 138–161. The texts of the sacramental prayers are found in a revelation Joseph Smith recorded in April 1830 and are published currently in Doctrine and Covenants 20:77–79. These prayers are among the few in the LDS Church that must be spoken exactly as they are written.

111. Brigham Young, untitled discourse, 8 Jan. 1865, *Journal of Discourses,* 11:39.

112. Heber C. Kimball, untitled discourse, 19 July 1863, *Journal of Discourses,* 10:245.

113. Heber C. Kimball, untitled discourse, 9 Nov. 1856, *Journal of Discourses,* 4:82.

114. Jedediah M. Grant, untitled discourse, 9 Nov. 1856, *Journal of Discourses,* 4:87. This sermon is also published in Sessions, *Mormon Thunder,* 243. Sessions' book contains the vast majority of Grant's Reformation era sermons and is an indispensable resource for students of the period.

115. "Journal of Homer Brown," entry for 9 Nov. 1856, MS 2181, LDS Archives.

116. Brigham Young to George Albert Smith, 26 Jan. 1857, MS 1322, box 5, folder 13, George A. Smith Collection, LDS Archives. It is unclear if LDS Church leaders knew that they were taking steps that resembled a mild form of the medieval Catholic practice of "interdict" in which church authorities denied the performance of the sacraments in a given region. The result of interdict was typically "to make people fear for the health of their souls because they were deprived of the sacraments." Swanson, *Religion and Devotion in Europe,* 296.

117. Mary C. Mansfield, *The Humiliation of Sinners: Public Penance in Thirteenth-Century France* (Ithaca, N.Y.: Cornell University Press, 1995), 5.

118. "Saints in Utah," *Deseret News* 6:261 (22 Oct. 1856).

119. Brigham Young to Silas Smith, 7 Dec. 1856, MS, CR 1234 1, box 3, Brigham Young Letterpress Copybook, 218.

120. Arrington, *Great Basin Kingdom,* 7.

121. Leonard J. Arrington, Feramorz Y. Fox, and Dean L. May, *Building the City of God: Community and Cooperation among the Mormons,* 2nd rev. ed. (Urbana: University of Illinois Press, 1992), 78.

122. Scholars have suggested several possible reasons. Peterson argued that Young was merely gauging the level of dedication among his people and that "he could not have been overly happy with the results." Peterson, "Mormon Reformation," 37. Arrington, Fox, and May offered several possible explanations, ranging from a simple lack of enthusiasm for the plan to a reluctance on Young's part to trust local bishops with the dispensation of stewardships. Arrington et al., *Building the City of God,* 77–78.

123. Stanley S. Ivins estimated that in 1856–1857 plural marriages were 65 percent higher than "in any other two years." By 1859, the number of plural marriages had dropped to less than one-fifth of the 1857 rate. Ivins, "Notes on Mormon Polygamy," 231–232. Although plural marriages increased, not all Mormons, even LDS leaders, responded with equal fervor to the call to marry more wives. Heber C. Kimball, a member of the church's governing First Presidency, married five wives in 1856–1857 while another prominent Mormon, William Clayton, took one additional wife in 1856 but did not marry again for ten years. Stanley B. Kimball, *Heber C. Kimball: Mormon Patriarch and Pioneer* (Urbana: University of Illinois Press, 1981), 230; Allen, "*No Toil nor Labor Fear,*" 202.

124. Muir, *Ritual in Early Modern Europe,* 73.

125. See Quinn, *The Mormon Hierarchy: Extensions of Power,* 243–258; Bagley, *Blood of the Prophets,* 51–52; Peterson, "Mormon Reformation," 61–62.

126. Kenney, *Wilford Woodruff's Journal,* entry for 16 Oct. 1856, 4:475.

127. John Smith to Joseph F. Smith, 4 Nov. 1856, MS 1325, box 8, folder 26, Joseph F. Smith Collection, LDS Archives. John Smith references his brother's mission because Joseph F. Smith was then serving as a proselytizing missionary in the Hawaiian islands.

128. Kenney, *Wilford Woodruff's Journal,* entry for 16 Oct. 1856, 4:475.

129. Benjamin F. Johnson, *My Life's Review: The Autobiography of Benjamin F. Johnson* (Provo, Utah: Grandin, 1997), 191.

130. Peterson also cited Johnson, but for some reason he replaced the phrase "and his servants" with an ellipsis, which tended to minimize the role of the church hierarchy in the process. Peterson, "Mormon Reformation," 112.

131. Cristina Bicchieri, *The Grammar of Society: The Nature and Dynamics of Social Norms* (New York: Cambridge University Press, 2006), 186.

132. Leonard J. Arrington, "Faith and Intellect as Partners in Mormon History," in *The Collected Leonard J. Arrington Mormon History Lectures* (Logan: Utah State University Special Collections and Archives, 2005), 14.

133. Albanese, *A Republic of Mind and Spirit,* 149–150.

134. Bicchieri, *Grammar of Society,* 196.

135. Ibid., 197.

136. Smith, *Imagining Religion,* 99–100.

137. James H. Martineau Journal, entry for 28 Apr. 1858; published in *An Uncommon Common Pioneer: The Journals of James Henry Martineau, 1828–1918,* ed. Donald G. Godfrey and Rebecca S. Martineau-McCarty (Provo, Utah: Brigham Young University Press, 2008), 81.

Conclusion

1. Stacey Chase, "The Last Ones Standing," *Boston Globe* (23 July 2006), www.boston.com/news/globe/magazine/articles/2006/07/23/the_last_ones_standing.

2. "President Gordon B. Hinckley Appears on Larry King Live," 8 Sept. 1998, LDS Newsroom. Hinckley died in 2008.

3. These insights into the relationship between Jonestown and Waco in the minds of members of the media and law enforcement are not mine. They are spelled out in Hall, "Public Narratives and the Apocalyptic Sect," 205–235.

4. One particularly interesting example could be added here. In June 1860, Brigham Young was discussing the violent treatment of a Brother Henifer, who apparently suffered at the hands of unspecified "persecutors." In response to the suggestion that Henifer's treatment was of "an unparalleled nature," Young responded that "at Haun's mill about 100 men ravished a young woman after tying her to a bench . . . and that was worse than whipping Henifer." While the October 1838 massacre of Mormons at Haun's Mill was indeed savage, there is no evidence to suggest that any attack such as the one mentioned by Young ever occurred. Collier, *Office Journal*, 101. For a discussion of the Haun's Mill massacre, see LeSueur, *The 1838 Mormon War in Missouri*, 162–168.

5. Scholars working in other fields have also noted the power of such narratives. See, for example, Sharot, *Messianism, Mysticism, and Magic*; Gregory, *Salvation at Stake*; and Castelli, *Martyrdom and Memory*.

BIBLIOGRAPHY

Manuscript Collections

Most of the sources cited are manuscripts, consulted either in the original or through microforms. For the location of specific manuscript items in each library or collection, please consult the notes. I made extensive use of the microform holdings at Indiana University's Herman B. Wells Library and of the comprehensive digital collections published as DVDs by the LDS Church's Historical Department, which were obtained via interlibrary loan.

Library and Archives of the Church of Jesus Christ of Latter-day Saints (LDS Archives), Salt Lake City, Utah
Library of Congress Shaker Collection (LCSC), Washington, D.C.
New York Public Library Shaker Manuscript Collection (NYPLSMC), New York City
New York State Library, Albany, New York
L. Tom Perry Special Collections (LTPSC), Brigham Young University, Provo, Utah
Western Reserve Historical Society Shaker Collections (WRHSSC), Cleveland, Ohio

Published Primary Sources

Beecher, Maureen Ursenbach, ed. *The Personal Writings of Eliza Roxcy Snow*. Salt Lake City: University of Utah Press, 1995.
"Beware of False Prophets." *Evening and Morning Star* (July 1833).
Bowers, Lucy. *Concise Statements Concerning the Life and Religious Views of the Shakers*. Mount Lebanon, N.Y.: United Society, 1896.
Brooks, Juanita, ed. *On the Mormon Frontier: The Diary of Hosea Stout*. Salt Lake City: University of Utah Press, 1964.
Cannon, George Q. "The Improvement of Our Species." *Western Standard* (7 Aug. 1857).
Cannon, George Q., and John Taylor. "An Epistle from the First Presidency to the Officers and Members of the Church of Jesus Christ of Latter-day Saints." *Woman's Exponent* 14 (15 Oct. 1885): 67.

"The Church of Christ—Today and in the Future." *Shaker Manifesto* 11:1 (Jan. 1881).

Clark, James R., comp. *Messages of the First Presidency.* Salt Lake City, Utah: Bookcraft, 1965–1970.

Collier, Fred, ed. *The Office Journal of President Brigham Young, 1858–1863,* book D. Hanna, Utah: Collier, 2006.

Cooper, James Fenimore. *Notions of the Americans, Picked Up by a Traveling Bachelor.* New York: Frederick Ungar, 1830.

Dunlavy, John. *The Manifesto; or, A Declaration of the Doctrines and Practices of the Church of Christ.* Pleasant Hill, Ky.: P. Bertrand, 1818.

"Editor's Easy Chair." *Harper's New Monthly Magazine* 20:19 (Apr. 1860): 689–701.

"An Epistle from Joseph Smith the Prophet to the Church of Jesus Christ of Latter-day Saints." *Times and Seasons* (1 Oct. 1842).

Evans, Frederick W. "Autobiography of a Shaker." *Atlantic Monthly* 23:168 (Apr. 1869): 410–422.

Foster, Charles A. "Tremendous Excitement—Unparalleled Outrage." *St. Louis Evening Gazette.* 12 June 1844.

"French Republicanism and American Democracy." *United States Democratic Review* 34:3 (Sept. 1854): 270–276.

"Great Reformation." *Deseret News* (Sept. 1856).

Green, Calvin, and Seth Y. Wells. *A Summary View of the Millennial Church,* 2nd ed. New York: C. Benthuysen, 1848.

Hallwas, John E., and Roger D. Launius, eds. *Cultures in Conflict: A Documentary History of the Mormon War in Illinois.* Logan: Utah State University Press, 1995.

Hatch, John P., ed. *Danish Apostle: The Diaries of Anthon H. Lund.* Salt Lake City, Utah: Signature, 2006.

Heath, Harvard S., ed. *In the World: The Diaries of Reed Smoot.* Salt Lake City, Utah: Signature, 1997.

Humez, Jean M., ed. *Mother's First-born Daughters: Early Shaker Writings on Women and Religion.* Bloomington: Indiana University Press, 1993.

"The Inauguration." *Oakland Daily Times* (5 Mar. 1881).

Jessee, Dean C., ed. *John Taylor's Nauvoo Journal.* Provo, Utah: Grandin, 1996.

Journal of Discourses of President Brigham Young, His Counselors, and Other Church Leaders. 26 vols. Liverpool: Latter-day Saints Book Depot, 1854–1886; lithograph ed., Los Angeles: Gartner Printing and Litho, 1956.

Kenney, Scott G., ed. *Wilford Woodruff's Journal, 1833–1898.* Salt Lake City, Utah: Signature, 1983.

Kimball, Stanley B., ed. *On the Potter's Wheel: The Diaries of Heber C. Kimball.* Salt Lake City, Utah: Signature, 1987.

Larson, Stan, ed. *A Ministry of Meetings: The Apostolic Diaries of Rudger Clawson.* Salt Lake City, Utah: Signature, 1993.

Loba, Frederick. "Utah and the Mormons." *New York Times* (7 May 1858).

"Matters and Things at Nauvoo." *Warsaw Signal* (8 May 1844).

McConkie, Mark L. *Remembering Joseph: Personal Recollections of Those Who Knew the Prophet Joseph Smith.* Salt Lake City, Utah: Deseret, 2003.

Meacham, Joseph. *A Concise Statement of the Principles of the Only True Church According to the Gospel of the Present Appearance of Christ.* Bennington, Vt.: Haswell and Russell, 1790.

"Minutes of a Quarterly Meeting Held in the City Bountiful." *Deseret News* (17–18 Nov. 1855).

"Minutes of a Quarterly Meeting Held in Kaysville." *Deseret News* (19 Dec. 1855).

"Minutes of a Quarterly Meeting Held in Tooele City, November 10–11, 1855." *Deseret News* (14 Nov. 1855).

"Mysticism." *New Englander and Yale Review* 5:19 (July 1847): 350–355.

Phelps, W. W. "Persecution." *Evening and Morning Star* (June 1832).

"Prospects of the Church." *Evening and Morning Star* (Mar. 1833).

Rathbun, Valentine. *Some Brief Hints of a Religious Scheme, Taught and Propagated by a Number of Europeans Living in a Place Called Niskeyuna in the State of New York, 1781*. Philadelphia: American Antiquarian Society, 1781.

Robinson, Charles Edson. *A Concise History of the United Society of Believers Called Shakers*. East Canterbury, N.H.: United Society, 1893.

"Romanists and the Roman Catholic Controversy." *New Englander and Yale Review* 2:6 (Apr. 1844): 239–246.

"Saints in Utah." *Deseret News* (22 Oct. 1856).

Savage, Minot J. "The Inevitable Surrender of Orthodoxy." *North American Review* 148:391 (June 1889): 719–721.

Sessions, Gene A. *Mormon Democrat: The Religious and Political Memoirs of James Henry Moyle*. Salt Lake City, Utah: Signature, 1998.

Sillito, John, ed. *History's Apprentice: The Diaries of B. H. Roberts*. Salt Lake City, Utah: Signature, 2004.

Smith, George A. Untitled address. *Deseret News* (18 Jan. 1855).

Smith, George D., ed. *An Intimate Chronicle: The Journals of William Clayton*. Salt Lake City, Utah: Signature, 1995.

Smith, Hyrum. "A History of the Persecution of the Church of Jesus Christ of Latter-day Saints in Missouri." *Times and Seasons* (1 Dec. 1839).

Smith, Joseph. *History of the Church of Jesus Christ of Latter-day Saints*, rev. ed. 7 vols. Salt Lake City, Utah: Deseret, 1980.

"Proclamation." *Nauvoo Neighbor* (22 June 1844).

Spicer, Henry. *Sights and Sounds: The Mystery of the Day: Comprising an Entire History of the American "Spirit" Manifestations*. London: Thomas Bosworth, 1853.

Stewart, Philemon. *A Holy, Sacred, and Divine Roll and Book: From the Lord God of Heaven, to the Inhabitants of the Earth: Revealed in the United Society at New Lebanon, County of Columbia, State of New York, United States of America, in 2 Parts*. Canterbury, N.H.: United Society, 1843.

Stone, W. L. "Matthias and His Impostures." *North American Review* 41:89 (Oct. 1835): 322–325.

Stuy, Brian, ed. *Collected Discourses*. Salt Lake City, Utah: BHS, 1987.

Taylor, John. "Patriarchal." *Times and Seasons* (1 June 1845).

———. "Retributive Justice." *Nauvoo Neighbor* (12 June 1844).

"They Will Never be Satisfied." *Deseret News* (6 Oct. 1890).

"Twelfth General Epistle of the Presidency of the Church of Jesus Christ of Latter-day Saints, to the Saints in the Valleys of the Mountains, and Those Saints Scattered Abroad Throughout the Earth." *Deseret News* (25 Apr. 1855).

Woodruff, Wilford. "Report of Quarterly Conference of Home Missions." *Deseret News* (24 Oct. 1855).

Wright, Eleazar [Richard McNemar]. *A Memorial of the Labors of Our Parents and Ministers, in Founding the Church in the West.* Watervliet, Ohio, 1834.

Young, Lorenzo Dow. *Fragments of Experience.* Salt Lake City, Utah: Juvenile Instructor Office, 1881.

Youngs, Benjamin S. *The Testimony of Christ's Second Appearing.* Lebanon, Ohio: Office of the Western Star, 1808.

Youngs, Benjamin S., Rufus Bishop, and Seth Y. Wells, eds. *Testimonies of the Life, Character, Revelations, and Doctrines of Our Ever Blessed Mother Ann Lee, and the Elders with Her; Through Whom the Word of Eternal Life Was Opened in This Day of Christ's Second Appearing: Collected from Living Witnesses.* Hancock, Mass.: J. Talcott and J. Deming, 1816.

Secondary Sources

Abercrombie, Nicholas, Stephen Hill, and Bryan S. Turner, eds. *The Penguin Dictionary of Sociology.* New York: Penguin, 2000.

Ahlstrom, Sydney E. *A Religious History of the American People.* New Haven, Conn.: Yale University Press, 1972.

Albanese, Catherine L. *Corresponding Motion: Transcendental Religion and the New America.* Philadelphia, Pa.: Temple University Press, 1977.

———. *A Republic of Mind and Spirit: A Cultural History of American Metaphysical Religion.* New Haven, Conn.: Yale University Press, 2007.

Alexander, Jeffrey C. *The Meanings of Social Life: A Cultural Sociology.* New York: Oxford University Press, 2003.

Alexander, Thomas G. "The Faith of an Urban Mormon." In *A Thoughtful Faith: Essays on Belief by Mormon Scholars,* ed. Philip L. Barlow. Salt Lake City, Utah: Cannon, 1986.

———. *Mormonism in Transition: A History of the Latter-day Saints, 1890–1930.* Urbana: University of Illinois Press, 1986.

———. "A New and Everlasting Covenant: An Approach to the Theology of Joseph Smith." In *New Views of Mormon History: Essays in Honor of Leonard J. Arrington,* ed. Davis Bitton and Maureen Ursenbach Beecher. Salt Lake City: University of Utah Press, 1987.

———. *Things in Heaven and Earth: The Life and Times of Wilford Woodruff, a Mormon Prophet.* Salt Lake City, Utah: Signature, 1991.

———. "Wilford Woodruff and the Mormon Reformation of 1855–1857." *Dialogue: A Journal of Mormon Thought* 25:2 (Summer 1992): 25–38.

Allen, James B. *"No Toil nor Labor Fear": The Story of William Clayton.* Provo, Utah: Brigham Young University Press, 2002.

Allen, James B., and Glen M. Leonard. *The Story of the Latter-day Saints.* Salt Lake City, Utah: Deseret, 1992.

Alston, William P. *Perceiving God: The Epistemology of Religious Experience.* Ithaca, N.Y.: Cornell University Press, 1991.

Altschuler, Glenn C., and Stuart M. Blumin. *Rude Republic: Americans and Their Politics in the Nineteenth Century.* Princeton, N.J.: Princeton University Press, 2000.

Anderson, Devery S., and Gary James Bergera, eds. *Joseph Smith's Quorum of the Anointed, 1842–1845: A Documentary History.* Salt Lake City, Utah: Signature, 2005.

———. *The Nauvoo Endowment Companies, 1845–1846: A Documentary History.* Salt Lake City, Utah: Signature, 2005.

Andrew, Laurel B. *Early Temples of the Mormons: The Architecture of the Millennial Kingdom in the American West.* Albany: State University of New York Press, 1977.

Andrews, Edward Deming. *The Gift to Be Simple: Songs, Dances and Rituals of the American Shakers.* 1940. Reprint. New York: Dover, 1962.

———. *The People Called Shakers: A Search for the Perfect Society.* 1953. Rev. ed. New York: Dover, 1963.

Arrington, Leonard J. *Brigham Young: American Moses.* New York: Knopf, 1985.

———. *Great Basin Kingdom: An Economic History of the Latter-day Saints, 1830–1900.* Cambridge, Mass.: Harvard University Press, 1958.

Arrington, Leonard J., and Davis Bitton. *The Mormon Experience.* New York: Knopf, 1979.

Bagley, Will. *Blood of the Prophets: Brigham Young and the Mountain Meadows Massacre.* Norman: University of Oklahoma Press, 2002.

Bainbridge, William S. "The Decline of the Shakers: Evidence from the United States Census." *Communal Societies* 4 (1984): 19–34.

Bainbridge, William Sims, and Rodney Stark. *A Theory of Religion.* New Brunswick, N.J.: Rutgers University Press, 1996.

Bell, Catherine. *Ritual: Perspectives and Dimensions.* New York: Oxford University Press, 1992.

Berger, Peter L. *The Sacred Canopy: Elements of a Sociological Theory of Religion.* New York: Anchor, 1967.

Berry, Brian J. L. *America's Utopian Experiments: Communal Havens from Long-Wave Crises.* Hanover, N.H.: University Press of New England, 1992.

Bitton, Davis. *George Q. Cannon: A Biography.* Salt Lake City, Utah: Deseret, 1999.

———. *Historical Dictionary of Mormonism,* 2nd ed. Lanham, Md.: Scarecrow, 2000.

———. "Joseph Smith in Mormon Folk Memory." *Restoration Studies* 1 (1980): 75–94.

———. "Mormon Catechisms." In *Revelation, Reason, and Faith: Essays in Honor of Truman G. Madsen,* ed. Donald W. Parry, Daniel C. Peterson, and Stephen D. Ricks. Provo, Utah: Foundation for Ancient Research and Mormon Studies, 2002.

Brewer, Priscilla J. *Shaker Communities, Shaker Lives.* Hanover, N.H.: University Press of New England, 1986.

Brooke, John L. *The Refiner's Fire: The Making of Mormon Cosmology, 1644–1844.* New York: Cambridge University Press, 1996.

Brown, Peter. *The Body and Society: Men, Women, and Sexual Renunciation in Early Christianity.* New York: Columbia University Press, 1988.

Buerger, David John. *The Mysteries of Godliness: A History of Mormon Temple Worship.* Salt Lake City, Utah: Signature, 1994.

Burkert, Walter. *Griechische Religion der archaischen und klassischen.* Stuttgart: Kohlhammer, 1977. Trans. John Raffan as *Greek Religion.* Cambridge, Mass.: Harvard University Press, 1985.

Bushman, Richard L. *Joseph Smith: Rough Stone Rolling.* New York: Knopf, 2005.

Campbell, Craig S. *Images of the New Jerusalem: Latter-day Saint Faction Interpretations of Independence, Missouri.* Knoxville: University of Tennessee Press, 2004.

Campbell, Eugene. *Establishing Zion: The Mormon Church in the American West, 1847–1869.* Salt Lake City, Utah: Signature, 1988.

Cannon, Donald Q., and Lyndon W. Cook, eds. *Far West Record.* Salt Lake City, Utah: Deseret, 1983.

Cannon, Kenneth L. "After the Manifesto: Mormon Polygamy, 1890–1906." In *The New Mormon History: Revisionist Essays on the Past,* ed. D. Michael Quinn. Salt Lake City, Utah: Signature, 1992.

Castelli, Elizabeth A. *Martyrdom and Memory: Early Christian Culture Making.* New York: Columbia University Press, 2004.

Christian, Lewis Clark. "Mormon Foreknowledge of the West." *BYU Studies* 21:4 (Fall 1981): 403–415.

———. "A Study of Mormon Foreknowledge of the American Far West Prior to the Exodus." Unpublished M.A. thesis, Brigham Young University, 1972.

Cohen, Anthony P. *Symbolizing Boundaries: Identity and Diversity in British Cultures.* Manchester, England: Manchester University Press, 1986.

Compton, Todd. *In Sacred Loneliness: The Plural Wives of Joseph Smith.* Salt Lake City, Utah: Signature, 1997.

Conkin, Paul K. *Cane Ridge: America's Pentecost.* Madison: University of Wisconsin Press, 1990.

Cook, Lyndon W. *The Revelations of the Prophet Joseph Smith: A Historical and Biographical Commentary on the Doctrine and Covenants.* Salt Lake City, Utah: Deseret, 1981.

Cook, Lyndon, and Andrew Ehat, eds. *The Words of Joseph Smith: The Contemporary Accounts of the Prophet Joseph Smith's Nauvoo Discourses.* Provo, Utah: BYU Religious Studies Center, 1980.

Cooper, Rex E. *Promises Made to the Fathers: Mormon Covenant Organization.* Salt Lake City: University of Utah Press, 1990.

Cott, Nancy F. *Public Vows: A History of Marriage and the Nation.* Cambridge, Mass.: Harvard University Press, 2000.

Dahl, Larry E., and Donald Q. Cannon, eds. *The Teachings of Joseph Smith.* Salt Lake City, Utah: Bookcraft, 1997.

D'Andrade, Roy G. "Schemas and Motivations." In *Human Motives and Cultural Models,* ed. Roy G. D'Andrade and Claudia Strauss. Cambridge: Cambridge University Press, 1992.

Daynes, Kathryn M. *More Wives than One: The Transformation of the Mormon Marriage System, 1840–1910.* Urbana: University of Illinois Press, 2001.

de Munck, Victor C. "Cultural Schemas of Celibacy." In *Celibacy, Culture, and Society: The Anthropology of Sexual Abstinence,* ed. Eliaa J. Sobo and Sandra Bell. Madison: University of Wisconsin Press, 2001.

DeWolfe, Elizabeth A. *Shaking the Faith: Women, Family, and Mary Dyer's Anti-Shaker Campaign, 1815–1867.* New York: Palgrave Macmillan, 2005.

Douglas, Mary. *Purity and Danger: An Analysis of Concept of Pollution and Taboo.* London: Routledge, 1966.

Ehrman, Bart D. *The Orthodox Corruption of Scripture: The Effect of Early Christological Controversies on the Text of the New Testament.* New York: Oxford University Press, 1993.

Eliade, Mircea. *The Sacred and the Profane: The Nature of Religion.* New York: Harcourt, 1959.

Ellis, Richard E. "The Market Revolution and the Transformation of American Politics, 1901–1837." In *The Market Revolution in America: Social, Political, and Religious Expressions, 1800–1880,* ed. Melvyn Stokes and Stephen Conway. Charlottesville: University of Virginia Press, 1996.

Erickson, Dan. *As a Thief in the Night: The Mormon Quest for Millennial Deliverance.* Salt Lake City, Utah: Signature, 1998.

Esplin, Ronald K. "'A Place Prepared': Joseph, Brigham and the Quest for Promised Refuge in the West." *Journal of Mormon History* 9 (1982): 85–111.

Filley, Dorothy M. *Recapturing Wisdom's Valley: The Watervliet Shaker Heritage, 1775–1975.* Albany, N.Y.: Albany Institute of History and Art, 1975.

Finke, Roger, and Rodney Stark. *The Churching of America 1776–2005: Winners and Losers in Our Religious Economy.* New Brunswick, N.J.: Rutgers University Press, 2005.

Firmage, Edwin B., and R. Collin Mangrum. *Zion in the Courts: A Legal History of the Latter-day Saints, 1830–1900.* Urbana: University of Illinois Press, 1987.

Flake, Kathleen "'Not to Be Riten': The Mormon Temple Rite as Oral Canon." *Journal of Ritual Studies* 9:2 (Winter 1995): 10–21.

Flood, Gavin. *The Ascetic Self: Subjectivity, Memory and Tradition.* Cambridge: Cambridge University Press, 2004.

Forsberg, Clyde L. *Equal Rites: The Book of Mormon, Masonry, Gender, and American Culture.* New York: Columbia University Press, 2003.

Foster, Lawrence. *Religion and Sexuality: The Shakers, the Mormons and the Oneida Community.* New York: Oxford University Press, 1982.

———. *Women, Family and Utopia: Communal Experiments of the Shakers, the Oneida Community, and the Mormons.* Syracuse, N.Y.: Syracuse University Press, 1991.

Foucault, Michel. *Discipline and Punish: The Birth of the Prison.* New York: Vintage, 1978.

Francis, Richard. *Ann the Word: The Story of Ann Lee, Female Messiah, Mother of the Shakers, the Woman Clothed with the Sun.* London: Fourth Estate, 2000.

Fredriksen, Paula. *From Jesus to Christ: The Origins of the New Testament Images of Jesus.* New Haven, Conn.: Yale University Press, 1988.

Garrett, Clarke. *Spirit Possession and Popular Religion: From the Camisards to the Shakers.* Baltimore, Md.: Johns Hopkins University Press, 1987.

Geertz, Clifford. "Religion as a Cultural System." In *The Interpretation of Cultures,* ed. Clifford Geertz. New York: Basic, 1973.

Girard, René. *Violence and the Sacred.* Trans. Patrick Gregory. Baltimore, Md.: Johns Hopkins University Press, 1992.

Glucklich, Ariel. *Sacred Pain: Hurting the Body for the Sake of the Soul.* New York: Oxford University Press, 2001.

Goff, Philip K. "Diversity and Religion." In *Themes in Religion and American Culture,* ed. Philip K. Goff and Paul Harvey. Chapel Hill: University of North Carolina Press, 2004.

Gold, Daniel. "Celibacy." In *The Encyclopedia of Religion,* ed. Mircea Eliade. New York: Macmillan, 1987.

Gordon, Sarah B. *The Mormon Question: Polygamy and Constitutional Conflict in Nineteenth-Century America.* Chapel Hill: University of North Carolina Press, 2002.

Gregg, Thomas. *The Prophet of Palmyra.* New York: Alden, 1890.

Gregory, Brad S. *Salvation at Stake: Christian Martyrdom in Early Modern Europe.* Cambridge, Mass.: Harvard University Press, 1999.

Gunn, Stanley R. *Oliver Cowdery: Second Elder and Scribe.* Salt Lake City, Utah: Bookcraft, 1962.

Gutjahr, Paul C. "The State of the Discipline: Sacred Texts in the United States." *Book History* 4 (2001): 335–370.

Haines, Michael R., and Richard H. Steckel. *A Population History of North America.* New York: Cambridge University Press, 2000.

Hall, John R. "Public Narratives and the Apocalyptic Sect, from Jonestown to Mt. Carmel." In *Armageddon in Waco: Critical Perspectives on the Branch Davidian Conflict,* ed. Stuart A. Wright. Chicago: University of Chicago Press, 1995.

Ham, F. Gerald. "Shakerism in the Old West." Ph.D. diss., University of Kentucky, 1962.

Hamilton, C. Mark. *Nineteenth-Century Mormon Architecture and City Planning.* New York: Oxford University Press, 1995.

Hansen, Klaus J. *Mormonism and the American Experience.* Chicago: University of Chicago Press, 1981.

———. *Quest for Empire: The Political Kingdom of God and the Council of Fifty in Mormon History.* East Lansing: Michigan State University Press, 1967.

Hardy, B. Carmon. *Solemn Covenant: The Mormon Polygamous Passage.* Urbana: University of Illinois Press, 1992.

Hatch, Nathan O. *The Democratization of American Christianity.* New Haven, Conn.: Yale University Press, 1990.

Hayes, John H. "The Tradition of Zion's Inviolability." *Journal of Biblical Literature* 82 (1983): 419–426.

Hervieu-Leger, Daniele. *Religion as a Chain of Memory.* Trans. Simon Lee. New Brunswick, N.J.: Rutgers University Press, 2000.

Hill, Marvin S. *Quest for Refuge: The Mormon Flight from American Pluralism.* Salt Lake City, Utah: Signature, 1989.

Hillerbrand, Hans J. "On Book Burnings and Book Burners: Reflections of the Power and Powerlessness of Ideas." *Journal of the American Academy of Religion* 74:3 (Sept. 2006): 593–614.

Homer, Michael W. "'Similarity of Priesthood in Masonry': The Relationship Between Freemasonry and Mormonism." *Dialogue: A Journal of Mormon Thought* 27:3 (Fall 1994): 2–113.

Hoopes, David S., and Roy Hoopes. *Mormon Apostle: The Story of Rudger Clawson.* New York: Madison, 1992.

Humphreys, Glen. "Missionaries to the Saints." *BYU Studies* 17:1 (Fall 1976): 74–100.

Iannaccone, Laurence R. "Why Strict Churches Are Strong." *American Journal of Sociology* 99:5 (Mar. 1994): 1180–1211.

Ivins, Stanley S. "Notes on Mormon Polygamy." *Western Humanities Review* 10 (Summer 1956): 229–239.

James, William. *The Varieties of Religious Experience.* 1902. Reprint. New York: Penguin, 1958.

Jary, David, and Julia Jary, eds. *The HarperCollins Dictionary of Sociology.* New York: HarperCollins, 1991.

Johnson, Benton. "On Church and Sect." *American Sociological Review* 28:4 (Aug. 1963): 539–549.

Johnson, Theodore E., ed. "'The Millennial Laws' of 1821." *Shaker Quarterly* 7 (1967): 35–58.

Kanter, Rosabeth Moss. *Commitment and Community.* Cambridge, Mass.: Harvard University Press, 1972.

Kenney, Scott G. "Before the Beard: The Trials of the Young Joseph F. Smith." *Sunstone* 120 (Apr. 2001): 20–42.

Kern, Louis J. *An Ordered Love: Sex Roles and Sexuality in Victorian Utopias: The Shakers, the Mormons and the Oneida Community.* Chapel Hill: University of North Carolina Press, 1981.

Knuth, Rebecca. "Systemic Book Burning as Evil?" In *Cultural Expressions of Evil and Wickedness: Wrath, Sex, Crime,* ed. Terrie Waddell. Amsterdam: Rodopi, 2003.

Larson, Gustive O. "The Mormon Reformation." *Utah Historical Quarterly* 26 (Jan. 1958): 45–63.

Leonard, Glen M. *Nauvoo: A Place of Peace, a People of Promise.* Salt Lake City, Utah: Deseret 2002.

LeSueur, Stephen C. *The 1838 Mormon War in Missouri.* Columbia: University of Missouri Press, 1987.

Marini, Stephen A. *Radical Sects of Revolutionary New England.* Cambridge, Mass.: Harvard University Press, 1982.

Marquart, H. Michael. *The Joseph Smith Revelations: Text and Commentary.* Salt Lake City, Utah: Signature, 1999.

Mauss, Armand L. *All Abraham's Children: Changing Mormon Conceptions of Race and Lineage.* Urbana: University of Illinois Press, 2003.

May, Dean L. "A Demographic Portrait of the Mormons, 1830–1980." In *The New Mormon History: Revisionist Essays on the Past,* ed. D. Michael Quinn. Salt Lake City, Utah: Signature, 1992.

McConkie, Bruce R. *Mormon Doctrine.* Salt Lake City, Utah: Bookcraft, 1966.

McRae, John R. *Seeing Through Zen: Encounter, Transformation, and Genealogy in Chinese Chan Buddhism.* Berkeley: University of California Press, 2003.

Moore, R. Laurence. *Religious Outsiders and the Making of Americans.* New York: Oxford University Press, 1986.

Moore, William D. "Interpreting the Shakers: Opening the Villages to the Public 1955–1965." *CRM: Journal of Heritage Stewardship* (Winter 2006): 1–6.

Morin, France, ed. *Heavenly Visions: Shaker Gift Drawings and Gift Songs.* Minneapolis: University of Minnesota Press, 2001.

Morris, Charles W. *Writings on the General Theory of Signs.* The Hague: Mouton, 1971.

Muir, Edward L. *Ritual in Early Modern Europe.* Cambridge: Cambridge University Press, 1997.

Murray, John E. "Human Capital in Religious Communes: Literacy and Selection of Nineteenth-Century Shakers." *Explorations in Economic History* 32 (1995): 217–234.

Nordhoff, Charles. *The Communistic Societies of the United States.* New York: Harper, 1875.

Numbers, Ronald L., and Jonathan M. Butler, eds. *The Disappointed: Millerism and Millenarianism in the Nineteenth Century.* Bloomington: Indiana University Press, 1987.

Olsen, Steve L. *The Mormon Ideology of Place: Cosmic Symbolism of the City of Zion, 1830–1846.* Provo, Utah: Joseph Fielding Smith Institute, 2002.

Patterson, Daniel W. *The Shaker Spiritual,* 2nd corrected ed. New York: Dover, 2000.

Pessen, Edward. *Jacksonian America: Society, Personality, and Politics.* Urbana: University of Illinois Press, 1985.

Peterson, Paul H. "The Mormon Reformation." Ph.D. diss., Brigham Young University, 1981.

Promey, Sally M. *Spiritual Spectacles: Vision and Image in Mid-Nineteenth-Century Shakerism.* Bloomington: Indiana University Press, 1993.

Quinn, D. Michael. "Latter-day Saint Prayer Circles." *BYU Studies* 19:3 (Fall 1978): 79–105.

———. "LDS Church Authority and New Plural Marriages, 1890–1904." *Dialogue: A Journal of Mormon Thought* 18:1 (Spring 1985): 96–105.

———. *The Mormon Hierarchy: Extensions of Power.* Salt Lake City, Utah: Signature, 1996.

———. *The Mormon Hierarchy: Origins of Power.* Salt Lake City, Utah: Signature, 1994.

———. "The Practice of Rebaptism at Nauvoo." *BYU Studies* 18:2 (Winter 1978): 1–7.

Quinn, D. Michael, ed. *The New Mormon History: Revisionist Essays on the Past.* Salt Lake City, Utah: Signature, 1992.

Roberts, B. H. *Life of John Taylor.* Salt Lake City, Utah: George Q. Cannon and Sons, 1892.

Rohrbough, Malcolm J. *The Trans-Appalachian Frontier: People, Societies, and Institutions, 1775–1850.* New York: Oxford University Press, 1978.

Romig, Ronald E., and John H. Siebert. "Jackson County, 1831–1833: A Look at the Development of Zion." *Restoration Studies* 3 (1986): 286–304.

Rosenberg, Charles E. *The Cholera Years: The United States in 1832, 1849, and 1866.* Chicago: University of Chicago Press, 1962.

Ruether, Rosemary Radford. *Goddesses and the Divine Feminine: A Western Religious History.* Berkeley: University of California Press, 2005.

Sasson, Diane. "Individual Experience, Community Control, and Gender: The Harvard Shaker Community during the Era of Manifestations." *Communal Societies* 13 (1993): 45–70.

———. *The Shaker Spiritual Narrative.* Knoxville: University of Tennessee Press, 1983.

Scott, James C. *Domination and the Arts of Resistance: Hidden Transcripts.* New Haven, Conn.: Yale University Press, 1990.

Sellers, Charles. *The Market Revolution: Jacksonian America, 1815–1846*. New York: Oxford University Press, 1992.

Sessions, Gene. *Mormon Thunder: A Documentary History of Jedediah Morgan Grant*. Urbana: University of Illinois Press, 1982.

Sharot, Stephen. *Messianism, Mysticism, and Magic: A Sociological Analysis of Jewish Religious Movements*. Chapel Hill: University of North Carolina Press, 1982.

Shepherd, Gary, and Gordon Shepherd. *A Kingdom Transformed: Themes on the Development of Mormonism*. Salt Lake City: University of Utah Press, 1984.

Shipps, Jan. *Mormonism: The Story of a New Religious Tradition*. Urbana: University of Illinois Press, 1985.

Smart, William B. *Mormonism's Last Colonizer: The Life and Times of William H. Smart*. Logan: Utah State University Press, 2008.

Smith, Jonathan Z. *Imagining Religion: From Babylon to Jonestown*. Chicago: University of Chicago Press, 1982.

———. *Map Is Not Territory: Studies in the History of Religions*. Chicago: University of Chicago Press, 1987.

———. *To Take Place: Toward Theory in Ritual*. Chicago: University of Chicago Press, 1987.

Spiro, Melford E. "Religion: Problems of Definition and Explanation." In *Anthropological Approaches to the Study of Religion*, ed. Michael Banton. London: Tavistock, 1966.

Stark, Rodney. *The Rise of Christianity: How the Obscure, Marginal Jesus Movement Became the Dominant Religious Force in the Western World in Just a Few Centuries*. New York: HarperCollins, 1996.

Stein, Stephen J. *The Shaker Experience in America: A History of the United Society of Believers*. New Haven, Conn.: Yale University Press, 1992.

———. "Shaker Gift and Shaker Order: A Study of Religious Tension in Nineteenth-Century America." *Communal Societies* 10 (1990): 102–113.

Swanson, R. N. *Religion and Devotion in Europe, c. 1215–c. 1515*. Cambridge: Cambridge University Press, 1995.

Tabor, James D. "Religious Discourse and Failed Negotiations: The Dynamics of Biblical Apocalypticism in Waco." In *Armageddon in Waco: Critical Perspectives on the Branch Davidian Conflict*, ed. Stuart A. Wright. Chicago: University of Chicago Press, 1995.

Taylor, Samuel W. *The Last Pioneer: John Taylor, a Mormon Prophet*. Salt Lake City, Utah: Signature, 2002.

Taysom, Stephen C. "A Uniform and Common Recollection: Joseph Smith's Legacy, Polygamy, and the Creation of Mormon Public Memory." *Dialogue: A Journal of Mormon Thought* 35:3 (Fall 2003): 113–144.

Thurman, Suzanne R. "The Order of Nature, the Order of Grace: Community Formation, Female Status, and Relations with the World in the Shaker Villages of Harvard and Shirley, Massachusetts, 1781–1875." Ph.D. diss., Indiana University, 1994.

———. "O Sisters Ain't You Happy?" *Gender, Family, and Community among the Harvard and Shirley Shakers, 1781–1918*. Syracuse, N.Y.: Syracuse University Press, 2002.

Turner, Victor. *The Ritual Process: Structure and Anti-Structure.* Ithaca, N.Y.: Cornell University Press, 1977.

Tweed, Thomas A. *Crossing and Dwelling: A Theory of Religion.* Cambridge, Mass.: Harvard University Press, 2006.

van der Leeuw, Gerardus. *Religion in Essence and Manifestation,* vol. 2. 1933. Reprint. New York: Harper and Row, 1963.

Van Wagoner, Richard S. *Mormon Polygamy: A History.* Salt Lake City, Utah: Signature, 1987.

Walker, Ronald W. *Qualities That Count: Heber J. Grant as Businessman, Missionary, and Apostle.* Provo, Utah: Brigham Young University Press, 2004.

Weisbrod, Carol. *The Boundaries of Utopia.* New York: Pantheon, 1980.

Westergren, Bruce N., ed. *From Historian to Dissident: The Book of John Whitmer.* Salt Lake City, Utah: Signature, 1995.

Whittaker, David J. "The Bone in the Throat: Orson Pratt and the Public Announcement of Plural Marriage." *Western Historical Quarterly* 18:3 (July 1987): 293–314.

Wilentz, Sean, and Paul Johnson. *The Kingdom of Matthias: A Story of Sex and Salvation in 19th Century America.* New York: Oxford University Press, 1994.

Wilson, Bryan R. "An Analysis of Sect Development." *American Sociological Review* 24:1 (Feb. 1959): 3–15.

Wolterstorff, Nicholas. *Divine Discourse: Philosophical Reflections on the Claim That God Speaks.* Cambridge: Cambridge University Press, 1995.

Wright, Stuart A., ed. *Armageddon in Waco: Critical Perspectives on the Branch Davidian Conflict.* Chicago: University of Chicago Press, 1995.

Yalom, Marilyn. *The History of the Wife.* New York: HarperCollins, 2001.

Young, Kimball. *Isn't One Wife Enough? The Story of Mormon Polygamy.* New York: Holt, 1954.

INDEX

Page numbers in *italics* refer to illustrations.

STEPHEN C. TAYSOM teaches in the Department of Religious Studies at Cleveland State University.